OpenGL®
Programming
on Mac OS® X

OpenGL®
Programming
on Mac OS® X
Architecture, Performance, and Integration

Robert P. Kuehne
J. D. Sullivan

✦✦Addison-Wesley

Upper Saddle River, NJ • Boston • Indianapolis • San Francisco
New York • Toronto • Montreal • London • Munich • Paris • Madrid
Capetown • Sydney • Tokyo • Singapore • Mexico City

Many of the designations used by manufacturers and sellers to distinguish their products are claimed as trademarks. Where those designations appear in this book, and the publisher was aware of a trademark claim, the designations have been printed with initial capital letters or in all capitals.

The authors and publisher have taken care in the preparation of this book, but make no expressed or implied warranty of any kind and assume no responsibility for errors or omissions. No liability is assumed for incidental or consequential damages in connection with or arising out of the use of the information or programs contained herein.

The publisher offers excellent discounts on this book when ordered in quantity for bulk purchases or special sales, which may include electronic versions and/or custom covers and content particular to your business, training goals, marketing focus, and branding interests. For more information, please contact:

> U.S. Corporate and Government Sales
> (800) 382-3419
> corpsales@pearsontechgroup.com

For sales outside of the United States, please contact:

> International Sales
> (317) 382-3419
> international@pearsontechgroup.com

 This Book Is Safari Enabled
The Safari® Enabled icon on the cover of your favorite technology book means the book is available through Safari Bookshelf. When you buy this book, you get free access to the online edition for 45 days.

Safari Bookshelf is an electronic reference library that lets you easily search thousands of technical books, find code samples, download chapters, and access technical information whenever and wherever you need it. To gain 45-day Safari Enabled access to this book:

- Go to http://www.awprofessional.com/safarienabled
- Complete the brief registration form
- Enter the coupon code 9LCJ-9EZD-XZE2-YYDP-PTV9

If you have difficulty registering on Safari Bookshelf or accessing the online edition, please e-mail customer-service@safaribooksonline.com.

Visit us on the Web: www.awprofessional.com

Library of Congress Cataloging-in-Publication Data

Kuehne, Robert P.
    OpenGL programming on Mac OS X : architecture, performance, and integration / Robert P. Kuehne,
    J. D. Sullivan.
        p. cm.
    Includes bibliographical references and index.
    ISBN-13: 978-0-321-35652-9 (pbk. : alk. paper)
    ISBN-10: 0-321-35652-7
    1. Computer graphics. 2. OpenGL. 3. Mac OS. I. Sullivan, J. D. II. Title.
    T385.K82 2007
    006.6'6 dc22

                                                                2007011974

> Pearson Education, Inc.
> Rights and Contracts Department
> 501 Boylston Street, Suite 900
> Boston, MA 02116
> Fax: (617) 671-3447

ISBN 13: 978-0-321-35652-9
ISBN 10:   0-321-35652-7
Text printed in the United States on recycled paper at Donnelley in Crawfordsville, Indiana.
First printing, December 2007

For my family
—Bob

For my family
—John

In memory of democracy

Contents

Chapter 9. The GLUT API for OpenGL Configuration   163

Chapter 10. API Interoperability   173

Chapter 11. Performance   195

Figures

Tables

Examples

The Mac is a computing platform that virtually defines ease of use, consistency, and effortless computing. The story of OpenGL on the Mac has been, shall we say, a bit more complex. With the arrival of OS X, the Mac platform supports even more ways of constructing OpenGL applications for the Mac. While there has been an apparent proliferation of OpenGL interfaces for the Mac, the platform itself has stabilized architecturally and programmatically and now offers the best developer and user experience in the industry for development of graphics applications. This is not just a statement of preference but an observation that, in many ways, the Mac is an OpenGL platform without peer. The Mac is a fun and efficient platform on which to develop applications, thanks to the set of OpenGL drivers at its core that support a rich and deep feature set, great performance, and deep integration in OS X. The Mac has excellent and usable tools for quickly monitoring OpenGL behavior, rapidly prototyping shaders, and digging deep to analyze OpenGL behavior in the application and driver. The Mac makes OpenGL development efficient and fun.

Although the development tools and environment are powerful and helpful, many corners of OpenGL on the Mac remain under-documented. A developer must choose among several development languages, user interface (UI) toolkits, window managers, and additional Mac APIs such as QuickTime and Core Image, yet still ensure that his or her software runs well on a variety of target Mac platforms. All of these factors can make using OpenGL on the Mac a challenging task even for developers who have been writing OpenGL applications on other platforms for years.

This book was put together with an eye toward simplifying and clarifying the ways in which OpenGL can be used on the Mac. It is our hope that by codifying all the information available about OpenGL on the Mac in one place and by presenting each interface with clarity and depth, developers will have a one-stop reference for all things OpenGL on the Mac.

Who Should Read This Book?

This book is intended for OpenGL programmers who wish to develop applications on Mac OS X. We target two categories of OpenGL programmers: those who are new to OpenGL on the Mac and those who want to explore the specific benefits of writing OpenGL programs on the Mac.

For those who are new to OpenGL on the Mac—either existing Mac developers or those coming from other platforms—we provide advice on cross-platform issues, portable interfaces, and ideas about choosing native interfaces for the Mac. Existing Mac developers will find a single-source reference guide to all OpenGL interfaces on the Mac. For developers wishing to explore the power and richness of the Mac, we provide complete details on Mac-specific OpenGL extensions and ways of integrating other Mac APIs (such as QuickTime and Core Image) into applications.

Organization

This text is intended to be useful as both a programming guide and a reference manual. The text contains several chapters focused on OpenGL on the Mac and other chapters that cover related graphics information. A few appendices are included to cover supplemental information in detail. The chapters are organized as follows:

Architecture Chapters 1 through 4 describe the hardware and software architectures of the Mac. This part of the book also presents an introduction to performance considerations as they relate to architecture.

Configuration and Integration Chapter 5 explores the interfaces to OpenGL on the Mac in detail. Those new to OpenGL on the Mac should begin here.

CGL, AGL, Cocoa, GLUT Chapters 6 through 9 explore details behind the individual APIs. Each API is covered in detail in its own chapter, and the APIs are compared and contrasted in each chapter. These chapters form the core of this book.

Interoperability Chapter 10 collects a variety of interesting OpenGL and other Mac API integration ideas. This chapter describes how to incorporate video in an application with QuickTime, perform image effects on textures or scenes with Core Image, and process CoreVideo data in an application.

Performance Chapters 11 and 12 describe the basics of analyzing performance of OpenGL applications and offer tips about where common problems may surface and how they might be resolved. Analysis, tools, architecture, data types, and solutions are covered.

Extensions Chapter 13 presents a guide to detecting, integrating, and using OpenGL extensions. This chapter introduces extension management principles and tools and provides details on how to perform such management specifically on the Mac.

Additional Resources

As both OpenGL and the Mac platform evolve, so must developers' applications. At our website, www.macopenglbook.com, we provide our example OpenGL code as well as other OpenGL-related resources. Additionally, we track and provide corrections for any errata and typos. Although we aspire to Knuth-like greatness, we are open to the idea that bugs may yet lurk within these pages. Should you find a possible gaffe, please bring it to our attention through our website.

This book has been a project long in the making, and rumblings of Leopard, Mac OS X 10.5, have been part of our plan since the beginning. However, due to information embargoes, the paucity of information available to the public, and publishing timelines, our best efforts at incorporating final, released Leopard-specific details are thwarted. Although we've accounted for most major changes to OpenGL programming for Leopard in this book, there was still some degree of flux for Leopard features at the time this book was published. Never fear, we've put together a detailed Leopard change synopsis for OpenGL, and accounted for the flux in Leopard on our website in an extra chapter. You'll find this bonus chapter at our website: www.macopenglbook.com.

A few words on Leopard that we can say at this time with authority: First, Leopard will provide OpenGL 2.0 and OpenGL ES support. OpenGL 2.0 is a great baseline for OpenGL developers, providing the most modern of OpenGL foundations upon which to develop. Also of interest is the inclusion of OpenGL ES in this release. ES stands for *embedded system*, and is a nice, stripped-down version of OpenGL, largely targeting handheld devices. At this time, if writing an application for a desktop system, it would still be most sensible to target OpenGL 2.0. However, if you're building and testing a cross-platform device that might be used for handheld devices, OpenGL ES would be a good OpenGL SDK to develop against. Second, Apple's tools for development and debugging are a lot more comprehensive in Leopard. XRay, in particular, integrates a variety of debugging tools in one information view, making it much easier to target certain types of bottlenecks, specifically those involving data transfer. Finally, Leopard brings a lot of bug-fixes and feature enhancements. We've got information on bits and pieces of the Leopard OpenGL throughout the book. But you'll have to read about the final and released version in our Leopard chapter on the website.

So, once you have this book in your hands, please go to the website and get the addendum. We think you'll be pleased with the detail and additional information it offers on the released version of Leopard. We consider it the definitive source of independent information for OpenGL on Leopard, Mac OSX 10.5. Get it by going to: www.macopenglbook.com.

Acknowledgments

The first edition of this book owes many thanks to many people, beginning with Bob's good friend, Dave Shreiner. Dave and Bob have taught numerous SIGGRAPH courses together over the years and worked together at SGI. Dave encouraged Bob to take on this project with Addison-Wesley and was instrumental in getting it off the ground and providing advice, reviews, and encouragement along the way.

The reviewers of the book performed heroic feats of editing and have made this book much better for their efforts. Many thanks go to Dave Shreiner, Paul Martz, Thomas True, Terry Welsh, Alan Commike, Michel Castejon, and Jeremy Sandmel.

Thanks, too, to the many other friends and relatives who contributed ideas, encouragement, and support. Finally, the authors would like to individually thank a few people.

J. D.'s Acknowledgments

I cannot fully express my gratitude for the support of my wife Samantha. She has been with me for the duration of this challenging project and always responded to the rough patches with compassion and a smile.

I also wanted to extend a special thanks to my friend Alex Eddy who reviewed this material with unmatched expertise on the subject matter of the current OS X OpenGL implementation, its history, and its incarnations.

Finally, I wanted to thank my parents Andrew and Sue, who never wavered in their support of my education and career. From their visionary gift in 1979 of a Timex Sinclair computer that started me down the road to software development to the present day, they have always been at my side.

Bob's Acknowledgments

Thanks very much to my wife, Kim, for her support, encouragement, and love. She's been my muse and a voice of reason throughout the often arduous process of shepherding a book from inception to publishing. I'd also like to thank my parents for getting me raised well, and without major injury, and for maintaining their encouragement throughout my life. Finally, thanks to my cats for keeping me warm, grounded, and focused on the essentials of life: food, sleep, and play.

About the Authors

Bob Kuehne is a graphics consultant and entrepreneur and currently works as the head of a graphics consultancy, Blue Newt Software. Blue Newt works with clients around the world to enhance their 3D graphics applications. Blue Newt helps clients move from fixed-function programming to shader applications, from single- to multi-pipe, multi-display systems, and from baseline OpenGL to scenegraphs as their needs change. Bob spends most of his time in modern OpenGL working with clients to design new applications, develop new features, and do performance engineering.

Before Blue Newt, Bob worked for nearly eight years at SGI in a variety of roles. His work included leading the OpenGL Shader project, creating demos for high-end multi-pipe graphics systems, and helping SGI developers create high-performance, high-quality applications.

Bob has worked in the graphics industry and with graphics systems for more than two decades and has been developing in OpenGL since it first existed. He has been a developer on the Mac since the early 1990s, when he was finally able to afford one. Bob has presented at numerous conferences over his career, including SIGGRAPH, Graphic Hardware, SGI Developer Forum Worldwide, and (the ex-conference) MacHack. He currently teaches OpenGL and scenegraph training courses around the world as part of his work for Blue Newt.

When Bob is able to be pulled away from his Mac and graphics work, you'll find him either playing volleyball or sailing with his wife. Please don't hesitate to email him: (rpk@blue-newt.com) or visit his website (http://www.blue-newt.com).

J. D. Sullivan is an OpenGL driver engineer who has been writing graphics software professionally for more than 15 years. His experience with OpenGL began with writing IrisGL applications for a finite element modeling and broadcast animation lab in 1992. His experience developing on the Macintosh platform began in 1988 with Symantec's Think C and a 16 MHz SE/30 that boasted 4MB of RAM and 1MB of video memory.

After three years working on a distributed renderer for the FEM and broadcast animation lab, J. D. joined Silicon Graphics, Inc., where he first focused on performance and feature differentiation of graphics applications from ISVs that were critical to SGI's business. A considerable portion of this work centered on medical and GIS imaging. He was one of the original four designers and implementers of SGI's Volumizer API, and he earned a design patent for high performance modulation of 3D textures. He then moved to SGI's Consumer Products Division, where he worked as part of the OpenGL software team during the bring-up of both the Cobalt and Krypton graphics chipsets.

Since SGI, J. D. has worked on the Mac as his primary development platform. He has been an OpenGL driver engineer for more than five years and serves on the OpenGL Architecture Review board.

Chapter 1

Mac OpenGL
Introduction

Welcome to OpenGL on Mac OS X! This book is designed to be your one-stop resource for all things OpenGL on the Mac. We wrote this book for Mac OpenGL developers such as you. We wrote it for ourselves, too—let us explain. We have always cherished having a comprehensive programming guide in hand that provides the continuity and context of programming environments. We also appreciate the concise, bulleted information found in most reference guides. The analog learning experience of sitting back in a comfortable chair with a clear mind and a cup of your beverage of choice is a great way to deeply understand the intention and usage of an API or programming environment. We invite you to sit back and enjoy learning what the exceptional pairing of the Mac OS and OpenGL have to offer.

This book will serve both existing Mac developers and those new to the platform. We are living proof of the former case: We've referenced it ourselves during the writing of the book itself! We've consolidated a lot of information from a variety of sources and our own experience into one complete guide. Developers who are new to the Mac platform should appreciate both the comprehensive nature of the material and the many comparisons and contrasts drawn with other programming environments and operating systems.

Given the long history of OpenGL on the Mac (which we discuss later in the book), you may be reading this book with an older application as your focus. With this in mind, we've included content covering all OpenGL-related APIs in OS X. The older APIs, however, may not be the preferred path for new development on the Mac, and we'll guide you accordingly. We cover all major OpenGL window-system APIs on the Mac in depth, but with enough guidance that even first-time Mac developers can get up to speed quickly.

Whatever type of developer you are, whatever the age of your code, and no matter how you arrived at this title, we welcome you and hope you find our book useful.

Why the Mac?

For those of you who are new to the Mac platform, we'd like to spend a moment explaining a few of the reasons why the Mac makes a great platform on which to develop your applications. Specifically, we'd like to explore some of the reasons that you would target Mac OS X for a new OpenGL application.

The Mac has had a long and rich history. In fact, Apple recently celebrated its thirtieth anniversary. The Mac has existed for more than 20 years of that 30-year span and has itself undergone many transformations over that time. Throughout it all, the Mac platform has exhibited a few key characteristics. Chief among those is one characteristic in particular that defines the Mac—style. You probably thought that we'd say "simplicity" or "consistency," but neither is as core to the Mac as style. You'd be right, however, in assuming that both simplicity and consistency are two key aspects of what makes developing for and using the Mac such an exceptional experience. And it's true that both consistency and simplicity are aspects of the overarching style that is the Mac. Nevertheless, we'd be doing a disservice to the Mac to suggest that there isn't substance behind that style, because there is. From its solid BSD underpinning through years of evolution in software APIs, the Mac has remained a robust platform.

From a user perspective, the Mac has always been, at its core, a smooth, fun, and stylish user experience. And now, with OS X, the Mac is also one of the best development platforms available.

From the developer side of the equation, things have not always been so elegant, of course. The Mac OS of the pre-OS X days was a much more "interesting" development experience. Beginning from their roots in Pascal and through their evolution into the C language, the OS 9 and its brethren from earlier days were a lot more challenging. Partly in response to these difficulties, NextStep, a start-up outgrowth of Apple in the early 1990s, worked hard to simplify the modern development experience, and the results of its work are now available in Mac OS X.

For us to describe the entire development history of the Mac would be a book by itself, but there's one key trend that the Mac has been tracking, on the development side as well as the userside: style. The latest Mac APIs for user interface (UI) development, for core application development, and, of course, for graphics development are really quite sane, well integrated, and fun to use. The intuitive user experience for which the Mac has always been known is for now a cornerstone of the development experience as well. The developer tools, such as XCode, Shark, and the various OpenGL debuggers and analyzers, bring a sense of efficiency, fun, continuity, and style to today's Mac developers.

So, back to the question of this section: Why the Mac? The authors of this book have developed applications for numerous platforms over the years—from Windows boxes, to generic Unix boxes, to SGI machines, Apple IIs, embedded systems, and many others. It's been our experience that, regardless of which platform you develop for, great tools and a great user experience make for great software. The answer to "Why the Mac?" is simple—the platform. Both elegant hardware and solid software make the goal of creating great software much easier to achieve. Once you've developed on the Mac, you'll probably want to develop all of your applications there first. You can get results so much more quickly, and with so much better overall quality, that it's truly eye-opening.[1] If you're not initially a member of our target audience for this book, we'd suggest that you give the Mac a try, developing a modern application from start to finish, and see if you don't agree.

Why OpenGL?

If you're reading this book, chances are that you already know why you are using OpenGL. But if you're reading this book and trying to make some decisions about which 3D API to use, we'll say a few words on why you should consider OpenGL.

The reasons are very similar to those as to why you'd choose the Mac platform. To reiterate, ease of development, ease of use, and solid, stylish tools make the Mac development process easy. OpenGL is no exception.

OpenGL has a long history, like the Mac. Although the history of OpenGL is covered in more detail later in the book, here's an abbreviated version. OpenGL was developed from the experience and foundation of IrisGL, an API for 3D graphics first developed by SGI. OpenGL was developed to bring a fresh set of eyes to the task of creating a clean, modern, and portable graphics API. The designers of OpenGL did an excellent job with an API that is nicely orthogonal in function, high performance in execution, and extensible in design.

It should be mentioned, too, that OpenGL is the only graphics API that exists on virtually every hardware platform you might want to develop, from cell phone to supercomputer. OpenGL exists on operating systems from Symbian to Mac OS X, and many others. No other graphics API has that sort of ubiquity, so if

---

1. We're not blind to the problems, mind you, but Apple is very responsive on the bug-fix side of things. And no, the Mac platform is not perfect: There are plenty of legacy APIs to be had. However, if you decide to write a modern Mac application, the development experience is hands-down better than on any other platform. It's quite simply a lot of fun.

you have visions of developing for multiple platforms, OpenGL is really your only option. Don't feel too bad about that mandate, though, because once you start working with OpenGL, you'll see that its performance is as good as any API out there.

In fact, from your perspective as a developer, one of the key strengths of OpenGL is the way in which you can learn core techniques once and then reapply them many times. For example, the way that you create and modify individual and batched graphics primitives is something that you can learn once and then apply to vertices, textures, shaders, and more. In many ways, OpenGL is a great match for the Mac, because both allow you to learn techniques once and reapply those same techniques repeatedly to many different object-types. Consistency of technique is a key aspect of why it is so easy to be productive on the Mac, and of why OpenGL is a great API to use.

Using an open standard graphics API like OpenGL means that its design today and in the future will incorporate all of the rich and diversified design considerations from various industry interests that only open standards can. Indeed, these diversified corporate and educational interests contributions are the very reason OpenGL runs on the widest array of devices. Furthermore, because design decisions are better decoupled from proprietary interests, the result is quite simply a better and more generalized design.

If you're new to the base OpenGL API, we won't be much help to you in this book because we're focused on Mac-specific infrastructure. However, there are other great books and resources on the subject out there. The canonical reference, the so-called Red Book [22], and the OpenGL website [2] provide a good foundation for OpenGL developers. There are also other, more compact guides, such as the recent *OpenGL® Distilled* [19]. The bibliography lists a few other reference books of note, including those describing in detail how to use OpenGL on other platforms [15, 18]. This book is a companion to those resources, focusing on the infrastructure, performance, and integration of OpenGL on the Mac.

The Book

What we describe in this book is the essence of OpenGL usage and integration on the Mac. We won't try to motivate you to choose the Mac or OpenGL further, but will rely on you to make your own informed decision after reading our text. We will describe in detail the rendering architecture used by Mac OS X and note how OpenGL integrates into it. We will explore in depth each of the major OpenGL interface APIs on the Mac, showing how to use each in a sample application and how to customize those applications for your specific needs. We will also explore the surrounding OpenGL infrastructure on the Mac, from tools to secondary APIs used to get data into OpenGL. Finally, we will attempt to bring a sensibility and a practicality to all of our discussions—not trying to explain everything there is in all APIs, examples, and tools, but just what's necessary and useful. We approach this entire topic from the perspective of an application developer who is trying to get a high-performance, great application developed on the Mac. OpenGL on the Mac is a large domain, but we have a good filter for what is important and have written this book with an eye toward ensuring the reader's enjoyment of this learning experience.

Chapter 2

OpenGL Architecture on OS X

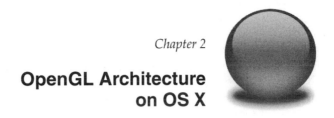

Overview

The Mac hardware platform has historically varied widely with regard to CPU, I/O devices, data busses, and graphics cards. The transition to Intel processors brings yet another step in this evolution to developers, who now have another Mac platform to consider with many different specifications. Despite the fact that the underlying hardware on the Mac differs so widely, the software architecture of OpenGL provides programmatic consistency for graphical applications across these varied configurations. OpenGL provides an abstraction layer that insulates application developers from having to develop specific logic for the unending array of systems and graphics devices.

At present, the Mac OS OpenGL implementation supports graphics devices from four vendors: ATI, Intel, NVIDIA, and VillageTronic. And, of course, the graphics drivers support either PowerPC or Intel CPUs feeding these devices. The Mac also supports a virtual graphics device that processes OpenGL rendering commands on the CPU of the system. This virtual device is canonically known as the "software renderer."

In this chapter, we'll explore the software architecture of the OpenGL on the Mac, including the history of OpenGL itself and the way in which the Mac software architecture supports flexible graphics application development using this API.

About OpenGL

To understand OpenGL on the Mac, let's begin by looking back at the evolution of OpenGL itself. Silicon Graphics (SGI) began development on OpenGL in 1990, with version 1.0 of the software being released in 1992. OpenGL was a logical evolution from its predecessor, IrisGL—named in accordance with the graphics hardware for which it was built. IrisGL was initially released by SGI in 1983. It included all of the necessary API entry points that, unlike OpenGL, handled windowing system tasks unrelated to actual graphics pipeline rendering. SGI soon realized that to grow its graphics workstation market share, the company needed to use a graphics API that was an industry standard. Ultimately, the applications that independent software vendors (ISVs) were producing were what sold the hardware they were building. By making IrisGL into an open standard (OpenGL), SGI could greatly help lower the ISVs' development costs to reach multiple platforms, which in turn would encourage them to adopt the use of the OpenGL API.

To make OpenGL an open standard, SGI formed the OpenGL Architecture Review Board (ARB) in 1991 to oversee and develop the specification with a broad range of industry interests in mind. The ARB includes both software- and hardware-focused vendors in the graphics industry with an interest in furthering an open graphics API standard.

In its simplest form, OpenGL is a specification document. To develop the OpenGL standard, a formal process has been established by which new functionality may be added to the OpenGL specification. But where do these extensions come from? Who decides they want one, and how do those new extensions get put into the standard?

New extensions to OpenGL are typically created by individual companies or organizations that are interested in including the new extension in the version of OpenGL they ship. These extensions are known as vendor extensions. They are specific to the company that created them and are named accordingly. For instance, an extension unique to Apple is the GL_APPLE_texture_range extension. Other extensions are named for the companies that formulated and specified them—for example, SGI, 3DLABS, or ATI.

Often ARB member companies will create parallel extensions—that is, two extensions with essentially the same functional purpose, but different interfaces. If these companies wish to collaborate on consolidating these similar specifications into a single unified proposal, they will often create a working group within the ARB so as to select the best aspects of each proposal and merge them into one. When an extension is supported by more than one ARB member, it is called an EXT extension. The GL_EXT_framebuffer_object extension, which is defined to do off-screen rendering, is an example of such an extension.

If a vendor or an EXT extension gains enough favor with the voting ARB members, it can be put to a vote to approve it as an ARB extension. With the approval of a two-thirds majority of the voting ARB members, the extension can gain ARB status. Often, vendor extensions go through a process of gaining acceptance

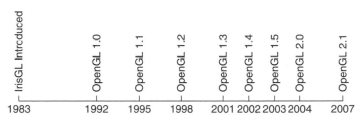

Figure 2-1 OpenGL Version History Timeline

as an EXT extension by other vendors before being promoted to the core specification. Each of these stages of the extension process allows for industry "soak time" to expose the extension's strengths and weaknesses. At every stage of the process—vendor, EXT, and ARB—the review board can (and often does) make changes to remedy any weaknesses that were uncovered through industry exposure.

As extensions are integrated into the core and other clarifying edits are made to the OpenGL specification, the document is revised and its version number updated. Version 1.0 of this specification was released in 1992, and Figure 2-1 details the timeline of versions since that time.

Each new revision of the core OpenGL API promoted extensions to core functionality, as shown in Table 2-1.

Table 2-1 Versions of OpenGL in Which Extensions Were Promoted to Core OpenGL

OpenGL Version	Extension
1.1	Blending logical operations `GL_EXT_blend_logic_op`
	Framebuffer-to-texture copies `GL_EXT_copytexture`
	Polygon offset `GL_EXT_polygon_offset`
	Subtexturing `GL_EXT_subtexture`
	Internal formats and component sizing for textures `GL_EXT_texture`
	Texture proxying `GL_EXT_texture`
	Replacement of output fragments by source texture values `GL_EXT_texture`
	Continued

Table 2-1 Versions of OpenGL in Which Extensions Were Promoted to Core OpenGL (*Continued*)

OpenGL Version	Extension
	Texture objects GL_EXT_texture_object
	Vertex arrays GL_EXT_vertex_array
1.2.1	ARB extensions introduced to promotion process
1.3	BGRA pixel format GL_EXT_bgra
	Range-bounded vertex draw elements GL_EXT_draw_range_elements
	Multisampling GL_ARB_multisample
	Multitexturing GL_ARB_multitexture
	Texture environment modes: Add, Combine, Dot3 GL_ARB_texture_env_{add|combine|dot3}
	Texture border clamp GL_ARB_texture_border_clamp
	Transpose matrix GL_ARB_transpose_matrix
1.4	Automatic mipmap generation GL_SGIS_generate_mipmap
	Blend squaring GL_NV_blend_square
	Depth textures GL_ARB_depth_texture
	Fog coordinates GL_EXT_fog_coord
	Multiple draw arrays GL_EXT_multi_draw_arrays
	Point parameters GL_ARB_point_parameters
	Secondary color GL_EXT_secondary_color
	Separate blend functions GL_EXT_blend_func_separate
	Shadows GL_ARB_shadow
	Stencil wrap GL_EXT_stencil_wrap

OpenGL Version	Extension
	Texture crossbar environment mode `GL_ARB_texture_env_crossbar`
	Texture LOD bias `GL_EXT_texture_lod_bias`
	Texture mirrored repeat `GL_ARB_texture_mirrored_repeat`
	Window raster position `GL_ARB_window_pos`
1.5	Buffer objects `GL_ARB_vertex_buffer_object`
	Occlusion queries `GL_ARB_occlusion_query`
	Shadow functions `GL_EXT_shadow_funcs`

2.0	Programmable shading
	`GL_ARB_shader_objects`
	`GL_ARB_vertex_shader`
	`GL_ARB_fragment_shader`

	Multiple render targets `GL_ARB_draw_buffers`
	Non-power-of-two textures `GL_ARB_texture_non_power_of_two`
	Point sprites `GL_ARB_point_sprite`
	Separate stencil `GL_ATI_separate_stencil`
2.1	Programmable shading Updated shading language to 1.20
	Pixel buffer objects `GL_ARB_pixel_buffer_object`
	sRGB textures `GL_EXT_texture_sRGB`

Mac OS X Implementation of the OpenGL Specification

Once an extension or a version of the specification has been completed and ratified by the required organization, the company or organization that will support the extension must then implement it. Naturally, there is some amount of delay between the publishing of a specification and a vendor's implementation of that published specification. We'll explore extensions in detail in Chapter 13.

Table 2-2 Mac OS Hardware Renderer Support for Versions of OpenGL

Mac OS Version	OpenGL Version	Renderer
10.2.8 Jaguar	1.3	Radeon 9600/9700/9800 Radeon 9000/9200 Radeon 8500 Radeon 7000/7200/7500 Geforce FX Geforce 4 Ti Geforce 3
	1.1	Apple Generic Renderer Geforce 2 MX/4 MX Rage 128
10.3.9 Panther	1.5	Geforce 6800 Geforce FX Radeon X800 Radeon 9600/9700/9800
	1.3	Radeon 9200 Radeon 9000 Radeon 8500 Radeon 7000/7200/7500 Geforce 4 Ti Geforce 3
	1.1	Apple Generic Renderer Geforce 2 MX/4 MX Rage 128
10.4.10 Tiger	2.0	Apple Float Renderer[a] Radeon HD 2400/HD 2600 Radon X1600/X1900[b] Geforce 8600M Geforce Quadro FX 4500[b] Geforce 6600/6800[b] Geforce FX[b]
	1.5	Radeon X800 Radeon 9600/9700/9800
	1.3	Radeon 9200 Radeon 9000 Radeon 8500 Radeon 7000/7200/7500 Geforce 4 Ti Geforce 3
	1.2	GMA 950
	1.1	Geforce 2 MX/4 MX Rage 128
		(*Continued*)

Table 2-2 Mac OS Hardware Renderer Support for Versions of OpenGL
(*Continued*)

Mac OS Version	OpenGL Version	Renderer
10.5 Leopard	2.1+	Apple Float Renderer
	2.0+	Radeon HD 2400/HD 2600 Radon X1600/X1900 Radeon X800 Radeon 9600/9700/9800 Geforce 8800/8600M Geforce Quadro FX 4500 Geforce 6600/6800 Geforce FX
	1.3	Radeon 9200 Radeon 9000 Radeon 8500 Radeon 7000/7200/7500 Geforce 4 Ti Geforce 3
	1.2	GMA 950
	1.1	Geforce 2 MX/4 MX

[a] This software renderer is limited to 1.21 compliance on PowerPC systems and was released supporting 2.1 on the newer 8600M and HD 2400/HD 2600 systems.

[b] These are limited to 1.5 compliance on PowerPC systems.

Table 2-2 illustrates the rather complex version landscape of the relationship between devices (hardware renderers), software renderers, and Mac OS X software releases. Version compliance for any hardware renderer or the latest software renderer may change (we hope increase only!) for any major or minor release of the Mac OS. Further, as the Tiger portion of the table shows, version compliance for the software renderer can vary in apparent relationship with the hardware renderer shipped for the system.

This apparent relationship is a false one, however. It merely reflects software improvements that accompanied hardware that had shipped later in the product cycle. In the software renderer case, its version will generally be consistent across all hardware configurations as is shown in the Leopard portion of the table.

Notice that the table references two different software renderers: the Apple Generic Renderer and the Apple Float Renderer. The Apple Float Renderer is simply a newer and much improved version of the Apple Generic Renderer. Both are referred to as "the software renderer." The software renderer was vastly improved in both performance and capabilities moving from Panther to Tiger and again moving from Tiger to Leopard.

As you can see in Table 2-2, no particular version of OpenGL is standard across all hardware in a particular release of Mac OS. Care must be taken when writing an OpenGL application to always ensure that your baseline OpenGL implementation version requirements are met independently of the Mac OS version.

Note that only the last minor release version of each major release of OS X is shown in Table 2-2. Minor releases in OS X are free downloads, so this table actually shows the "version potential," if you will, for each of these major releases. To obtain OpenGL version information for other minor releases, you must first choose a pixel format with the hardware or software renderer in which you are interested. Once you have created a context with the pixel format of interest, you can retrieve the OpenGL version of the selected renderer as follows:

```
char *opengl_version_str =
    strdup( (const char *) glGetString( GL_VERSION ) );
// The OpenGL version number is the first
// space-delimited token in the string
opengl_version_str = strtok( opengl_version_str, " " );
if( !strcmp( opengl_version_str, "2.1" ) )
{
    // OpenGL 2.1 Specific Application Configuration
}
else if ( !strcmp( opengl_version_str, "2.0" ) )
{
    // OpenGL 2.0 Specific Application Configuration
}
else
{
    // Configuration for other versions of OpenGL
}
free( opengl_version_str );
```

OpenGL Feature Support

Every graphics card has different capabilities with regard to support of OpenGL features. Naturally, the more advanced and modern the graphics card, the more support it has for OpenGL features natively on its graphics processing unit (GPU). Perhaps a bit surprisingly, the software renderer often has the most full-featured support of OpenGL of the possible devices. As a result, and so as to maintain compliance with the OpenGL specification, the software renderer is often called upon by Mac OS OpenGL to handle rendering tasks that the GPU installed in the system cannot. Thus, in many cases, even older Macs have relatively modern versions of OpenGL running on them. However, this also means that you may want to test the performance of crucial graphics features of your application (perhaps the more modern features) on a variety of Macs to ensure they meet your performance needs.

Software developers for OpenGL on the Mac OS don't have the luxury of writing applications that will function on only graphics cards from a single graphics vendor. Fortunately, the additional burden of communicating with different devices is largely shouldered by the implementation of OpenGL on the Mac OS. At the same time, the decision to tailor an application for peak performance or the cutting edge frequently requires reliance on features of specific graphics cards. The choice to specialize is a decision that lies in the hands of the developer and must always be weighed against the size of the customer base that will use the application and have the graphics devices so targeted. We'll explore in Chapter 13 how to take advantage of specific extensions for either performance reasons or feature enhancements.

The architecture of OpenGL on Mac OS also provides developers with a degree of consistency between the two windowing systems available to Mac users: Quartz and X11. Under either windowing system, the Mac OS OpenGL implementation can support multiple heterogeneous graphics cards concurrently and provide a virtualized desktop among multiple graphics devices. This greatly simplifies application development when compared to creating and maintaining display connections for each device installed in the system.

API Layers

OpenGL is defined as an abstracted software interface to graphics hardware. As with most operating systems, OpenGL on the Mac OS is a software layer that interfaces with hardware. Applications and other APIs depend on this layer to provide a common interface to the varied graphics hardware they wish to control. Unlike many operating systems, the Mac allows explicit selection of specific rendering paths and has a few other unique features as well.

On Mac OS, the dependencies between the graphics driver stack layers, and sometimes even just the names of those layers, can be tough to get a handle on. Although OpenGL is defined to remain separate from the windowing system of the operating system on which it runs, OpenGL must implicitly interface with it to observe the rules of drawing in a windowed environment. This need for interaction has a variety of implications, from application performance to window selection, and we'll explore those in later sections. The layering of the various APIs on Mac OS X occurs in a specific way to allow this window–system integration and permit a bit of legacy interoperability. Hence, a few choices must be made when deciding how to open a window for OpenGL rendering on the Mac.

Windowing systems primarily operate on a data structure known in OS X as a "surface." Surfaces are a logical construct that includes the memory and metadata required to act as a destination for rendering. These surfaces may correspond to visible pixels on the display or they may be invisible or off-screen surfaces maintained as a backing store for pixel data. On the Mac OS, four APIs manage or interact with surfaces:

- Core Graphics
- CGL (Core OpenGL)
- AGL (Apple OpenGL)
- AppKit (or Cocoa)

Of these, only Core Graphics is not an OpenGL-specific interface. Of the OpenGL-specific windowing (or surface)-related interfaces, CGL is the lowest logical layer. It provides the most control when managing the interface between OpenGL and the windowing system. GLUT is the highest-level and easiest to use of these layers but has limited UI capabilities. This is followed by the App-Kit (Cocoa) classes, which provide the highest-level fully functional windowing interface to OpenGL on OS X. AGL lies somewhere in between these two extremes and is used primarily by legacy applications or applications that draw their own user interface rather than using the Quartz window system components defined in AppKit. Figure 2-2 is a basic diagram that shows the interaction of these software layers.

There are some simple relationships between the layers in Figure 2-2 and some not-so-simple relationships. For instance, AGL depends on and is defined in terms of CGL commands. Pretty clear so far—this seems like a simple layering with AGL atop CGL. But if you actually look at the CGL headers, there is no (exposed) way for you to perform windowed rendering in CGL! If you're doing *only* full-screen or off-screen rendering, you can work exclusively with CGL commands.

The point here is that there is more to these APIs than meets the eye, and that the exposed API doesn't necessarily allow you the same functionality that the internal APIs can themselves access. We'll go into more detail about the relationships among these APIs in Chapter 5.

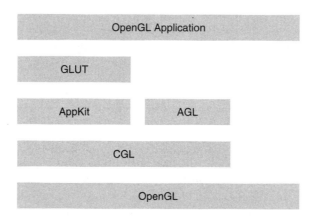

Figure 2-2 AGL, CGL, and AppKit Layered with OpenGL

The Mac OS OpenGL Plug-In Architecture

One important thing that the engineers at Apple responsible for the OpenGL implementation realized early in development was that the computing landscape is constantly under change. Consider just the six major versions of Mac OS X that have emerged since 2001 (Table 2-3). Whether it's market conditions, technical capabilities, costs, or other factors, the OpenGL implementation on OS X has to adapt to a changing environment. Further, because the OS depends so heavily on OpenGL, the implementation has many eyes on its performance. In short, the OpenGL implementation needs to be adaptable, error free, and high performance.

To adapt to the changing environment and to mitigate circumstances that give rise to bugs, the Mac OS OpenGL implementation has been modularized as a plug-in architecture at multiple levels (Figure 2-3). At the highest level, the OpenGL interface is managed as a dispatch table of entry points. These entry points can be changed out according to hints or other environmental factors. The most common reason for changing these entry points arises when you are using CGL macros to reduce the overhead of calling into the OpenGL API itself. (Chapter 6 provides more discussion of CGL macros.)

Beneath the dispatch table, another plug-in layer exists. On OS X, this is referred to as the OpenGL engine layer. This logical abstraction layer is responsible for handling all of the device-independent OpenGL state. The OpenGL engine layer checks the error state, maintains any client state required by the OpenGL specification, and is responsible for assembling OpenGL commands into a buffer for submission to the underlying renderer. By logically separating this set of functionality at the OpenGL engine layer, entire OpenGL engines can be loaded or unloaded so as to most efficiently leverage the underlying CPU platform. The multithreaded OpenGL engine announced at WWDC 2006 and available for Leopard is an example of a functional module that can be selected for the OpenGL engine interface.

Below the OpenGL engine exists another plug-in architecture for loading renderers. These driver plug-ins are the most dynamic set of the various plug-in

Table 2-3 Timeline of Mac OS X Releases, Drawing APIs, and Windowing APIs

Mac OS Version	Code Name	Release Date
10.0	Cheetah	March 24, 2001
10.1	Puma	September 25, 2001
10.2	Jaguar	August 24, 2002
10.3	Panther	October 24, 2003
10.4	Tiger	April 29, 2005
10.5	Leopard	October, 2007

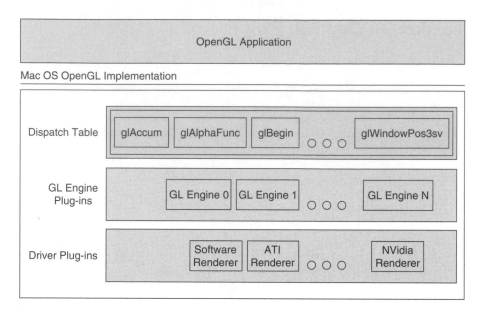

Figure 2-3 The Mac OS OpenGL Plug-in Architecture

layers, for two reasons:

- Plug-ins are selectable directly by the application at pixel format selection time.
- Plug-ins are changed out according to the physical screen on which the application resides.

Underlying your OpenGL application at any given time is a chain of logical modules linked together to service your application according to its needs and the environment in which the application is running.

Renderers

In the Mac OS drawing layers, we've started from the top and discussed what Apple calls the "Windowing Layer." Any drawing or drawing state calls made into AGL, CGL, and the Cocoa Classes are deemed "Windowing Layer" calls.

Beneath this layer, and getting closer to the metal, is the Renderer Layer. A renderer is the primary term used to describe the software object (or structure) that graphics applications will interface with to perform rendering on OS X. Each renderer represents a set of capabilities in terms of being able to process and execute OpenGL commands. Renderers may or may not be associated with a hardware device. They are configured, created, maintained, and destroyed in CGL.

Earlier we discussed the very capable software renderer—a purely software path for rendering OpenGL commands. Hardware renderers are associated with specific hardware devices and accordingly have the graphics processing capabilities of those devices. One of the more notable capabilities of today's graphics cards is their ability to drive multiple physical displays. Accordingly, the renderers associated with these devices support multiple displays as well. In OS X, each physical display has an associated software virtual screen. Renderers are always associated with exactly one virtual screen. Macs configured with more than one graphics card will always have more than one virtual screen.

Note that the Mac OS provides a mechanism to configure a virtualized desktop from more than one graphics device. This virtual desktop allows users to drag applications across the boundaries of the displays supported by the installed display devices seamlessly. For your application, this means that an OpenGL window can be dragged from one virtual screen to another, each of which has different rendering capabilities! In this event, CGL will automatically switch the renderer you are interacting with to a renderer representing the new territory that your application now occupies.

This feature has obvious implications if this new renderer does not have the same capabilities as your original renderer. If your application then proceeds to draw but now lacks the capabilities it relies upon to render, all kinds of unpleasant things could be displayed! For example, one consequence might be that your application is running on a renderer that has half the texture resources, or that your application is running with a surface that doesn't have stencil capability. If you relied on having stencil capability for some form of pixel test, your application may not be able to get those results computed on this new renderer. In the texture case, your application may suddenly begin swapping textures in and out of graphics memory with each frame, yielding dramatically slower performance. Of course, the most extensive set of consequences from changing virtual screens could relate to a raw OpenGL capability change. It's possible that an OpenGL extension you were using on one screen will be unavailable on another screen.

Fortunately, the Mac OS X software architecture will switch renderers for your application to meet its needs automatically. For example, if the user moves your application's window from a screen supported by a higher-performance graphics device such as a high-end ATI Radeon to a screen supported by a lesser-performance graphics device, Mac OS X OpenGL can switch from using the Intel GPU to its native software renderer and perform your rendering on the host CPU. This performance is much slower, of course, but at least it provides your application with logic capable of producing the correct output.

Whenever an application crosses a virtual screen boundary, it must make a call to synchronize its OpenGL context across the two different renderers. In other words, the context should be synchronized whenever your application windows are moved. This is due to the fact that in addition to the OpenGL context that you manage, every OpenGL application has a context that is maintained in the OpenGL runtime engine. This context holds all of the application's OpenGL rendering state. The renderer for each virtual screen also contains a context of rendering state.

When an application crosses a virtual screen boundary, the renderer is implicitly changed by CGL. At this time the new renderer doesn't know what's going on with the application's rendering state. The explicit or implicit call to CGLUpdateContext serves to synchronize the new renderer state to that of the application context. The call to CGLUpdateContext or aglUpdateContext must be done explicitly with Carbon applications but is done implicitly, on your behalf, with Cocoa applications.

A word of caution here: Because implicit calls are made by the AppKit classes that modify the internal graphics context state of a renderer, serious thread safety issues arise that must be considered. If, for instance, your application has a drawing thread that is modifying your application context, while in another thread your NSOpenGLView instance is implicitly issuing calls to synchronize your application context with that of the renderer, memory corruption and a crash will likely result. To avoid these thread safety issues, CGLLockContext and CGLUnlockContext can be called to resolve thread contention issues. You can find out more about these functions in Chapter 6.

In addition to context synchronization, there is another key aspect to handling virtual screen changes. If you plan to allow your application to move between virtual screens (that is, between different graphics devices), you must create a pixel format that is compatible with all graphics cards installed on the system. In CGL, this is done by using a display mask (the kCGLPFADisplayMask attribute). You'll find more information on display masks in Chapter 6.

So we now must consider this common question: "What happens when my application is straddling two different renderers?" In this case, whichever renderer's virtual screen has the majority of the application's OpenGL windows real estate is called upon to perform the rendering in full. In other words, if your application has an OpenGL rendering area, and that window straddles two virtual screens, the virtual screen/renderer that would be responsible for rendering more than 50 percent of those pixels renders *all* the pixels. The remaining pixels that are on the minority virtual screen are filled in by a copy operation from the renderer associated with the majority virtual screen. There are obvious performance consequences when such copying takes place. The good news is that there is no performance penalty for having and using multiple virtual screens as long as your application's OpenGL rendering area resides entirely within one of them.

Choosing a renderer is the first logical step in creating an OpenGL application for Mac OS. Several APIs are available to set up renderers on Mac OS, including GLUT, CGL and AGL, and you can also use the OpenGL-capable Cocoa View classes defined in AppKit. These methods of setting up a renderer for your application are described in detail in Chapters 6, 7, and 8, respectively.

Drivers

The lowest layer in the rendering software hierarchy is the driver layer. This layer contains all of the device-specific logic for the installed graphics hardware of the system. The driver layer buffers rendering commands and rendering state commands until it becomes necessary to send them across the system bus to the graphics hardware. The graphics hardware will then respond to the commands by changing its rendering state, uploading or downloading data to system memory, or rendering to the display. The driver also performs caching of recently used data, manages data flow for cached data (e.g., display lists, vertex buffers, and textures), and essentially does all the talking to and from the hardware.

As an application writer, it is important that you understand the basic functions of the driver layer when you are tuning performance or, on occasion, submitting bug reports. When using diagnostic tools from the CHUD framework (discussed in detail later), you may see functions show up in a trace that are clearly reminiscent of a particular type of graphics hardware. We'll discuss and interpret traces into the OpenGL drivers in Chapter 11.

Summary

The software architecture of OpenGL on Mac OS X reflects both the history and the future of OpenGL as well as the diverse and ever-changing Mac hardware platform itself.

From the dispatch table down to the device-specific driver modules, a basic understanding of the logical modules of the OpenGL implementation on Mac OS X is the key to efficient usage of the software architecture as a whole. Understanding these software modules and their interactions will aid you in debugging and allow you to make the most effective choices when configuring your application.

Chapter 3

Mac Hardware
Architecture

Overview

We'll now step back from the software side of things and look at hardware. Most modern personal computers have at least two large processors in them; a central processing unit (CPU) and a graphics processing unit (GPU—a term coined in the late 1990s). In 2001, the number of transistors in GPUs caught up with and surpassed the number within CPUs. Although this feat is in large part a result of parallel logic in the GPUs, it still speaks loudly to the fact that more and more processing in today's computers is happening on the GPU. These are exciting times to be a graphics developer!

Now that there are more transistors on the GPU than on the CPU, graphics developers have been looking at many different ways to push computation to the GPU. This trend toward more processing on the GPU was greatly catalyzed by the introduction of programmable shaders in the late 1990s. Shading and high-level shading languages opened the door to performing more generalized computing tasks on the GPU. A necessary complement to complex shading was a place to store those high-precision results. That need gave rise to the development of floating-point framebuffers. The lack of precision storage was a significant barrier to generalized computing on the GPU but is no longer an obstacle. Furthermore, recent GPUs have been chipping away at other barriers, such as conditionals, loops, rendering to multiple surfaces simultaneously, and entirely virtualized shading engines. General-purpose computing on GPUs (GPGPU) is a growing topic of importance in the graphics world.

The overall hardware architecture of today's Macs consists of one or more CPUs with memory, a GPU with memory, and a bus over which the two communicate. Macs, like PCs, have a CPU northbridge and southbridge. The northbridge is the

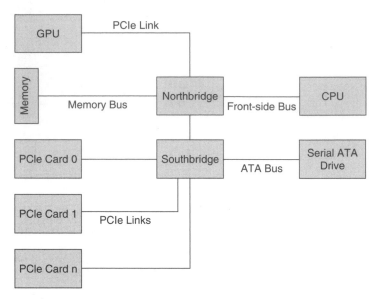

Figure 3-1 Prototypical System Architecture Diagram

pathway to the memory controller and memory. The southbridge is the pathway to all other devices installed in the system, including PCI, AGP, and PCI Express (Peripheral Component Interconnect) devices such as graphics cards.

In this chapter, we'll dig into the hardware architecture of modern and historical Macintoshes to provide context relevant to graphics developers. We'll point out some obvious bottlenecks and some ways of considering data flow within a system so as to maximize graphics performance. Armed with a few observations about hardware and how your software interacts with it, you'll be much better prepared for developing high-performance applications now and in the future.

Figure 3-1 presents a schematic of a typical system's architecture. The reason we point this out, even at this very abstract level, is to help you understand where your graphics data lives and flows in a modern Mac. Understanding how the CPU in your Mac communicates with and transfers data to and from the GPU will help you optimize your graphics applications on Mac OS.

Data Flow and Limitations

It's important to understand hardware architecture when evaluating how a graphics application runs on a specific system. We will cover performance-tuning case studies and methods in Chapter 11 but felt it worthwhile to discuss some macro-level concepts of graphics software performance considerations here in the hardware architecture chapter. Our intention is to identify some of the general classes of performance problems that graphics applications face and to suggest how well (or badly) the available hardware solves these problems. Specifically, it's necessary to understand the fundamental limits of the various processing units, buffers, and busses through which the application's data will pass.

There are two primary types of data in OpenGL: pixels and vertices. Each type of data has a different logical flow through the system and can, therefore, be subjected to different hardware and software limitations. We'll begin where your data originates, and walk through the process of getting that data to the GPU for rendering.

We'll first look at your chunk of data, either pixels or vertices, to be rendered. We'll assume that you've not loaded your data yet, so it currently lives on a disk somewhere. Beginning by loading your data from disk, if there is not enough system memory to hold the data resident, then you must take the disk I/O limit into account.

Once the data is in the system memory, a memory bandwidth limit between the CPU and the memory itself becomes important. Understanding system caching and using it efficiently is key here. If the data is being streamed, managing the caches becomes less significant. However, if you are frequently revisiting the same data, keeping the CPU caches "hot" is critical to application performance.

When the data is in the primary cache of the CPU, the next limitation may well be the instruction throughput, which relates directly to the clock rate of the CPU itself. This constraint (and more loosely memory and cache access) is often described as being "CPU bound." Being CPU bound has two forms: bound by code inside the application or bound by code inside the graphics system software of the Mac.

After being processed by the CPU, the data is transferred to the GPU. During this process, it may encounter a bandwidth limit between CPU and GPU. When your application hits this limit, it is referred to as "upload limited" (sometimes "download limited," depending on if you view things differently) based on the constraints of both setting up and transferring data between the host and graphics processor.

Once your data is on the GPU, however, the graphics processor can directly process the uploaded data for display or store it in VRAM. If the application overcommits the VRAM by, for instance, defining a great deal of vertex, texture, or framebuffer objects, the data will be continuously paged in, as needed, from the host CPU/memory subsystem. The upload limit becomes a key bottleneck at this point.

We have now described the various forms of bottlenecks that can arise in getting your data from the disk to the graphics. To review, the main data flow bottlenecks your application will face from the system perspective are as follows:

- Disk I/O
- Memory I/O
- CPU I/O
- GPU I/O

Modern graphics cards internally look a lot like the host CPU architecture. That is, they have a memory controller, sometimes several processors, a main memory with various caches, busses connecting the various components, and a bunch of other plumbing.

Let's consider the processing of vertex data first. On older graphics cards, the notion of being "transform limited" was quite common. This limit describes the required time to transform in space, clip, and light vertices in the scene. With the degree of parallelism in today's CPU, this has become a less common bottleneck for all but the heaviest users of geometry. However, shaders now allow people to perform increasingly complex calculations during vertex transformation, so this bottleneck should not be discounted—you can still become bottlenecked by this phase.

The other primary data type, pixels (or texels, as pixels are known if they consist of texture data), encounters performance limits during rendering as well. When an application has to rasterize or "fill" a large amount of screen real estate, the application may become "fill limited." The term "fill" originates from the need to fill polygons with pixels when drawing them. These rasterization-stage output pixels are known as fragments in OpenGL. However, fill doesn't necessarily just refer to the fragments that you see; it also implies all the secondary data that is rendered per pixel, including stencil, depth, alpha, and other capabilities of the visual you're using. In short, a lot of secondary data is moved around for every pixel that ends up reaching the fragment engines, and too many fragments being processed can lead to a fill limitation. Fill-limited applications are quite common these days, although not necessarily for your application. As always, you will need to evaluate your specific application for this risk.

The ultimate destination of the data in a graphics application is the display on which it will be shown. These devices have their own limits in terms of refresh rate or response time that will affect how fast you can render your graphics. A common performance problem with graphics applications and monitor refresh rate occurs when your application only achieves frame rates that are some integer multiple of the refresh rate. For example, your monitor may be refreshing at 60Hz, but your application only sees 30Hz or 20Hz; that is, you never see

27Hz, or 34Hz, or 19Hz—only integer multiples. This is due to an effect called "frame rate quantization," which we'll explore briefly in Chapter 11.

Problem Domains

Each domain from which a graphics application originates tends to have its own points of early saturation limits for general-purpose graphics hardware like the Mac. Here are some examples:

- Gaming: CPU bound when computing the physics of the characters and objects in their scenes.
- Video editing: Upload limited when manipulating multiple high-definition streams of video during transitions between video streams.
- CAD, CAE, and modeling: Transform limited. This software will take constructive solid geometry or surface models and create incredibly dense meshes of tetrahedra or other 3D primitives for the purpose of stress analysis by finite element engines. Each of these 3D primitives is represented by polygons that must be transformed to manipulate the model.
- Medical imaging/volume rendering: Fill limited. Arrays of 2D image scans from medical or seismic, oil and gas equipment are reconstructed into three dimensions by this software for analysis. These arrays of images are rasterized into large polygons for display and impose an enormous fill burden on the system.

It is important to approach graphics application development with a good understanding of the limits of your domain and to design your application, its logic, and its data structures accordingly. Keep in mind that once you eliminate a bottleneck, some other portion of the system will inevitably provide a new bottleneck: It's always an iterative process, and one in which you'll need to invest some time to get the best results.

Know Thine OS Requirements

Any modern application you write will likely have to support multiple versions of the Mac OS. It's obviously easiest to support only one version, but your customers will likely have multiple versions, which you must then accommodate. If your application is expected to run on multiple Mac OSs such as Panther, Tiger, or Leopard, each will have a different set of features, capabilities, and baseline requirements. For your application, whether based on OpenGL or not, understanding these baselines will have consequences for your software. For this reason, each of these operating systems is published with a set of minimum system requirements. Naturally, the minimum configuration is the most restrictive system that you will have to support and is what your application should be most concerned about. This section explores some of these baselines and explains their implications for your application.

CPU and Clock Rate

Consider this minimum configuration example with regard to CPU and clock rate: On Mac OS 10.3 (also known as Panther), the minimum required CPU is a 300MHz G3 processor, 128MB of RAM, and no explicit requirements on VRAM of the graphics card. What does it mean to you if the system has a G3 processor? Aside from clock rates being lower, we know that a G3 processor has no vector engines to process AltiVec code. If your application requires intense vector code to sustain a minimum frame rate of 30 frames per second (FPS), it's not going to perform well—or maybe even at all—on a G3. (Note that G3 support was dropped in Leopard.)

Also, you should recognize that the lack of a vector engine will create some nonlinearities in what might be expected of a system based on its clock rate alone. For instance, if performance on a G3-based system was estimated simply by scaling the performance on a test run carried out on a G4, you may be in for some surprises. To further aggravate these results, the Mac OS software *itself* relies heavily on the AltiVec engines wherever possible. In the absence of these vector units, the performance bottleneck of your application could shift from somewhere in the graphics processing to the CPU.

How about having a G4 as a minimum requirement? A G4 does get you some on-chip vector engines, but does your application do a great deal of high-precision or 64-bit math? If so, then the G4 may not be sufficient, but G5 and IA64-capable Intel CPU performance results are going to be very good.

Establishing the processor baseline will also give you some clues about the available graphics bandwidth of the system. For instance, no Mac system with a G3 processor supports greater than AGP 1x. No Mac system with a G4 processor supports greater than AGP 4x. G5 processor-based Macs support up to AGP 8x and PCI Express. Intel-based Macs support PCI Express throughout the product line and have different characteristics for memory bandwidth as well. The point here is that it's important to consider the data rates that your application may request of (and realistically attain from) the system. By knowing the basic system CPU, you can make a few assumptions about how much bandwidth is available.

Bus

Two primary busses come into play with today's Mac computers: the memory bus and the graphics bus.

Memory

The physical data path between main memory, the CPU, and other subsystems is known as the memory bus. The memory bus is the primary path over which data flows when it is being loaded to and from a disk, a network, or graphics. Memory bus speeds are implicitly related to the performance of the CPU, so knowing one gives insight into the other. Historically, there has always been an even multiplier between the clock rate of the memory bus and that of the CPU such as a 2.5GHz processor using a 1.25GHz bus.

A very common scenario where the memory bus affects applications is as a result of implicit data copies. By "implicit," we mean that within the framework, the OpenGL runtime engine and graphics drivers make copies of your data during the processing of that data for rendering. You don't explicitly do anything in your application except use a data type that has to be transformed into a card-native format. Several additional copies of your data may be created, causing both valuable memory and valuable memory bus bandwidth to be used.

Consider the architecture of a theoretical system containing two processors (one CPU and one GPU) and two banks of memory (RAM and VRAM). The memory for graphics data is initially allocated by the application itself and passed to one of the OpenGL functions. When the OpenGL function is called, the OpenGL runtime engine may make a copy of the data, the graphics driver may make a copy of the data, and a copy of the data may be created in VRAM. With so many data copies taking place, the memory bus becomes very busy.

For more information on controlling when and where data is copied in the Mac OS OpenGL implementation, see the texture range extension and vertex data copy information in Chapter 11.

Graphics

The latest graphics bus available on the Mac platform as of this writing is PCI Express. Prior to PCI Express, modern Macs used the AGP (Advanced Graphics Port) bus. The AGP bus has been around since 1997, when it was originally developed by Intel. As we discussed a bit in the prior section on memory busses, there's a strong correlation between CPU type and graphics bus type. Table 3-1 shows this correlation.

The bandwidth numbers listed in Table 3-1 describe the theoretical maximum throughput numbers. None of these numbers accounts for the protocol (AGP or PCI Express) overhead implicit in managing the bus traffic. For instance, the theoretical maximum bandwidth for 16-lane PCI Express is approximately 3.4GB/s when accounting for bus protocol overhead. If you then include the overhead of managing and transferring OpenGL command and data packets,

Table 3-1 Processor Type and Graphics Bus Pairing

CPU	Bus	Bandwidth (MB/s)
G3	AGP 1X	256
G4	AGP 4X	1024
G5	AGP 8X	2048
G5	16-lane PCI Express	4096
CoreDuo/Core2Duo	16-lane PCI Express	4096
Xeon	16-lane PCI Express	4096

the realizable data bandwidth throughput to these devices is approximately 2.2GB/s on modern hardware.

Despite the copious amounts of bandwidth available on modern hardware, the graphics bus can still become a bottleneck. This problem is much less likely if proper care is used to manage data copying, as described previously. However, if you're downloading or updating a movie, or animating geometry, you will most likely be transferring data per frame—there is no way around that. There are only two solutions when the limits of the graphics bus are reached. First, you can send less data using lower-fidelity images, compressed textures, or decimated models. Alternatively, you can distribute the graphics data transfers over a longer time span. That is, you can spread the data you're downloading among multiple frames of rendering. You sometimes see the results of a technique like this as a progressive improvement in image fidelity over several frames rendered, as more and higher-fidelity models and textures are transferred and rendered.

A third bus also has relevance for graphics programmers: the bus bandwidth available on the actual graphics card on which you're rendering. Most modern graphics hardware have much faster busses than either the graphics or memory busses described thus far. Typically, these are approximately an order of magnitude faster than their counterparts farther upstream. Current GPUs have memory bandwidths in the 10s of gigabytes per second. In most applications, you probably won't be bound by this bus, but, as always, it's possible to get bottlenecked here as well. Never say never! It's vastly more common to see an application have difficulties managing data computation, copies, and transfer to the graphics card.

Video Memory: VRAM

Video memory on graphics hardware is a complex and opaque topic. Modern graphics cards have lots of video memory—amounts that for old-timers in the computing industry were once large amounts to have on complete computing systems, let alone subsystems like graphics. Even so, these large buffers are used for lots of tasks, including not just display of resultant images but also storage of various graphics data, from textures to geometry to the framebuffer itself. We'll explore some of the issues you should consider about VRAM from a hardware perspective in this section.

Why does Mac OS 10.2 (also known as Jaguar) have a minimum VRAM requirement, while Mac OS 10.1 does not? With the introduction of OS X and Quartz 2D, Apple moved from a simple planar windowing environment to a composited 3D window system. Today, everything you see—windows, icons, the dock, and so on—is floating in 3D space on the Mac desktop. What once were simple pixel maps now have representation as textures in VRAM.

This means that the OS is capable of a unique and rich user experience, albeit at a cost. Quartz 2D, the main system 2D graphics rendering engine, is also an OpenGL application and competes with your application for some of the same graphics system resources.

Leopard continued to push forward with OpenGL usage, introducing Quartz 2D Extreme, which fully accelerated the Quartz layer in OpenGL. This feature of the OS has pushed VRAM requirements into another echelon previously unknown to personal computer operating systems. Quartz 2D Extreme is more or less a wholesale replacement of the CPU/RAM backing store of the user desktop. Virtually everything displayed on your screen is rendered and stored on the GPU—even individual glyphs are cached in VRAM! Undoubtedly, with the enormous computing potential of modern GPUs and ever-larger VRAM configurations of these GPUs, the trend toward shifting the burden of the visual process to the GPU is expected to continue. If it does, you can expect the video card minimum specifications to rise accordingly in the future.

The VRAM consideration is less important for full-screen applications that essentially take over the graphics hardware, as they can swap out all the other visual data from the GPU. However, if your application runs in a window, you must take care to ensure it doesn't require all of the OS's minimum VRAM requirements to run. If so, you'll end up competing with the OS frequently for precious GPU resources and consequently suffer poor performance.

RAM

Beginning with Mac OS Tiger, the minimum system RAM requirements were raised from 128MB to 256MB. In one sense, this led to a sigh of relief from application developers—that is, unless you had less free memory on your 256MB-configured Tiger or Leopard system than was available on your 128MB-configured Panther system. Historically, each new version of the OS has used more than the previous version. Monitoring and quantifying the available system memory in a minimally configured and quiescent Mac using the utility application Activity Monitor or Big Top can give you a basis for determining how much free memory you can reasonably expect to have available. Doing so early in your development cycle may help you later diagnose memory-related performance headaches.

Summary

Graphics application writers should have a solid understanding of the often well-known hardware limitations for the software they are writing or intend to write. If your application will handle a great deal of vertices, you should anticipate the effects of potential transform or shader limitations for these vertices and design your software and data structures accordingly. Similarly, if your application is heavier on the back end of the OpenGL pipeline, where heavy rasterization is required, you can program defensively for those limits. In either case, knowing the overall VRAM requirements of your application, the VRAM requirements of Mac OS X itself, and the available VRAM of the target hardware is as important to application performance as a consideration of the general system's RAM.

The hardware landscape for Macs is quite diverse. Nevertheless, it's essential to get a handle on these configurations so that you can develop applications that are highly optimized, yet usable on a rather diverse class of Mac hardware.

Chapter 4

Application
Programming
on OS X

Overview

The OS X revolution of the Mac operating system began in 2001. Darwin, the open-source core of OS X, is derived from Berkeley Systems Division (BSD) Unix. The introduction of a Unix core has had a profound—and arguably positive—effect on software developers for the platform. Along with the time-tested and industry standardized architecture of Unix, its multiprocessing capabilities, and advanced virtual memory semantics came the diverse and powerful shell programming environment, libraries, and tools familiar to Unix application developers. The addition of scripting environments such as Perl, Ruby, and Python can further catalyze the development and testing process.

The X11 window system is also supported on OS X. With an industry standard OS kernel, windowing system, and graphics API, graphics applications written on other Unix platforms can be ported to OS X with relative ease.

Mac OS X Versions

Mac OS X has gone through several major iterations and many more minor iterations during its life so far. Each minor release number for OS X represents a large chunk of functionality. Releases such as 10.1, 10.2, and 10.3 represent at least a year of engineering time for Apple. Another way to think of it is that each time there's a new cat—such as Panther, Tiger, or Leopard—assigned to a designated OS X, it represents a substantial software release for the OS.

In the developer community, and sometimes even in the popular press, these major-release versions are interchangeably referred to by their code names. Because we have been working on Mac OS X for years, these names are an innate part of our lexicon, but we want to make sure we're not confusing you,

Table 4-1 Mac OS X Versions and Code Names

Version Number	Code Name
10.0	Cheetah
10.1	Puma
10.2	Jaguar
10.3	Panther
10.4	Tiger
10.5	Leopard
10.6	Ocelot? Manx? Margay? Serval?

dear reader. So, for your viewing, edification, and entertainment, we present in Table 4-1 a list of the Mac OS version numbers and release names current as of this publishing. For fun, we've added some speculative suggestions for future versions, too.

System Configuration

You can determine which GPU core your machine has by using the Apple System Profiler. Go under the Apple menu and select "About this Mac ...". Click the "More Info ..." button. Under the hardware list, you will see a category for PCI/AGP cards. An ATI part will have a label such as `ATY,Radeon X1600`. We'll discuss in detail both how this information can be programmatically queried and how these tools work later in this book. Specifically, programmatic inquiry of hardware capabilities is discussed in Chapter 13, and tools for inspecting and analyzing your OpenGL code and environment are explored in Chapter 11.

Power Management

The Mac OS can be configured so as to conserve power by putting the CPU, the display, and the hard drive to sleep. Many application writers do not need to be concerned about the sleep semantics on the Mac. If, however, your application needs to respond to the sleep, powering-up, or powering-down events, we thought we would include some of the essentials here.

From a device driver perspective, consideration of power management can be rather complex. Fortunately, for user applications, the task is much simpler. The power management API is designed to accommodate a hierarchical set of power domains. For application development, the root power domain, which covers all system sleep and power-on events, is all you will likely need to consider.

For symmetry, it is easiest to consider power-on events as wake-up events. Sometimes, these events may be misunderstood to mean the system has powered up from an off state, based on the naming conventions used. In reality, a wake-up event means that the system is coming out of a low-power mode and is notifying your application of that state change.

So now that we have the sleep and wake-up terminology straight, let's consider sleep events. There are two kinds: active sleep events, which are generated from the user selecting the "Sleep" option in the Apple menu, and idle sleep events, which occur in response to an inactive system. Example 4-1 shows an example of power management code on the Mac.

Example 4-1   Power Management on OS X

```
#include <stdio.h>
#include <mach/mach_interface.h>
#include <mach/mach_init.h>
#include <IOKit/pwr_mgt/IOPMLib.h>
#include <IOKit/IOMessage.h>

io_connect_t  root_port;

void callback(void *x, io_service_t y,
              natural_t messageType,
              void *messageArgument)
{
    float z = *((float *) x);

    printf("z = %6.2f\n", z);

    switch ( messageType )
{
    case kIOMessageSystemWillSleep:
        printf("SystemWillSleep\n");
        // Here can either cancel or allow
        // IOCancelPowerChange(root_port, (long) messageArgument);
        IOAllowPowerChange(root_port,(long)messageArgument);
        break;
    case kIOMessageCanSystemSleep:
        printf("CanSystemSleep\n");
        // Here can either cancel or allow
        IOCancelPowerChange(root_port, (long) messageArgument);
        // IOAllowPowerChange(root_port,(long)messageArgument);
        break;
    case kIOMessageServiceIsTerminated:
        printf("ServiceIsTerminated\n");
        break;
    case kIOMessageServiceIsSuspended:
        printf("ServiceIsSuspended\n");
        break;
    case kIOMessageServiceIsResumed:
        printf("ServiceIsResumed\n");
        break;
```

```
        case kIOMessageServiceIsRequestingClose:
            printf("ServiceIsRequestingClose\n");
            break;
        case kIOMessageServiceIsAttemptingOpen:
            printf("ServiceIsAttemptingOpen\n");
            break;
        case kIOMessageServiceWasClosed:
            printf("ServiceWasClosed\n");
            break;
        case kIOMessageServiceBusyStateChange:
            printf("ServiceBusyStateChange\n");
            break;
        case kIOMessageServicePropertyChange:
            printf("ServicePropertyStateChange\n");
            break;
    case kIOMessageCanDevicePowerOff:
        printf("CanDevicePowerOff\n");
        break;
    case kIOMessageDeviceWillPowerOff:
        printf("DeviceWillPowerOff\n");
        break;
    case kIOMessageDeviceWillNotPowerOff:
        printf("DeviceWillNotPowerOff\n");
        break;
    case kIOMessageDeviceHasPoweredOn:
        printf("DeviceHasPoweredOn\n");
        break;
    case kIOMessageCanSystemPowerOff:
        printf("CanSystemPowerOff\n");
        break;
    case kIOMessageSystemWillPowerOff:
        printf("SystemWillPowerOff\n");
        break;
    case kIOMessageSystemWillNotPowerOff:
        printf("SystemWillNotPowerOff\n");
        break;
    case kIOMessageSystemWillNotSleep:
        printf("SystemWillNotSleep\n");
        break;
    case kIOMessageSystemHasPoweredOn:
        printf("SystemHasPoweredOn\n");
        break;
    case kIOMessageSystemWillRestart:
        printf("SystemWillRestart\n");
        break;
    case kIOMessageSystemWillPowerOn:
        printf("SystemWillPowerOn\n");
        break;
    default:
        IOAllowPowerChange(root_port, (long) messageArgument);
        printf("messageType %08lx, arg %08lx\n",
                (long unsigned int)messageType,
                (long unsigned int) messageArgument);
    }
```

```
}

int main(int argc, char **argv)
{
    IONotificationPortRef   notify;
    io_object_t             anIterator;
    float x = 5.81;

root_port = IORegisterForSystemPower (&x,&notify,callback,&anIterator);

if ( root_port == 0 )
{
    printf("IORegisterForSystemPower failed\n");
    return 1;
}
CFRunLoopAddSource(CFRunLoopGetCurrent(),
                   IONotificationPortGetRunLoopSource(notify),
                   kCFRunLoopDefaultMode);

    printf("waiting...\n\n");

    CFRunLoopRun();

    return 0;
}
```

Two OS X frameworks are central to the handling of sleep events: CoreFoundation and IOKit. In particular, CoreFoundation is responsible for dispatching sleep and other system events. IOKit is used, in this case, to register your application as a listener for these events.

The first step in the example is to write a callback routine that will handle power management events that conform to the `IOServiceInterestCallback` prototype:

- `userData` is data that can be sent to the handler when registering the callback with `IORegisterForSystemPower`.
- `service` is the IOService whose state changed and resulted in the callback being invoked.
- `msg` is the actual `msg`, or type of power event.
- `msgArg` is qualifying information for the message that, practically speaking, is used to respond to the power event.

As far as this callback is concerned, aside from any housekeeping your application may want to do, there are two possible responses the system is looking for: allowing the power state change or disallowing the power state change. This is where things get deceiving. The truth is that the only time you can disallow a power state change is when an idle sleep event occurs. In this case, your application will be sent a `kIOMessageCanSystemSleep` message. In response to this message, your application can cancel the power state change with a call to `IOCancelPowerChange`.

In other words, if the user asks the system to sleep from the Apple menu, calling `IOCancelPowerChange` will have no effect. In fact, for an active sleep request on the part of the user, your application will not receive a `kIOMessageCanSystemSleep` message as an event. You can, however, delay the power event in any sleep scenario. If you choose not to respond to a power event with either `IOAllowPowerChange` or `IOCancelPowerChange`, the system will wait 30 seconds before effecting the power state change. By adding a default condition on the power event switch, you will avoid this 30-second delay on messages that you had not explicitly written logic to handle.

The second and final step specific to handling power events is to request notifications of them from the CoreFoundation run loop. When a sleeping Mac wakes up, your power event handler will first receive a `kIOMessageSystemWillPowerOn` message and shortly after will receive a `kIOMessageSystemHasPoweredOn` message.

For graphics applications, it is a good idea to consider calling `CGLUpdate-Context` when your application receives power-on events. If, for instance, a display was removed from the system while it was sleeping, the system will do an implicit renderer change if your application was occupying the display that was removed. In this case, you want to force a synchronization between the OpenGL context of your application and that of the new renderer.

Filesystem

There are a few surprises in store for Unix users who move to the Mac OS for the first time. From a user or an application developer perspective, the biggest difference is case insensitivity in the most common filesystem, HFS (and HFS+). The problem to be aware of here is that HFS is case preserving but not case sensitive. Thus, to the filesystem, you can create and save a file named `Foo`, but later access that file by opening `foo`. That makes for some tricky errors, if you're not aware of that distinction. The Mac also supports a number of other filesystems natively, including a few that are both case sensitive *and* case preserving. Again, when accessing files on the Mac, it's imperative to ensure that the file you asked for is really the file you received.

From an administrative perspective, the tools used to manage and configure the filesystem on the Mac OS are likely to be considerably different from the tools available on other Unix workstations you may have used, simply due to the diversity of filesystems available.

Finding, Verifying, and Filing Bugs

Occasionally, while writing or porting your OpenGL application to OS X, you may suspect you've found a bug in the OpenGL implementation or other parts of the Mac OS. One great thing about the Apple OpenGL team is that they want to help you succeed with your application on the Mac. With a collaborative effort, you'll get great results.

If you're inclined to file an OpenGL bug, here are a few tips to support your report. First, check the GL error state when you're finished rendering a frame. You can do so by adding the code to your application and recompiling or, even easier, use the OpenGL Profiler application to break on OpenGL errors for you. You can simply open the breakpoint view and check the "Break on Error" option. Your goal in this step is to ensure that you're not causing an OpenGL error. That is, you're trying to validate that the bug actually lies in the rendering, not in your usage of OpenGL.

The next step you can take to provide fortifying data for a bug report is to try the new software renderer. You do so by selecting the `kCGLRendererGenericFloatID` as your renderer ID. See Chapters 6, 7, and 8 for more information on choosing different renderers.

Once you've chosen the software renderer, compare the results you got when rendering with the hardware renderer you were using. If the results are the same, the problem most likely lies in your software rather than in Apple's. If they're different, Apple will want to know about it.

You can also try your application out on different cards from different vendors to fortify your bug report. In particular, you may want to test your application on one machine—say, a laptop with an ATI part—and then compare the results with running your application on another machine—for example, a desktop that has an NVIDIA part.

To qualify your bug a step further, and if you have the machines at your disposal, you can test your application on different GPU cores from the same graphics hardware vendor. By and large, if you've tested your application on one GPU core from a specific vendor, you're going to get the same results on other GPUs that use the same core.

When filing bugs, it's imperative that you've verified that your application is not relying on undefined behavior. Apple sees many bug reports filed where a developer has written code that depends on OpenGL behavior that is explicitly declared as undefined in the OpenGL specification. When behavior is specified to be undefined, all bets are off. You truly don't know what you're going to get for a rendering, and Apple isn't going to be able to fix your problem.

Perhaps even more common than bugs filed where applications rely on undefined behavior are bugs filed that state "Application X runs on OS 10.x.y, but not on OS 10.x.z," where z is a later revision than y. From a developer's perspective, this can feel like a certainty that there is a bug in OS 10.x.z. This may well be the case, but consider this: The Mac OS OpenGL implementation gets stricter in its compliance with the OpenGL specification (and arguably better) with each release. If an application begins to misbehave after a software update, often this is because the application wasn't strictly adhering to the OpenGL specification. That said, it's entirely possible a regression was introduced with the software update; again, Apple is eager to hear about such a problem.

A closely related cousin to this type of filing is the bug that is filed with the rationale that "It works on this other platform; therefore it must be broken on OS X." This may be the case. It may also be the case that the other platform is more lax in its compliance with the specification and is allowing behavior that it probably shouldn't. In any case, this is a great data point for a bug filing but isn't the proverbial "nail in the coffin" for identifying the source of the bug.

Suppose you've done some due diligence, and now you're ready to file a bug. Here are some tips to get satisfaction for your efforts. First, realize there are a few layers of Apple engineers involved when it comes to bug processing. When a bug report is filed, it is screened by the developer program to see if it can resolve the problem. If not, the report will be sent to the appropriate engineering group within Apple. That group will also have a screener. The engineering group screener knows what everyone is working on within the group and will dispatch the bug to the appropriate engineer. By now, I hope you can see where I'm going with this: Given the many people and many schedules involved, it can take quite a while to validate and assign your bug.

You will want to short-circuit this process as much as possible by providing as much essential information as possible. Honing your bug report, as described earlier, by trying different renderers, trying different graphics cards, checking the GL error state, and so on is a great start. The next thing is to specify the precise steps to reproduce the bug. If you have a very complex environment requiring a sophisticated license mechanism or hardware dongles, see if you can pry the problem out of this environment and make it reproducible in a more simple setting.

Other essential information includes the OS X build number, which can be obtained by clicking the "Version ..." text of the "About This Mac" dialog you can bring up from the Apple menu. Also, provide information on the graphics hardware that is installed on the test system.

One final note on bug filing: Try to attain the holy grail of bug reporting—a small test application. Sometimes this is impractical, but often it's not too hard to create a small application with the offending OpenGL state that produces the problem. Don't hesitate to ask Apple for template applications that can be augmented to create a test application. The company has templates that use all of the windowing system interfaces to OpenGL on Mac OS X: CGL, AGL, and Cocoa.

With a smart and informative title, some coverage testing as described earlier, steps to reproduce the bug, and a test application, you'll skip the maximum number of people and get the best turnaround time for your bug report.

Threading

A thread on OS X, and on many other operating systems, contains all the required state elements for executing instructions on a processor. Threads have an associated call stack, have their own set of register states, and share the virtual address space of the process in which they are created.

Threads are quite lightweight and high performance. Provided you give them some work to do, thread switching and synchronization overhead can be amortized with relative ease. In this manner, threads are the doorway to full utilization of multiprocessor Mac computers, which, unlike with some platforms, has been a common configuration for many years.

At the lowest level, OS X threading is implemented as Mach threads. This level, however, is generally not interesting for application development and should be avoided if possible. Above Mach threads, OS X conforms to the industry standard POSIX threading model. If you're porting from other platforms, OS X's use of POSIX threads can be a real relief. POSIX threading is the foundation of threading logic for application developers working on OS X.

Depending on whether your application is a Carbon application or an Objective-C Cocoa application, there are different abstraction layers for threading above the POSIX interface.

For Carbon, there are two threading packages: Threading Manager and Multiprocessing Services. Both of these threading packages are part of the Core-Services framework. Multiprocessing services allows pre-emptive scheduling of threads. Threading Manager will schedule threads cooperatively, sharing the available resources among the threads.

Cocoa applications can and should leverage the NSThread class for pre-emptively scheduled threads. This is part of the Foundation framework.

Threading Manager, Multiprocessing Services, and NSThread are all built on top of the POSIX threading interface in OS X. This, in turn, is built on top of the Mach threading interface (Figure 4-1).

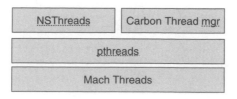

Figure 4-1 Threading Layer Cake: Thread Packages, on Top of POSIX, on Top of Mach Threads

For OpenGL applications on OS X, only a single thread may generate OpenGL commands for a given OpenGL context at one time. This, with some consideration, is somewhat self-evident. Consider the rendering output you would get if you interleaved rendering commands and OpenGL state changes from two different threads at one time!

One of the more insidious threading problems for OpenGL applications on OS X arises with the use of the Cocoa NSOpenGLView class. This class does some implicit CGL and OpenGL calls and will modify the OpenGL context accordingly. These implicit calls most frequently occur when your application window is updated or resized. If your application creates a new thread that is distinct from the main NSApplication thread and starts issuing OpenGL calls on this thread, voila! A thread contention problem is created.

To avoid threading issues of this sort, Apple added the entry points CGLLockContext and CGLUnlockContext as of OS X Tiger (10.4). If you wish to perform OpenGL rendering or state changes in a thread that you've created in your Cocoa application that uses an NSOpenGLView, you must bracket those calls with calls to CGLLockContext and CGLUnlockContext to avoid contention issues between the main thread and your ancillary thread.

Data Parallel Computation: SIMD

This section focuses on the programming paradigm know as Single Instruction, Multiple Data (SIMD). In this model, data that has an intrinsic parallelism—say, a color, vertex, or normal—has a computation applied to each of its elements in parallel. Put differently, one instruction is applied to multiple data elements simultaneously.

PowerPC

Modern PowerPC processors (i.e., G4 and later) have vector processing units dubbed AltiVec units that work as we just described. That is, AltiVec instructions are vector instructions that allow the application of the same operation to multiple data elements, in parallel. In some cases, if the data elements are large enough, the instructions may operate on a single data element or even a portion of a data element.

AltiVec units have a set of burly registers that are 128 bits in size. For the math-adept among us, that's four single-precision floating-point values that can be processed per pass. AltiVec instructions work best on big chunks of data. AltiVec units can issue instructions that operate on as small a chunk of data as a byte. There are only a very few bit-level operations.

Not only are AltiVec-enabled functions fast at processing streaming data or big data elements and fun to write (hee-hee), they are also faster at loading and storing memory. The AltiVec instruction set is very well specified but takes some skill to master. In particular, clever methods for economically loading the same value into multiple data elements (byte, half-word, word, double) of an AltiVec register are out there if you look for them. Apple's Developer website is a great place to start [12].

The engineers at Apple bust out the AltiVec and SSE big guns whenever serious performance and maximum efficiency needs to happen. You can, too, if you have data that will fit that operational model, as the performance benefits of a vectorized algorithm can be significant. Just keep in mind that if your application is expected to run on a G3 system, you'll need to code an alternative to your AltiVec logic. In Chapter 11, we'll investigate a tool that can help you generate optimized code for AltiVec and SSE (which is introduced in the next section). Any Mac with a G4 or later is AltiVec- or SSE-capable. Thus, if you're writing new code targeting newer Macs, consider these SIMD instruction sets for intensive CPU processing. A detailed discussion of SIMD programming is beyond the scope of this book, so for now we'll simply provide you with a code sample at http://www.macopengl.com that can help you determine whether your CPU has SIMD capabilities.

Intel

Streaming SIMD Extensions or SSE were introduced in 1999 by Intel. Numerous versions of SSE exist (e.g., SSE, SSE2, SSE3), but the basic idea is the same as with AltiVec coding: Vectorize your algorithm, and implement it as a chunk of SSE assembly in your code. As with AltiVec, this is obviously not a graphics function per se but may be related to your OpenGL development. For example, if your application does compression or decompression of video, audio, or other streaming data, and then displays this information on screen, you might want to investigate SSE as a way of accelerating your codecs.

Apple provides two good references if you're interested in learning the details behind SSE. First, the performance analysis tool Shark, as described in Chapter 11, is a good way to see what's going on in your code and find hints about what might be candidates for vectorization. Shark also contains a very nice SSE reference, containing all of the commands, their arguments, and results. Apple's second reference to SSE is found on the web, as part of its overall developer tools [13]. Both resources will help you understand the commands and their usage.

Chapter 5

OpenGL Configuration and Integration

This chapter explores in detail how to configure the necessary infrastructure to begin drawing with OpenGL. Specifically, it describes use of the various Macintosh APIs to window systems and off-screen render areas, and it examines how to configure each API for the type of OpenGL data you plan to render. If you've jumped to this chapter to get details on a particular API, skip the introduction and dig right in. If you've arrived here wondering which API is right for you, you'll probably want to read the overview first to learn about the differences among the many windowing APIs to OpenGL on Mac OS X.

The OpenGL configuration APIs presented here are classified into two groups: Mac-specific APIs and cross-platform APIs supported on the Mac. Although there are many interfaces to the window system and OpenGL configuration, all APIs function using the same core ideas and ultimately run on the same drivers. In essence, each of these interfaces uses the same concepts for its configuration, though the details and capabilities of each are different.

We begin with the Mac-specific APIs, presented roughly in order of modernity, from most to least modern. This is by no means a sorting meant to imply preference—you should use whichever API best meets your application's needs. However, many of the examples later in this book do express a preference and are written in Objective-C/Cocoa. Quite frankly, it's the best UI toolkit out there, and it's really fun to write applications using it.

Let's begin by reviewing the high-level concepts involved for all flavors of OpenGL APIs on the Mac.

API Introductions and Overview

The Mac has a rich history of 2D and 3D graphics, and the sheer number of API choices for drawing bears this out. Despite the many choices available, these APIs differ both in design and implementation, so it's not too difficult to determine which is right for you. This section discusses each API specifically with the idea in mind that you'll be integrating it into an application. That means the choices among these APIs largely revolve around how well they will integrate with the rest of your application in general, and your windowing system in particular. OpenGL is used consistently among these APIs, and the standard OpenGL API is how you'll be rendering graphics data. But when considering OpenGL setup, configuration, and window management, the various APIs differ dramatically.

We'll begin by looking at each API and discussing the applicability of each, and then dig into the details in later chapters.

Mac-Only APIs

Four key APIs for 3D graphics are available only on the Mac: Quartz Services, Core OpenGL (CGL), Apple OpenGL (AGL), and Cocoa OpenGL (NSGL). If you're starting with a blank sheet of paper and writing an application from the ground up for the Mac, one of these APIs is where you'll want to focus your energy for integrating OpenGL. Architecturally, both Cocoa OpenGL and AGL are layered on top of CGL. For applications that require more comprehensive access to the underlying infrastructure, direct access is always possible from either Cocoa or AGL.

Quartz Services

Quartz Services is part of the Core Graphics framework. It succeeds the Macintosh Display Manager and convention associated with DrawSprocket. The Quartz Services API controls systemwide parameters for configuring the display hardware on a Macintosh computer. You may be interested in setting the following parameters from your OpenGL application:

- Refresh rate
- Resolution
- Pixel depth
- Display capture
- Gamma setting (display fades)

Quartz Services also provides services for applications that do remote operation of OS X. We won't cover this topic in our book.

In short, this API provides the functionality needed for your OpenGL application to communicate with the Macintosh Quartz Window Server.

Core OpenGL

CGL is the foundation layer of the Quartz windowing system interface to the OpenGL API. As with most foundation-layer APIs, CGL allows the greatest amount of flexibility and control over how your OpenGL application is configured, albeit at the cost of greater complexity.

The most important limitation—and one that neither AGL nor the Cocoa interface to OpenGL has—is that there is no way to build a windowed OpenGL application using only CGL. A CGL-only application can render full-screen or off-screen images only.

Because AGL and Cocoa are layered on top of CGL, you may freely mix CGL calls with an AGL application or a Cocoa application. Be aware that when doing so, you have to be careful not to introduce bugs because your AGL or Cocoa calls are undoing or redoing the same tasks as CGL.

In most cases you'll find that AGL and Cocoa interfaces should provide enough flexibility and control so that direct use of CGL is not required.

Apple OpenGL

AGL is the Carbon interface to OpenGL on the Mac. Carbon is a set of C-level APIs to most Mac systems, and is the foundation of many an older Macintosh application. Carbon is by no means a deprecated API set; in fact, quite the opposite is true. Carbon-layer APIs tend to be the first place you see lots of new functionality for the Mac. You can also create full-featured, modern, Mac OS X applications written entirely in Carbon. But the goal here is not to motivate to you to either use or not use Carbon but rather to help you decide whether this API is of relevance to you. The quick litmus test for using AGL is this: If you have a Carbon application into which you're adding OpenGL, then AGL is the API for you.

Cocoa OpenGL

Cocoa is the hip, newer,[1] and remarkably powerful user-interface API on the Mac, as anyone following the Mac scene since OS X knows. If you're writing an application from scratch on the Mac, Cocoa makes it very easy to get a pretty

---

1. Or old, depending on how much attention you paid to the brief NeXT empire. Cocoa's heritage comes directly from NeXT, right down to the prefix NS that prepends every Cocoa API entry.

complex application up and running quickly. Cocoa offers other benefits as well, but it's the most modern of the user-interface choices on the Mac, with all the associated object-oriented benefits you'd expect. Interestingly, many of the Mac APIs for many other things start as lower-level APIs and are later incorporated into high-level Cocoa classes that do a lot of the painful configuration work for you. NSMovieView, for example, takes care of all of the QuickTime setup and configuration necessary to get a movie loaded, playing, and on screen. Similarly, NSOpenGLView takes care of all of the basic OpenGL infrastructure setup and configuration so that you can launch into writing OpenGL code directly. It's a reasonably simple decision at this point: If you're writing for a new or an existing Cocoa application, you should use the Cocoa OpenGL API. Taking a broader view, Cocoa is the best place to begin if you're starting a new application from scratch on the Mac.

Cross-Platform APIs Supported on the Mac

If you've made it this far, you likely have an application that you're bringing to the Mac from another platform, or you want a simple, low-impact way of setting up an OpenGL rendering area on the Mac. Either way, the next two options provide ways for you to quickly get an application from another platform running on the Mac.

GLUT

The OpenGL Utility Toolkit (GLUT) is a toolkit encapsulating OpenGL setup and configuration (and many other things) that has existed for many years, on many platforms. GLUT provides hooks for easily setting up a window, drawing to it, capturing input device data such as mouse and keyboard events, and even some extra goodies such as basic 3D shape rendering. GLUT also runs on just about any platform you can think of—and if it doesn't, the source code is available so you can make it run there.

So far, so good! However, while GLUT is great for getting an application up and running, it's most useful as a test bed or demonstration system, as it provides a lot of functionality but doesn't integrate so seamlessly with other native window elements on most platforms. Nevertheless, because of GLUT's simplicity and portability, it's very easy to find GLUT-based code examples that compile and run on the Mac. In fact, Apple ships a set of GLUT examples in its developer tools.

When should you use GLUT? If you're developing some code that you need to run on many platforms but that doesn't require a complex UI, GLUT is appropriate. If you're doing anything more complex than a keyboard or simple menu interface, the Mac-specific OpenGL APIs and windowing systems are the place to look.

X11

The last major API set for graphics on the Mac is an old standby, X11. X11 APIs for windowing and OpenGL have existed for many years, and Apple fully supports a set of them through its X11 SDK. If you're bringing an application from another Unix platform to the Mac, it's likely that the application uses X11 at its core. Apple has taken great effort with OpenGL and X11 on the Mac to ensure that OpenGL runs at full speed within X, and because of this excellent performance, a straightforward port of a legacy X11 application to the Mac is often a very viable route to take. This strategy will get an application up and running on the Mac, but the look and feel of that application won't fit well with the rest of the Mac experience. Even so, this is an expedient path to bringing an application to the Mac.

If you've got a code base that uses X11, then the X11 set of APIs is the right path for you. By contrast, if you're starting from scratch on the Mac, or porting an application to the Mac and want to ensure the best look and feel, then one of the Mac-only APIs is the right place to begin.

API Introduction and Overview Wrap-Up

In summary, there are five API choices for opening a window, choosing a pixel format, creating a rendering context, and issuing OpenGL commands on the Mac. Now that we've introduced the five Apple-supported APIs for doing OpenGL setup and configuration on the Mac, we'll explore a bit of the history behind these window system integration APIs and describe each of them in detail.

Configuration API Relationships

There are two types of windows on OS X: Carbon windows and Cocoa windows. AGL provides the integration between OpenGL and Carbon windows. AppKit provides the integration between OpenGL and Cocoa windows (NSWindows). Unlike AGL and the AppKit interface to OpenGL, CGL has no corresponding window type and, accordingly, no window event mechanism defined. As a result, windowed OpenGL applications must rely on either AGL and the Carbon framework or the AppKit framework to provide access to their respective windows and the event mechanisms behind them.

The CoreGraphics framework, which is located in the /System/Library/ Frameworks/ApplicationServices.framework/CoreGraphics.frame work directory, is the lowest-level interface to the Quartz window system on OS X. CGL, AGL, and AppKit all depend on CoreGraphics for integration with the windowing system. Whether the windows are visible, invisible, or full-screen doesn't affect this dependency. Typically, only the Quartz Services API of the CoreGraphics framework will be called upon by your OpenGL application.

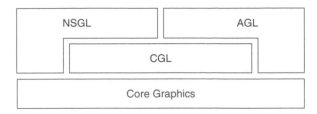

Figure 5-1 OpenGL Configuration API Dependencies

Even these calls may be unnecessary because Carbon and AppKit provide an abstraction for all of the window–server integration your API will likely need. Exceptions to this rule may arise when you are controlling the event stream directly or when you are requesting or setting windowing system-wide parameters such as obtaining the ID of the main display, setting the display pixel depth or resolution, or modifying display gamma values.

The dependency layering gets more interesting when you consider that AGL and AppKit both rely on the CGL interface to OpenGL itself. To summarize, AppKit, AGL, and CGL depend on CoreGraphics, and AppKit and AGL depend on CGL. This means the dependency relationship isn't a simple layering. It looks more like the hierarchy shown in Figure 5-1.

Note that Figure 5-1 doesn't reveal anything about the layout of the directory structure of the frameworks within the /System/Library/Frameworks directory of OS X. AGL and AppKit are easy to understand: They have their own frameworks and reside in the /System/Library/Frameworks directory. CGL is part of OpenGL and, therefore, is contained in the /System/Library/ Frameworks/OpenGL.framework directory. Core Graphics is perhaps the most difficult to find. Ruining the surprise, you can find this framework in the /System/Library/Frameworks/ApplicationServices.framework/ frameworks directory. You'll find this information important for linking but probably even more crucial when you want to browse headers.

Table 5-1 summarizes the APIs, short names, nicknames, and framework paths discussed in this section. Note that all frameworks are relative to /System/ Library/Frameworks, the standard Apple framework path.

Table 5-1 API and Framework Locations

Long Name	Function Prefix	Nickname	Framework Path
Cocoa	NS	AppKit	AppKit.framework
Carbon	AGL		AGL.framework
Core OpenGL	CGL		OpenGL.framework
CoreGraphics	CG		ApplicationServices.framework

Sharing OpenGL Data Between Contexts

To conserve VRAM and bandwidth throughout the system, it is a good idea to share data across contexts whenever possible. Sharing resources across contexts is one of the most commonly discussed topics in the OpenGL ARB, and with good reason. Sharing falls under the purview of the windowing system interface to OpenGL. These shared resources are created, managed, and destroyed by OpenGL. ARB members, in a sense, represent different windowing systems because they come from IHVs and ISVs that are working with different platforms. The convergence of all this information makes this one hot topic for debate.

When ARB members meet to discuss the sharing of objects across contexts in OpenGL, the GLX specification is often at the center of that discussion. Because these design discussions are almost always independent of any particular windowing system, the GLX specification, in a sense, becomes required reading for any developer who works on OpenGL—not just those developers who are developing applications under the X11 window system. If you have uncertainty about behavior regarding shared objects, consult the GLX specification—the architects of OpenGL do.

The following data can be shared across contexts:

- Display lists
- Texture objects
- Vertex array objects
- Vertex buffer objects
- Shader objects
- Pixel buffer objects
- Framebuffer objects

Sharing OpenGL resources across contexts is also a hot topic for developer discussion lists. This concern could well originate from the fact that sharing is not currently in part of the OpenGL specification (though it is in OpenGL Longs Peak). As a result, OpenGL implementations follow some guidelines for shared objects but do not have to adhere to any strict rules.

The biggest controversy seems to be the following question: What happens when an OpenGL object is deleted or modified in one context while being concurrently referenced by another? For modifications, this question becomes: When are the changes of an object in one context reflected in another context that is sharing it? In the case of deletion, this conversation breaks down into two questions: Should the object be deleted or should the ID for the object be removed from the object namespace? If the shared object ID is deleted from the namespace in one context but another context continues to reference the object, what happens when a new object ID is then requested in either context?

The Apple OpenGL implementation maintains a reference count for shared objects. For most shared objects, this count is kept according to bind calls to those objects. In the vertex array object and framebuffer object cases, the reference counts are kept according to the attachment state of these objects. For display lists, the reference count is maintained with respect to the `glEndList` call. Thus, if context A is using a certain display list, while context B is concurrently redefining the contents of that display list, the change made by context B will not be visible to context A until context B commits the changes with a call to `glEndList`.

When a shared object is deleted, the Mac OpenGL implementation internally tags it for deletion and the object's ID is immediately made free in the namespace. When the reference count for this tagged object reaches zero, the object itself is deleted from memory.

If the reference count of a shared object tagged for deletion has not reached zero and the now-freed object ID is reused, things get more complicated. If context A deletes shared texture 2, binds shared texture 2 again, and then redefines its contents, the share context B, which is still bound to texture 2, will be referring to the original texture object that was backing texture ID 2. If share context B then rebinds that same texture 2, because the binds are the reconciliation point, it will now refer to the new texture that was defined for texture ID 2 back in context A.

Things get *really* complicated if the shared object state is queried in the midst of all of these concurrent operations. Again, this isn't a problem unique to the Mac OpenGL implementation, but consider this scenario:

- Context A and context B share texture object 2.
- Context B is currently bound to texture object 2.
- Context A calls `glDeleteTexture(2)`.
- Context B calls `glGet(GL_TEXTURE_BINDING)`; the return value is 2.
- If context A and context B now check the contents of texture object 2, they get different answers.
- Context B calls `glIsTexture(2)`; the return value is `GL_FALSE`.

Now if context B rebinds to that same texture object 2, it will no longer be referring to the original texture object because context A deleted it and the binds are the reconciliation point. So, rebinding to the same object ID gives you a different object.

To avoid ever confronting the confusion of the preceding scenario, it's a good idea to strictly conform to the OpenGL specification when it comes to shared object management. OpenGL applications are solely responsible for maintaining the integrity of shared objects across contexts. This is not a surprising requirement as this situation is completely analogous to critical regions when doing multithreaded programming.

The GLX specification has more information regarding this popular topic among ARB members if you're interested.

Framebuffers

When an OpenGL application performs its rendering, the output of that rendering is directed to a buffer that contains the resulting pixels. In the language of the OpenGL specification, the official name of this buffer is a framebuffer. Given all of the other terminology sometimes used to describe this buffer, such as window, pbuffer, logical buffer, and off-screen buffer, it is good to be clear about the meaning of this term: A framebuffer is a destination for rendering. Whether or not this buffer is visible and where this buffer physically resides are not part of its definition.

Also, it's important to distinguish a framebuffer from a framebuffer object. A framebuffer object is a container of framebuffer meta-information rather than the framebuffer itself. An analogue is a texture object, which is a convenient reference to a parcel of texture data but not the actual data itself. OpenGL is actually a really well-designed system, much like the Mac. Although its use involves many terms and interfaces, once you've mastered a few key concepts, you can reuse them again and again. Thus the distinction between a hypothetical OpenGL type foo and a foo-object is always the same across the API: The -object is a handle to the base type and all its associated configuration state.

Another way to think of a framebuffer is as a collection of logical buffers arranged in a stacked or stratified manner. Each logical buffer is a scalar field containing values specific to this "layer" in the rendered output. Examples of these logical buffers are color buffers (red, green, blue, or alpha), depth buffers, stencil buffers, and accumulation buffers. An individual 1-pixel column through each of these layers is known as a *fragment*. The related concepts of frame-buffers and fragments are important in understanding both what's written and perhaps what's read from the framebuffer when your OpenGL commands are completed. There are performance considerations here as well, which we'll examine in later chapters.

Each scalar in these logical buffers is represented by some number of bits. For instance, an 8-bit red color buffer contains width*height 8-bit scalar values, and a 32-bit depth buffer contains width*height 32-bit depth values. The composition of these mixed-size or same-size logical buffers makes up a frame-buffer. Figure 5-2 depicts a typical framebuffer.

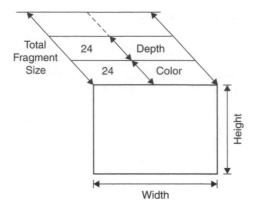

Figure 5-2 Framebuffer Strata

Framebuffers are a core resource for OpenGL. They, along with texture objects, vertex array objects, shader objects, and other OpenGL resources, must be created, managed, and destroyed. To allocate, configure, and size them, their attributes must be described. The set of attributes that describe a framebuffer is collectively known as the framebuffer's pixel format. Pixel format is the terminology most commonly used to describe this idea on the Mac OS because that is how it is referred to in the CGL interface. Given that X11 also runs on the Mac OS, the term "visual" is used to describe the layout of a framebuffer. We'll stick with "pixel format" for our discussion, however.

Chapter 6

The CGL API
for OpenGL
Configuration

Overview

Since the transition from IrisGL to OpenGL, this graphics API has been independent of the windowing system of the operating system on which it runs. This
aspect of the API was the primary redesign requirement of IrisGL to make it an
open standard and multiplatform, rather than running on just the Iris workstations on which it originated.

When windowing functionality was first written out of the IrisGL API, it needed
a new home. This home is GLX, the interface between OpenGL and X11. Shortly
after this transition, WGL was created as an interface between OpenGL and
Windows.

On OS X, the original interface developed between the Quartz windowing
system and OpenGL was called CGL, short for Core OpenGL. The AGL
(Apple GL) interface for Carbon applications was written later and is layered
on top of CGL. Similarly, when Cocoa arrived, classes and data structures were
developed, again on top of CGL, to provide Cocoa applications with an OpenGL
interface.

Thus CGL lies at the heart of the window system interfaces to OpenGL on OS X
and, in fact, is part of the OpenGL framework. Because of this, you might think
that, like the foundation of other layered APIs like Xlib or perhaps Win32, CGL
can do all that the higher layers can do and more, albeit with more effort on the
part of the software engineer. This is mostly true, with one important exception:
Only full-screen or off-screen OpenGL applications can be written using exclusively CGL. For windowed applications, the AGL or Cocoa interface to OpenGL
is required.

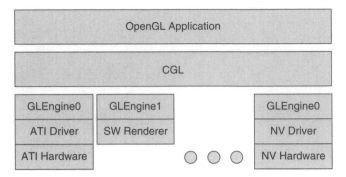

Figure 6-1   CGL Renderer Selection

Because CGL lies beneath both AGL and the Cocoa interface to OpenGL, you can freely use CGL in combination with either an AGL application or a Cocoa application. CGL may also be freely used with GLUT applications because the OS X GLUT implementation relies on Cocoa, which in turn relies on CGL. The only invalid combination of these four interfaces is to use the AGL or Carbon interface to OpenGL in combination with the Cocoa interface to OpenGL.

Generally speaking, you will find that both AGL and Cocoa provide enough flexibility that you may not need any of the additional control that CGL allows. If you're doing simple prototyping of graphics techniques, you'll probably find GLUT to be the easiest API with which to get up and running.

CGL shares many things with other windowing interfaces to OpenGL: pixel format selection, context creation and manipulation, and a pbuffer interface, to name a few. On OS X, CGL also has to shoulder the burden of requirements that arise out of having a plug-in renderer architecture that supports a heterogeneous set of installed graphics devices (Figure 6-1). Dragging a window from one display to another is a simple matter if both displays are being driven by a single graphics device; it's quite another matter if the displays are on different devices with widely varying capabilities. On any OpenGL implementation, the context state that is maintained internally is a reflection of the capabilities of the underlying hardware. Imagine how that context state varies when you drag a window from a display supported by a high-end graphics device built by one graphics hardware vendor to a display supported by a low-end device built from another!

Linking with CGL is easy; it's part of `OpenGL.framework`, which is typically found in `/System/Library/Frameworks` but may also be in a path specific to your SDK installation. Because CGL is part of the OpenGL framework, its headers are found in the Headers directory of the OpenGL.framework directory. Commonly used CGL headers include CGLTypes.h, CGLRenderers.h, and CGLMacros.h. We'll talk more about these headers in this chapter.

Error Handling

CGL error handling is based on the values returned from each of the CGL functions. All CGL functions return 0 when successful. Upon failure, a number of different return values may be returned that describe the nature of the failure. The full list of possible error values is part of the CGLError enum and can be found in /System/Libraries/Frameworks/OpenGL.framework/Headers/CGLTypes.h:

```
/*
 ** Error return values from CGLGetError
 */
typedef enum _CGLError {
    kCGLNoError             = 0,      /* no error */
    /* invalid ... */
    kCGLBadAttribute        = 10000, /* pixel format attribute */
    kCGLBadProperty         = 10001, /* renderer property     */
    kCGLBadPixelFormat      = 10002, /* pixel format          */
    kCGLBadRendererInfo     = 10003, /* renderer info         */
    kCGLBadContext          = 10004, /* context               */
    kCGLBadDrawable         = 10005, /* drawable              */
    kCGLBadDisplay          = 10006, /* graphics device       */
    kCGLBadState            = 10007, /* context state         */
    kCGLBadValue            = 10008, /* numerical value       */
    kCGLBadMatch            = 10009, /* share context         */
    kCGLBadEnumeration      = 10010, /* enumerant             */
    kCGLBadOffScreen        = 10011, /* offscreen drawable    */
    kCGLBadFullScreen       = 10012, /* offscreen drawable    */
    kCGLBadWindow           = 10013, /* window                */
    kCGLBadAddress          = 10014, /* pointer               */
    kCGLBadCodeModule       = 10015, /* code module           */
    kCGLBadAlloc            = 10016, /* memory allocation     */
    kCGLBadConnection       = 10017  /* CoreGraphics connection */
} CGLError;
```

Pixel Format Selection

A pixel format is simply a set of attribute–value pairs that describe the desired configuration for the framebuffer. All graphics hardware has limitations in terms of the allowable framebuffer configurations it supports. For instance, a specific video card may support an RGBA, 8 bits per component, double-buffered pixel format, but it may not support an RGBA, 12 bits per component, double-buffered pixel format. Because of these differences, pixel format APIs such as CGL provide a selection mechanism that attempts to match a set of requested attributes as closely as the underlying renderer can support.

The CGL pixel format API consists of three entry points for creating, querying, and destroying pixels:

```
CGLChoosePixelFormat
CGLDescribePixelFormat
CGLDestroyPixelFormat
```

CGLChoosePixelFormat

CGLChoosePixelFormat creates a pixel format using a NULL-terminated mixed array of attributes and, if applicable, the attribute's value. Let's look at Example 6-1, which shows how to create a simple pixel format, before we dive into the details of all the possible pixel format attributes.

Example 6-1 CGLChoosePixelFormat Usage

```
#include <OpenGL/CGLTypes.h>
...
    CGLPixelFormatAttribute attribs[] =
    {
        kCGLPFADoubleBuffer,
        kCGLPFAColorSize,          24,
        kCGLPFADepthSize,          16,
        kCGLPFAMinimumPolicy,
        NULL
    };

    CGLPixelFormatObj pixelFormatObj;
    long numPixelFormats;
    CGLError cglError;

    cglError = CGLChoosePixelFormat( attribs, &pixelFormatObj,
                &numPixelFormats );

    if(cglError != kCGLNoError)
    {
        printf("Unable to create pixel format." \
                "Error is: 0x%0x\n", cglError);
    }
```

Notice that the pixel format attribute constants are prefaced with "kCGLPFA." The "k" specifies that the value is a global constant. "CGL," well, that just means CGL. "PFA" stands for pixel format attribute.

Pixel format attributes are scalars that may be integer quantities or Boolean values. In our example, kCGLPFADoubleBuffer and kCGLPFAMinimumPolicy are Boolean values. There's a certain asymmetry in specifying Boolean versus non-Boolean values, but you can't argue that it doesn't save on typing: Rather than having a value of `true` or `false` explicitly listed for Boolean attributes, they are simply specified when true and not specified when false.

The design of Apple's pixel format API is subtractive in nature. That is, you can think of your attribute array as a set of constraints for the list of possible pixel formats that will match, rather than trying to build up a pixel format containing only these features.

```
typedef enum _CGLPixelFormatAttribute {
    kCGLPFAAllRenderers          =    1,
    kCGLPFAOffScreen             =   53,
    kCGLPFAFullScreen            =   54,
    kCGLPFAAuxDepthStencil       =   57,
    kCGLPFAColorFloat            =   58,
    kCGLPFASupersample           =   60,
    kCGLPFASampleAlpha           =   61,
    kCGLPFARendererID            =   70,
    kCGLPFASingleRenderer        =   71,
    kCGLPFANoRecovery            =   72,
    kCGLPFAAccelerated           =   73,
    kCGLPFARobust                =   75,
    kCGLPFABackingStore          =   76,
    kCGLPFAMPSafe                =   78,
    kCGLPFAWindow                =   80,
    kCGLPFAMultiScreen           =   81,
    kCGLPFACompliant             =   83,
    kCGLPFADisplayMask           =   84,
    kCGLPFAPBuffer               =   90,
    kCGLPFARemotePBuffer         =   91,
    kCGLPFAVirtualScreenCount    =  128,
} CGLPixelFormatAttribute;
```

Policies and Buffer Sizing

Each of the policies used in pixel format selection is a scoring system to nominate matching pixel format candidates.

The policy attributes `kCGLPFAMinimumPolicy` and `kCGLPFAMaximumPolicy` are applicable only to the color, depth, and accumulation buffer sizes. If you specify the minimum policy, then these attributes must have at least the value specified with the attribute. In our example, we've requested that the pixel format be chosen using only pixel formats that are double buffered, have at least 24 bits for the R/G/B color channels, and that there be at least 16 bits for the depth buffer.

Here is the set of policy attributes:

```
kCGLPFAMinimumPolicy
kCGLPFAMaximumPolicy
kCGLPFAClosestPolicy
```

The minimum policy sets the low bar for acceptance, but there is another asymmetry here: `kCGLPFAMaximumPolicy` doesn't set the high bar for acceptance. Instead, it means that if `kCGLPFAColorSize`, `kCGLPFADepthSize`, or `kCGLPFAAccumSize` is specified with a non-zero value, then the largest possible corresponding buffer size will be chosen for your pixel format object.

`kCGLPFAClosestPolicy` is applicable to only the color buffer size attribute `kCGLPFAColorSize`; it does not consider the size specified for the depth or accumulation buffers. With this attribute, the color buffer size of the returned pixel format object will most closely match the requested size. This policy is most similar to the behavior that the X11 window system uses when choosing visuals.

As you may have gathered by now, `kCGLPFAMinimumPolicy` is the default policy for buffer sizing. Also, notice that neither of the nondefault policies `kCGLPFAMaximumPolicy` and `kCGLPFAClosestPolicy` is applicable to the `kCGLPFAAlphaSize` or `kCGLPFAStencilSize` attribute. Apply a little deductive reasoning and we have a new rule: The pixel format matching semantics for `kCGLPFAAlphaSize` and `kCGLPFAStencilSize` follow the `kCGLPFAMinimumPolicy` behavior only.

Render Targets

You may have noticed when running a game or other full-screen application that only the primary display (the display with the Apple menu bar) is captured for the full-screen application. The reason for this is that full-screen rendering is supported only with a single renderer on the Mac OS. Therefore, if you include the `kCGLPFAFullScreen` attribute to qualify your pixel format, only renderers capable of supporting full-screen rendering will be considered and `kCGLPFASingleRenderer` is implied.

Mutually exclusive to `kCGLPFAFullScreen` are the `kCGLPFAOffScreen` and `kCGLPFAWindow` attributes. On some platforms, the term "hidden window" or "invisible window" is used when describing an off-screen destination. On the Mac OS, if you're rendering off screen, according to this mutual exclusivity you're not rendering to a window.

If you wish to restrict the list of renderers that will match your format to those that can render off screen, specify the `kCGLPFAOffScreen` attribute. However, be wary of this attribute if you are at all concerned about the performance of your off-screen rendering. There are three ways to do off-screen rendering on the Mac OS. If that's not confusing enough, with the introduction of the framebuffer object specification in OpenGL, there are now four. See Chapter 5 for more information.

Finally, if you wish to restrict the renderer list to only those renderers that can render on screen in a window, specify the kCGLPFAWindow attribute in your format array.

Multisampling

If multisampling is desired, set the kCGLPFASampleBuffers attribute to 1 to indicate a preference for a multisample buffer. Set the kCGLPFASamples attribute to the number of samples desired for each pixel. The policy attributes are not applicable to these two multisampling attributes.

Stereo

For stereo rendering, also known as quad-buffering, the token kCGLPFAStereo is used. This option produces a pixel format that contains two double-buffered drawables, logically a left and a right, with a stereo offset to produce a 3D projected rendering. If you haven't experienced the LCD shutter glass type of stereo rendering, it is as if the scene is floating in space in front of the physical surface of the display. The stereo effect is achieved by providing two buffers (left and right), each with a separate perspective frustum. Each frustum is offset by the inter-ocular distance or, in English, the distance between your eyes.

The NVidia Quadro FX 4500, which was introduced in 2005, was the first hardware introduced on the Mac platform to support stereo in a window. The alternative to stereo in a window is full-screen stereo. For any Mac configured with hardware released prior to the FX 4500, kCGLPFAStereo implies kCGLPFAFullScreen, which in turn implies kCGLPFASingleRenderer.

Selecting a Renderer

Another way of selecting a renderer is by explicitly choosing one for your application. There are a number of possibilities when it comes to selecting a renderer by ID, enumerated in the file CGLRenderers.h. You use the kCGLPFARendererID attribute to select your own renderer ID. Here is a snapshot of the evolving list of possible renderer IDs:

```
kCGLRendererGenericID
kCGLRendererGenericFloatID
kCGLRendererAppleSWID
kCGLRendererATIRage128ID
kCGLRendererATIRadeonID
kCGLRendererATIRageProID
kCGLRendererATIRadeon8500ID
kCGLRendererATIRadeon9700ID
kCGLRendererGeForce2MXID
```

```
kCGLRendererGeForce3ID
kCGLRendererGeForceFXID
kCGLRendererVTBladeXP2ID
kCGLRendererIntel900ID
kCGLRendererMesa3DFXID
```

The star of this show is the Apple software renderer, which was released as part of Tiger. If you wish to use or test certain functionality that your hardware doesn't support, you can use this renderer. The new software renderer is specified using kCGLRendererGenericFloatID. You may hear this renderer described as "the float renderer" because of its support for floating-point framebuffers and pixel formats. This software renderer is highly tuned for the Mac platform. It uses a great deal of hand-tuned and hand-scheduled PowerPC and Intel assembly. The performance of this renderer, though not comparable to that of a dedicated hardware renderer, is quite astonishing.

The software renderer is a great tool to use when you are debugging your application. If, for instance, you believe your OpenGL logic is correct yet the rendering doesn't appear correct, try changing your renderer to the software renderer. The software renderer allows you to cross-check the vendor-specific renderers to determine whether your application has a bug that is specific to a certain graphics card. If you see correct results in the software renderer but not in the vendor-specific renderer, or vice versa, it's time to file a bug report and let Apple have a look at it. Keep in mind, however, that OpenGL is not a pixel-exact specification, and minor differences between rendered images are always possible, and even likely. However, gross differences are likely bugs—so please file them.

There are two other renderer IDs that correspond to software renderers. The software renderer preceding the current float renderer is referenced using kCGLRendererAppleSWID. This older renderer is neither as fast nor as full featured as the new software renderer but could prove useful as another check when debugging or comparing results. Aside from this scenario, this renderer should not be used unless you wish to hamstring your application performance.

kCGLGenericID

kCGLGenericID corresponds to the original software renderer written for OS X. If you are experiencing difficulty with the new software renderer and your application doesn't use features beyond OpenGL 1.2, you may have better luck with this original renderer. Although not as highly tuned, the old software renderer is better tested by virtue of its age alone. This older software renderer can also be used as yet another data point in fortifying a bug submission if you suspect a problem with one of the hardware renderers.

```
kCGLRendererAppleSWID
```

Arguably, this renderer ID should not be published. It serves as a placeholder (and a questionable one at that) for graphics driver writers for OS X.

```
kCGLRendererATIRage128ID
kCGLRendererATIRadeonID
kCGLRendererATIRageProID
kCGLRendererATIRadeon8500ID
kCGLRendererATIRadeon9700ID
kCGLRendererATIRadeonX1000ID
kCGLRendererGeForce2MXID
kCGLRendererGeForce3ID
kCGLRendererGeForceFXID
kCGLRendererGeForce8XXXID
kCGLRendererVTBladeXP2ID
kCGLRendererIntel900ID
kCGLRendererMesa3DFXID
```

If you wish to restrict pixel format matching to a device-specific hardware renderer, you may use the list above to do so. When you ask for a specific renderer ID of this sort, your software will run only on the requested hardware. On other devices, your pixel format selection will fail.

Most graphics application developers are familiar with the ATI, NVIDIA, and Intel graphics hardware described in the renderer ID strings above. Less familiar is the kCGLRendererVTBladeXP2ID ID, which corresponds to the Village-Tronic hardware renderer.

kCGLRendererMesa3DFXID is outdated and will eventually be removed from the list of renderer IDs.

Context Management

The CGL type CGLContextObj is the fundamental data type for an OpenGL context on the Mac. CGL contexts are created as follows:

```
CGLError CGLCreateContext(CGLPixelFormatObj pixelFormat, CGLContextObj
sharedContext, CGLContextObj *ctx);
```

Contexts may be duplicated with a call to

```
CGLError CGLCopyContext(CGLContextObj src, CGLContextObj dst, unsigned long
stateMask);
```

The stateMask parameter should be set using a bitwise OR of the enum values used with the OpenGL call glPushAttrib. It provides a handy mechanism to filter which state elements you wish to copy from the source context to the destination context.

Specifying GL_ALL_ATTRIB_BITS for your state mask will yield as close as possible to a duplicate of your source context. The faithful reproduction of the copy is limited only by the scope of state encapsulated by the glPushAttrib/glPopAttrib state management API within OpenGL. Various OpenGL state elements, such as feedback or selection settings, cannot be pushed and popped. The OpenGL specification has a detailed description of this state management API if you need to further scrutinize the details of your context copy.

To free a context and set the current context to NULL use, call

```
CGLError CGLDestroyContext(CGLContextObj ctx);
```

Setting or getting the current context in CGL is a simple matter of calling

```
CGLError CGLSetCurrentContext(CGLContextObj ctx);
```

or

```
CGLContextObj CGLGetCurrentContext(void);
```

You may find CGLGetCurrentContext() to be the most useful entry point in the API. It's very handy for debugging CGL, AGL, and NSOpenGLView-based OpenGL applications. You can simply insert this call in your code anywhere downstream of context initialization and use the result for the full gamut of reasons you use contexts. It's quite handy for debugging configuration-related issues.

Context Parameters and Enables

Like any logical object, a CGLContextObj has an associated set of parameters that are scoped to the context itself. Some parameters are read/write; others are read-only and simply allow the application to inspect the running configuration of the context. Here's a code fragment from the CGLTypes.h file on a Tiger system that lists the valid context parameter values:

```
/*
** Parameter names for CGLSetParameter and CGLGetParameter.
*/
typedef enum _CGLContextParameter {
    kCGLCPSwapRectangle     = 200,
    /* 4 params. Set or get the swap rectangle {x, y, w, h}  */
    kCGLCPSwapInterval      = 222,
    /* 1 param.  0: Don't sync, n: Sync every n retrace  */
    kCGLCPDispatchTableSize = 224,
    /* 1 param.  Get the dispatch table size */
    kCGLCPClientStorage     = 226,
    /* 1 param.  Context specific generic storage */
    kCGLCPSurfaceTexture    = 228,
    /* 3 params. SID, target, internal_format */
    kCGLCPSurfaceOrder      = 235,
    /* 1 param.  1: Above window, -1: Below Window */
```

```
    kCGLCPSurfaceOpacity      - 236,
    /* 1 param.  1: surface is opaque (default), 0: non-opaque */
    kCGLCPSurfaceBackingSize = 304,
    /* 2 params. Width/height of surface backing size */
    kCGLCPSurfaceSurfaceVolatile = 306,
    /* 1 param.  Surface volatile state */
    kCGLCPReclaimResources      = 308,
    /* 0 params. */
    kCGLCPCurrentRendererID      = 309,
    /* 1 param.  Retrieves the current renderer ID */
    kCGLCPGPUVertexProcessing    = 310,
    /* 1 param.  Currently processing vertices with GPU (get) */
    kCGLCPGPUFragmentProcessing  = 311
    /* 1 param.  Currently processing fragments with GPU (get) */
} CGLContextParameter;
```

Context parameters are set with

```
CGLError CGLSetParameter(CGLContextObj ctx, CGLContext Parameter
parameterName, const long *params);
```

and retrieved by

```
CGLError CGLGetParameter(CGLContextObj ctx, CGLContext Parameter
parameterName, long *params);
```

Notice that for each of the valid parameter values is prefaced by the string "kCGL" followed by "CP". "CP" stands for context parameter, but this note will help you distinguish this CGL constant from others. Each value passed to CGLSetParameter is either a parameter with a value specific to the parameter or a Boolean enabled parameter that is controlled by calls to

```
CGLError CGLEnable(CGLContextObj ctx, CGLContextEnable enableName);
CGLError CGLDisable(CGLContextObj ctx, CGLContextEnable enableName);
```

A list of CGL context enables, also from CGLTypes.h, follows:

```
/*
** Enable names for CGLEnable, CGLDisable, and CGLIsEnabled.
*/
typedef enum _CGLContextEnable {
    kCGLCESwapRectangle      = 201,
    /* Enable or disable the swap rectangle           */
    kCGLCESwapLimit          = 203,
    /* Enable or disable the swap async limit       */
    kCGLCERasterization      = 221,
    /* Enable or disable all rasterization          */
    kCGLCEStateValidation    = 301,
    /* Validate state for multi-screen functionality */
    kCGLCESurfaceBackingSize = 305,
    /* Enable or disable surface backing size override */
    kCGLCEDisplayListOptimization = 307
    /* Ability to turn off display list optimizer */
    } CGLContextEnable;
```

Read/Write Parameters

`kCGLCPSwapRectangle`

If your application occupies much more screen space (whether the full screen or windowed) than you are typically drawing to, a `kCGLCPSwapRectangle` may be specified as an optimization hint for OpenGL. When a swap rectangle is defined, the Mac OpenGL implementation may be able to optimize your application by only swapping the back to the front buffer in the region defined by this swap rectangle. As with any hint, this behavior is not guaranteed. Furthermore, the region outside the swap rectangle may be swapped (or flushed) by the Quartz windowing system itself. This is often the case in a compositing situation where windows overlap.

`kCGLCPSwapInterval`

The swap interval parameter allows applications to control the frequency at which the buffers are swapped in a double-buffered application. The swap interval allows your application to tie buffer swaps to the retrace rate of the display. This behavior is often desirable for real-time applications that wish to guarantee a specific frame rate rather than running "as fast as they can." This mechanism allows synchronization of your application with an external device that generates interrupts at a fixed time interval.

If the swap interval setting is 0, swaps are executed as early as possible without regard to the refresh rate of the monitor. For any swap interval setting n that is greater than 0, buffer swaps will occur every nth refresh of the display. A setting of 1 will, therefore, synchronize your buffer swaps with the vertical retrace of the display. This is often referred to as vertical blank synchronized or "VBL sync'd."

`kCGLCPClientStorage`

The client storage parameter allows for associating a single 32-bit value with a context. Essentially this parameter allows applications to piggy-back an arbitrary pointer or other 4-byte value onto the context so as to allow logical grouping of data with a context.

`kCGLCPSurfaceTexture`

Surface texturing in OS X allows texturing from a drawable object that is associated with a context. Thus, surface texturing is yet another mechanism to render to a texture on OS X. Given the availability of pbuffer texturing and now framebuffer objects, the now twice superseded surface texturing approach is the oldest, least flexible, and least well-maintained render-to-texture method on the Mac. If we haven't dissuaded you yet, read on . . .

Surface texturing is typically done using AGL or GLUT, as both of these APIs provide a direct interface to set up surface texturing—`aglSurfaceTexture` and `glutSurfaceTexture`, respectively. The Mac OpenGL surface texturing API requires a surface ID. If you're intent on using CGL only in your application (recommended solely as an academic exercise, and not for production code), your surface texturing will be limited to using pbuffers as the drawable source of the surface texture itself. There are no other surface IDs obtainable through CGL.

See Chapter 7 for more information on surface texturing.

`kCGLCPSurfaceOrder`

`kCGLCPSurfaceOrder` is used to control the overlay ordering of visible drawables on the desktop. A value of 1 (the default) orders the surface in front of existing windows. A value of −1 orders the surface behind existing windows.

`kCGLCPSurfaceOpacity`

`kCGLCPSurfaceOpacity` is used by the Quartz windowing system when compositing the drawable associated with the current context. `kCGLCPSurfaceOpacity` is a Boolean value describing whether the surface is opaque (1) or has transparency (0).

`kCGLCPReclaimResources`

`kCGLCPReclaimResources` provides application writers with the flexibility to free all data allocations associated with the current context. These resources include memory allocated for

- Draw pixels (textures used for faster drawing)
- Display lists
- Texture objects
- Vertex buffer objects
- Vertex array objects
- Any device-specific data

Because the memory is released and pointers nullified for all of these resources, you should expect a slowdown in your application if you subsequently use OpenGL entry points that create, modify, or use the data described in the list above.

Typically, `kCGLCPReclaimResources` is used when the context usage is expected to be much simpler after the resources have been freed. For instance, perhaps your application no longer intends to use vertex buffer objects, vertex array objects, or display lists but still makes calls to `glDrawPixels()`. In this case, it's worth the small amount of setup overhead needed to reestablish the internal draw pixels state, given that you'll be freeing a great deal of memory associated with the other object types in the OpenGL driver.

Read-Only Parameters

`kCGLCPDispatchTableSize`

Used internally by OS X and tools for memory allocation.

`kCGLCPSurfaceBackingSize`

Used to retrieve the amount of memory allocated to support the drawable attached to the current context.

`kCGLCPSurfaceSurfaceVolatile`

Used internally by OS X for efficient surface management.

`kCGLCPCurrentRendererID`

Use as an argument to CGLGetParameter to retrieve the ID of the current renderer.

`kCGLCPGPUVertexProcessing`

Use to determine whether the GPU associated with the renderer will be used for vertex shading.

`kCGLCPGPUFragmentProcessing`

Use to determine whether the GPU associated with the renderer will be used for fragment shading.

Renderer Information

Obtaining information about the renderers available on a Mac is a four-step process. Here, we'll show a simple example and then elaborate on the four steps needed to complete this task and describe possible variations at each step. Many readers will be able to just glance at the example and get all the information they need. If so, you can skip the individual steps. In any case, immediately following the steps is a full description of the complete set of renderer properties. Most developers will be interested in reading through this list to determine the applicability to their application.

Now the example:

Example 6-2 Creating and Inspecting Renderer Info Objects

```
#include <OpenGL/OpenGL.h>
#include <OpenGL/gl.h>
#include <OpenGL/glext.h>
#include <CoreGraphics/CGDirectDisplay.h>
#include <stdio.h>
#include <stdlib.h>
```

```
int main(int argc, char **argv)
{

    // Grab the display mask for the main display
    // using kCGDirectMainDisplay
    // (steps 1 & 2 of 4)
    CGOpenGLDisplayMask displayMask =
        CGDisplayIDToOpenGLDisplayMask( kCGDirectMainDisplay ) ;
    CGLPixelFormatAttribute attribs[] =
    {
        kCGLPFAFullScreen,
        kCGLPFADisplayMask,
        displayMask,
        0
    };

    CGLPixelFormatObj pixelFormatObj ;
    CGLContextObj contextObj ;
    CGLRendererInfoObj rendererInfoObj;
    long i, numPixelFormats, rendererCount, vram, texMem, rendererID ;

    // Create the context
    CGLChoosePixelFormat(attribs, &pixelFormatObj, &numPixelFormats);
    CGLCreateContext(pixelFormatObj, NULL, &contextObj) ;
    CGLDestroyPixelFormat(pixelFormatObj) ;
    CGLSetCurrentContext(contextObj);

    // Now that we have a context, populate the
    // rendererInfoObj instance (step 3)
    CGLQueryRendererInfo(displayMask, &rendererInfoObj, &rendererCount);

    // Iterate over all of the renderers
    // contained in the rendererInfoObj instance (step 4)
    for(i = 0; i < rendererCount; i++)
    {
        CGLDescribeRenderer(rendererInfoObj, i, kCGLRPRendererID,
          &rendererID);
        CGLDescribeRenderer(rendererInfoObj, i, kCGLRPVideoMemory,
          &vram);
        CGLDescribeRenderer(rendererInfoObj, i, kCGLRPTextureMemory, &texMem);
        printf("Renderer ID: 0x%lx \n\t%16s %ld b "\
               "(%0.2f MB) \n\t%16s %ld b  (%0.2f MB)\n\n",
            rendererID, "Video Memory:", vram,
            vram / (1024.0f * 1024.0f), "Texture Memory:",
            texMem, texMem / (1024.0f * 1024.0f));
    }
    return 0;
}
```

Example 6-2 shows the simplest and most commonly used form of each of the steps. Now let's look at some of the options and details where the four steps could vary.

Step 1: Obtaining Display IDs

The first step is to obtain the display ID associated with the renderer you're interested in inspecting. The Quartz Services API provides several routines for obtaining display IDs:

- `CGMainDisplayID`
- `CGGetOnlineDisplayList`
- `CGGetActiveDisplayList`
- `CGGetDisplaysWithPoint`
- `CGGetDisplaysWithRect`

`CGMainDisplayID` is the simplest of these calls. Its prototype is

```
CGDirectDisplayID CGMainDisplayID(void);
```

In a sense, a call to `CGMainDisplayID`, in the context of obtaining renderer information, is redundant (and slow). If it is just the main display ID you wish to use, the constant `kCGDirectMainDisplay` is defined for this purpose.

Displays on a Mac system employ a global coordinate system to describe positional information independent of a specific device and display pairing. The main display is defined as the display in this global coordinate space with its screen location at (0,0).

Mac systems can perform display mirroring to display the same information on two monitors. Alternatively, the display preferences pane allows you to configure multiple monitors in an extended desktop mode. As a point of reference, in extended desktop mode, the display with the menu bar is the main display of the system.

All other display retrieval functions, aside from `CGMainDisplayID` in the Quartz Services API, return a list of displays. To obtain a list of displays that can be rendered to, use

```
CGDisplayErr CGGetActiveDisplayList( CGDisplayCount activeDisplayArraySize,
CGDirectDisplayID *activeDisplayArray, CGDisplayCount activeDisplay-
ReturnCount);
```

This function uses the common data retrieval entry point parameters of an array, the allocation size of the array, and a pointer for the return count of matching items.

For a broader list of all displays connected to a system, call

```
CGDisplayErr CGGetOnlineDisplayList( CGDisplayCount onlineDisplayArraySize,
CGDirectDisplayID *onlineDisplayArray, CGDisplayCount onlineDisplay-
ReturnCount);
```

`CGGetOnlineDisplayList` will return active displays, mirrored displays, and sleeping displays. To distinguish this function from `CGGetActiveDisplayList`, mirrored displays may or may not be drawable and sleeping displays are not drawable.

Display IDs can also be obtained based on spatial parameters:

```
CGGetDisplaysWithPoint( CGPoint point, CGDisplayCount displayArraySize,
CGDirectDisplayID *displayArray, CGDisplayCount displayReturnCount);

CGGetDisplaysWithRect( CGRect rect, CGDisplayCount displayArraySize,
CGDirectDisplayID *displayArray, CGDisplayCount displayReturnCount);
```

In the point case, the display list will contain a single display in extended desktop mode. In mirrored mode, the display list may contain multiple displays that encompass the same point. In the rect case, the display list returned will be all displays intersected by the specified rectangle and behaves as the point case does for mirrored mode.

Step 2: Obtaining an OpenGL Display Mask from a Display ID

The second step in the process of obtaining renderer information is to obtain an OpenGL display mask. This step is a simple matter of calling

```
CGOpenGLDisplayMask CGDisplayIDToOpenGLDisplayMask( CGDirectDisplayID
display);
```

This function is invertible, if you will, by calling `CGOpenGLDisplayMaskToDisplayID` or `CGGetDisplaysWithOpenGLDisplayMask`. These routines use OpenGL display masks to obtain display IDs. OpenGL display masks are created using display IDs and work in the same manner as the other display ID retrieval entry points. Their signatures are as follows:

```
CGDirectDisplayID CGOpenGLDisplayMaskToDisplayID( CGOpenGLDisplayMask mask);

CGDisplayErr CGGetDisplaysWithOpenGLDisplayMask( CGOpenGLDisplayMask mask,
CGDisplayCount displayArraySize, CGDirectDisplayID *displayArray, CGDisplay
Count *displayReturnCount);
```

Step 3: Obtain Renderer Info Objects

Step 3 takes us from the Quartz Services API back to CGL. You must now retrieve a `CGLRendererInfoObj` from CGL. This is done with a call to

```
CGLError CGLQueryRendererInfo( CGOpenGLDisplayMask displayMask, CGLRenderer
InfoObj *rendererInfoObj, long *rendererCount);
```

Note that in the case of `CGLQueryRendererInfo`, despite the presence of the `rendererCount`, the `rendererInfoObj` parameter is not an array. Instead, `rendererInfoObj`, upon return from this function, will contain information about all of the renderers matching the OpenGL display mask.

The `displayMask` parameter is a 32-bit quantity. To obtain renderer information about all renderers in the system, set all bits in `displayMask` to 1, or 0xFFFFFFFF.

Step 4: Probing the Renderer Information Object for Information

The `CGLRendererInfoObj` data type is an opaque pointer to a structure. To extract information from this structure, use

```
CGLError CGLDescribeRenderer( CGLRendererInfoObj rendererInfoObj, long
rendererIndex, CGLRendererProperty property,  long *value);
```

Seeing this function begs the obvious question: How do I obtain the number of renderers referenced by the renderer info object? The answer to this question is the same as for the question dealing with obtaining information about the renderers themselves. That is, use an enumeration value from the `CGLRendererProperty` enumerated array:

```
typedef enum _CGLRendererProperty {
    kCGLRPOffScreen            =  53,
    kCGLRPFullScreen           =  54,
    kCGLRPRendererID           =  70,
    kCGLRPAccelerated          =  73,
    kCGLRPRobust               =  75,
    kCGLRPBackingStore         =  76,
    kCGLRPMPSafe               =  78,
    kCGLRPWindow               =  80,
    kCGLRPMultiScreen          =  81,
    kCGLRPCompliant            =  83,
    kCGLRPDisplayMask          =  84,
    kCGLRPBufferModes          = 100,
    kCGLRPColorModes           = 103,
    kCGLRPAccumModes           = 104,
    kCGLRPDepthModes           = 105,
    kCGLRPStencilModes         = 106,
    kCGLRPMaxAuxBuffers        = 107,
    kCGLRPMaxSampleBuffers     = 108,
    kCGLRPMaxSamples           = 109,
    kCGLRPSampleModes          = 110,
    kCGLRPSampleAlpha          = 111,
    kCGLRPVideoMemory          = 120,
    kCGLRPTextureMemory        = 121,
    kCGLRPRendererCount        = 128,
    } CGLRendererProperty;
```

The renderer count is obtained using the property `kCGLRendererCount`.

Let's go through the remaining `CGLRenderProperties`:

`kCGLRPOffScreen`

Boolean indicating whether the renderer supports off-screen rendering.

`kCGLRPFullScreen`

Boolean indicating whether the renderer supports full-screen rendering.

`kCGLRPRendererID`

The renderer ID being "described" by `CGLDescribeRenderer`.

`kCGLRPAccelerated`

Boolean indicating whether the renderer is hardware accelerated.

`kCGLRPRobust`

In the event that your current renderer is a hardware renderer, `kCGLRobust` indicates whether it can fall back to software in the event that one of the limits of the renderer is exceeded. `kCGLRPRobust` is a renderer selection attribute. That is, if `kCGLRobust` is set to `true` at pixel format selection time, only renderers that cannot fall back to software will be returned in the match list.

The vast majority of applications should ignore this attribute. It has historical relevance for situations where two hardware devices, each with an attached display, were installed in the system. If the less capable of these devices had one of its limits exceeded (`GL_MAX_TEXTURE_SIZE`, for instance), and `kCGLRobust` was set to `true`, the more capable device would be used as a fallback renderer. If `kCGLRobust` was set to `false`, the less capable device would fall back to the software renderer to handle the situation where its limits were exceeded.

`kCGLRPBackingStore`

Boolean indicating whether the renderer can provide a back buffer, for color information, that is the size of the drawable object associated with the context using the renderer. If set to `true`, `kCGLRPBackingStore` guarantees that the contents of this back buffer are valid after a call to `CGLFlushDrawable` is made.

`kCGLRPMPSafe`

Historical Boolean indicating whether the renderer is thread safe. This renderer property is no longer used, as all renderers are now thread safe.

`kCGLRPWindow`

Boolean used only by the AGL or Cocoa API that describes whether the renderer is capable of rendering to a window. As CGL does not render to windows, this renderer property should be irrelevant to your application.

`kCGLRPMultiScreen`

Boolean indicating whether the renderer is currently driving multiple displays.

`kCGLRPCompliant`

Boolean indicating whether the renderer is OpenGL compliant.

kCGLRPDisplayMask

The display mask describing the physical displays to which the renderer is capable of rendering. Display masks are managed by the Direct Display API, which is part of the Core Graphics API. See Steps 1 and 2 in Renderer Information earlier in this chapter (pages 70–71) for information on display masks.

kCGLRPBufferModes

The bitwise OR of buffer mode bits for the renderer. The list of buffer mode bits includes

- kCGLSingleBufferBit
- kCGLDoubleBufferBit
- kCGLMonoscopicBit
- kCGLStereoscopicBit

kCGLRPColorModes and kCGLRPAccumModes

Both kCGLRPColorModes and kCGLRPAccumModes are bitwise ORs of formats supported by the renderer. They share the same list of constants:

```
kCGLRGB444Bit        0x00000040
/* 16 rgb bit/pixel,    R=11:8, G=7:4, B=3:0              */
kCGLARGB4444Bit      0x00000080
/* 16 argb bit/pixel,   A=15:12, R=11:8, G=7:4, B=3:0     */
kCGLRGB444A8Bit      0x00000100
/* 8-16 argb bit/pixel, A=7:0, R=11:8, G=7:4, B=3:0       */
kCGLRGB555Bit        0x00000200
/* 16 rgb bit/pixel,    R=14:10, G=9:5, B=4:0             */
kCGLARGB1555Bit      0x00000400
/* 16 argb bit/pixel,   A=15, R=14:10, G=9:5, B=4:0       */
kCGLRGB555A8Bit      0x00000800
/* 8-16 argb bit/pixel, A=7:0, R=14:10, G=9:5, B=4:0      */
kCGLRGB565Bit        0x00001000
/* 16 rgb bit/pixel,    R=15:11, G=10:5, B=4:0            */
kCGLRGB565A8Bit      0x00002000
/* 8-16 argb bit/pixel, A=7:0, R=15:11, G=10:5, B=4:0     */
kCGLRGB888Bit        0x00004000
/* 32 rgb bit/pixel,    R=23:16, G=15:8, B=7:0            */
kCGLARGB8888Bit      0x00008000
/* 32 argb bit/pixel,   A=31:24, R=23:16, G=15:8, B=7:0   */
kCGLRGB888A8Bit      0x00010000
/* 8-32 argb bit/pixel, A=7:0, R=23:16, G=15:8, B=7:0     */
kCGLRGB101010Bit     0x00020000
/* 32 rgb bit/pixel,    R=29:20, G=19:10, B=9:0           */
kCGLARGB2101010Bit   0x00040000
/* 32 argb bit/pixel,   A=31:30  R=29:20, G=19:10, B=9:0  */
kCGLRGB101010_A8Bit  0x00080000
/* 8-32 argb bit/pixel, A=7:0  R=29:20, G=19:10, B=9:0    */
kCGLRGB121212Bit     0x00100000
/* 48 rgb bit/pixel,    R=35:24, G=23:12, B=11:0          */
```

```
kCGLARGB12121212Bit 0x00200000
/* 48 argb bit/pixel,   A=47:36, R=35:24, G=23:12, B=11:0 */
kCGLRGB161616Bit    0x00400000
/* 64 rgb bit/pixel,    R=63:48, G=47:32, B=31:16         */
kCGLRGBA16161616Bit 0x00800000
/* 64 argb bit/pixel,   R=63:48, G=47:32, B=31:16, A=15:0 */
kCGLRGBFloat64Bit   0x01000000
/* 64 rgb bit/pixel,    half float                        */
kCGLRGBAFloat64Bit  0x02000000
/* 64 argb bit/pixel,   half float                        */
kCGLRGBFloat128Bit  0x04000000
/* 128 rgb bit/pixel,   ieee float                        */
kCGLRGBAFloat128Bit 0x08000000
/* 128 argb bit/pixel,  ieee float                        */
kCGLRGBFloat256Bit  0x10000000
/* 256 rgb bit/pixel,   ieee double                       */
kCGLRGBAFloat256Bit 0x20000000
/* 256 argb bit/pixel,  ieee double                       */
```

For all of the preceding constants, the color components occupy some multiple of 16 bits. In most, the pixel size is simply the sum of the component widths. In some, such as kCGLRGB444Bit, the pixel occupies more than the required 12 bits but is always stored in the low-order bits of the nearest 16-bit boundary—in this case, 16 bits.

The relevant information in these constants is the component sizes themselves. These sizes provide information on the level of quantization of the pixel data you should expect to see when using a framebuffer configured in this format. There is no programmatic interface through OpenGL or CGL to retrieve the data—with the bit positions as they are described here remaining intact—from the framebuffer. The layout of these pixels as they are retrieved from the framebuffer is controlled by tokens in OpenGL.

kCGLRPDepthModes and kCGLRPStencilModes

Both kCGLRPDepthModes and kCGLRPStencilModes are bitwise ORs specifying the number of respective bits that are supported by the renderer. The range of possible values includes

- kCGL0Bit
- kCGL1Bit
- kCGL2Bit
- kCGL3Bit
- kCGL4Bit
- kCGL5Bit
- kCGL6Bit
- kCGL8Bit
- kCGL10Bit
- kCGL12Bit
- kCGL16Bit
- kCGL24Bit
- kCGL32Bit
- kCGL48Bit
- kCGL64Bit
- kCGL96Bit
- kCGL128Bit

`kCGLRPMaxAuxBuffers`

The maximum number of auxiliary buffers supported by the renderer.

`kCGLRPMaxSampleBuffers`

The maximum number of independent sample buffers supported by the renderer. This renderer property generally reduces to a Boolean value. If a multisample buffer exists for the renderer, `kCGLRPMaxSampleBuffers` will be set to 1; otherwise, it is set to 0.

`kCGLRPMaxSamples`

For multisampling, `kCGLRPMaxSamples` indicates the maximum number of samples per pixel that are supported by the renderer.

`kCGLRPSampleModes`

Bitwise OR of sampling modes supported by the renderer. The constants available for `kCGLRPSampleModes` include `kCGLPFAMultisample`, `kCGLPFASupersample`, and `kCGLPFASampleAlpha`.

`kCGLRPSampleAlpha`

When multisampling, this Boolean indicates whether the alpha component, along with the color components, is multisampled.

`kCGLRPVideoMemory`

Indicates the number of bytes of video memory on the graphics card associated with the renderer. For software renderers where host memory is used for video memory, 0 is reported as this attribute's value.

`kCGLRPTextureMemory`

Indicates the number of bytes of texture memory configured on the graphics card associated with the renderer. Often this number will be some number less than video memory, where the difference is accounted for in allocations for framebuffer memory. For software renderers, where host memory is used for texture memory, 0 is reported as this attribute's value.

Sharing OpenGL Objects Across CGL Contexts

Sharing data across contexts is done by specifying a share context at `CGLCreateContext` time. `CGLCreateContext` is defined in `CGL.h`:

```
CGLError CGLCreateContext( CGLPixelFormatObj pix, CGLContextObj shareCtx,
CGLContextObj *newCtx);
```

`CGLCreateContext` also has an external definition in `OpenGL.h` of the `OpenGL.framework`.

To successfully share data across contexts, the contexts must share the same renderer. Another way of expressing this requirement is to say that the contexts must have the same virtual screen list. A virtual screen is defined as the pairing of one renderer and its associated set of physical displays. Given that there is only one renderer per virtual screen, having the same virtual screen list means having the same renderer. To determine the virtual screen list from a context, use

```
CGLError CGLGetVirtualScreen(CGLContextObj ctx, long *screen);
```

To determine the renderer ID from this virtual screen, use

```
CGLError CGLDescribePixelFormat(CGLPixelFormatObj pix, long pix_num,
CGLPixelFormatAttribute attrib, long *value);
```

If the renderer IDs are the same between the contexts, data sharing will be successful.

If your application has multiple contexts, it is more likely that you will also have multiple threads. If so, remember to bracket your OpenGL calls in each thread with calls to `CGLLockContext()` and `CGLUnlockContext()` to prevent state collisions.

Drawables

Depending on which company representative you speak to, which conference you're attending, the context of the meeting you're in, or perhaps even the time of day or the weather, different people in 3D graphics frequently use different terms for pretty much the same thing. One graphics concept that has many names is the memory and state used and established as a destination for rendering. In some places, it's referred to as a drawable; while in others, a surface or perhaps a framebuffer. CGL refers to this rendering destination as a drawable.

There are three recognized types of drawables in CGL: pbuffers, off-screen buffers, and full-screen buffers. The most fundamental operation for drawables is associating them with a CGL context, which establishes the destination for rendering for OpenGL commands issued when that context is current. These association functions are `CGLSetPBuffer`, `CGLSetOffscreen`, and `CGLSetFullscreen`. Removing the drawable association with a context is done with a call to

```
CGLError CGLClearDrawable(CGLContextObj ctx);
```

For double-buffered drawables, swapping the contents of the back buffer to the front buffer is done by calling

```
CGLError CGLFlushDrawable(CGLContextObj ctx);
```

`CGLFlushDrawable` causes an implicit flush of the OpenGL command stream. The results of all previously submitted OpenGL commands are then executed and reflected in the back buffer prior to it being copied to the front buffer.

As with most OpenGL implementations, performing complex application logic immediately following a call to swap buffers is a good way to take advantage of the latency inherent in the swap. The Mac OpenGL implementation has the additional flexibility of specifying a swap interval. Read the details of the context parameter `kCGLCPSwapInterval` on page 66 for more information on how the swap interval affects the timing of the buffer swap.

Now let's discuss each of three drawable types in more detail.

Pixel Buffers

Pixel buffers (pbuffers) are accelerated off-screen rendering drawables that are defined in many OpenGL configuration APIs like CGL. These buffers exist because drawables, for any OpenGL implementation, have been resource managed by the window system. This put them outside the realm of core OpenGL.

Aside from being a destination for rendering, CGL pbuffers can be used as a source for texturing. Combine these two aspects, and you have the ability to render to textures, which is useful in many graphics applications. More so than textures of equivalent size, pbuffers are large resources and should be managed with care so as not to introduce memory or performance problems in your applications. Rendering to them requires either switching the drawable of your CGL context or doing a context switch from your main rendering context to a context you've dedicated to the pbuffer. Neither of these operations is particularly cheap.

Fortunately, pbuffers have been handily superseded by the introduction of framebuffer objects in OpenGL 2.0. The framebuffer object extension to OpenGL was one of the largest and most carefully considered additions in OpenGL's history. Therefore, there is no reason to use pbuffers for new software development on the Mac. Of course, there is plenty of existing software that uses the pbuffer API, so it's worthy of discussion here.

The pbuffer API in CGL consists of the entry points seen in Table 6-1.

To create a new pbuffer, use

```
CGLError CGLCreatePBuffer(long width, long height, unsigned long target,
unsigned long internalFormat, long maxLevel, CGLPBufferObj *pbuffer);
```

Notice the `target` and `internalFormat` parameters. `target` may be either GL_TEXTURE_2D, GL_TEXTURE_RECTANGLE_EXT, or GL_TEXTURE_CUBE_MAP.

Table 6-1 CGL Pbuffer Functions

Function	Description
CGLCreatePBuffer	Creates an AGL pixel buffer for use with an OpenGL texture type
CGLDestroyPBuffer	Destroys an AGL pixel buffer
CGLDescribePBuffer	Gathers information about an AGL pixel buffer
CGLGetPBuffer	Queries a context for the pixel buffer attached to it
CGLSetPBuffer	Sets the pixel buffer to be the target for the specified context
CGLTexImagePBuffer	Binds a pixel buffer as a texture; analogous to glTexImage2D

internalFormat may be either of the two basic internal OpenGL texture formats, GL_RGBA or GL_RGB. These two parameters give good insight into why pbuffers exist in the CGL interface. They were specifically designed for rendering to textures—so much so that there isn't a simplified interface for creating them that is texturing agnostic!

Continuing with the texturing theme, the width and height parameters must be powers of 2 when using either a GL_TEXTURE_2D or GL_TEXTURE_CUBE_MAP target. Also, width must equal height for GL_TEXTURE_CUBE_MAP targets, because they must be square.

The last parameter constraint, also a texturing consideration, deals with mipmaps. The maxLevel parameter must be commensurate with the number of possible mipmap levels when using the provided width and height parameters. If the number of mipmap levels is less than the value specified in maxLevel or if any of the aforementioned constraints is violated, CGLCreatePBuffer will return kCGLBadValue.

Freeing a pbuffer and its resources entails a simple call to

```
CGLError CGLDestroyPBuffer(CGLPBufferObj pbuffer);
```

Given that it has only one argument, only one thing can go wrong with this call: If the pbuffer argument is NULL, kCGLBadAddress will be returned.

Getting information about an existing pbuffer is done using

```
CGLError CGLDescribePBuffer(CGLPBufferObj obj, long *width, long *height,
unsigned  long *target, unsigned long *internalFormat, long *maxLevel);
```

Each of the pointer arguments to CGLDescribePBuffer is used by this function to fill in its corresponding value. The values for these parameters are fixed at the time the pbuffer was created, so there should be no concerns while debugging that another CGL call has altered the configuration of the pbuffer. Again, only a NULL pbuffer object parameter will cause CGLDescribePBuffer to return its single possible error condition: kCGLBadAddress.

To associate a pbuffer with a CGL context for rendering, call

```
CGLError CGLSetPBuffer(CGLContextObj ctx, CGLPBufferObj pbuffer, unsigned
long face, long mipmapLevel, long virtualScreen);
```

Like most APIs, CGL defers as much work as it can until as late as is logically possible. This is the case with the relationship between CGLCreatePBuffer and CGLSetPBuffer. Despite its name, CGLCreatePBuffer doesn't do nearly as much work to establish a drawable for rendering as CGLSetPBuffer does. This difference arises because you must call CGLSetPBuffer to associate it with a CGL context before rendering into it. This makes sense, because there is no CGL context argument to the CGLCreatePBuffer function.

In addition to the context association, CGLSetPBuffer configures the current face and level settings for pbuffers with targets of the respective types.

The virtualScreen argument to CGLSetPBuffer requires the most care when setting it. Recall that there is one renderer per virtual screen. This argument serves to establish the renderer to be used when rendering to this pbuffer. Often, you'll wish to use the same renderer that is associated with your CGL context to render to your pbuffer. This can be done inline with a simple call to CGLGetVirtualScreen:

```
CGLGetVirtualScreen(CGLContextObj ctx, long *screen)
```

Using the same renderer as your main rendering context is essential for best performance when texturing from your pbuffer. If the renderer used for your context and pbuffer differs, it will likely result in a copy of the texture-level data from the local storage of one renderer to the other. Pbuffers hold a lot of data, so this copy may well cause considerable performance and memory problems for your applications.

Once a pbuffer has been associated with a CGL context for rendering, you can call

```
CGLError CGLGetPBuffer(CGLContextObj ctx, CGLPBufferObj *pbuffer, unsigned
long *face, long *mipmapLevel, long *screen);
```

to retrieve information about the pbuffer associated with ctx. If the target of the pbuffer is GL_TEXTURE_CUBE_MAP, face will be set to the cube map face of the pbuffer. Otherwise, face will be set to zero. The level will be set to the mipmap level that was last specified in a call to CGLSetPBuffer.

Texturing with Pixel Buffers as the Source

If you wish to specify that your pbuffer is to be used as the current texture, call

```
CGLError CGLTexImagePBuffer(CGLContextObj ctx, CGLPBufferObj pbuffer,
unsigned long sourceBuffer);
```

The semantics for this call are the undisputed champion of complexity of all calls in CGL, and with good reason. CGLTexImagePBuffer is most similar to one of the glTexImage(N)D calls of OpenGL. That is, it defines the texture source for the currently bound texture ID to use the contents of the pbuffer for rendering.

The ctx argument refers to the main rendering context that is using the pbuffer as a data source for texturing. It does not refer to a context that you may have dedicated to your pbuffer (which you would have then specified in a call to CGLSetPbuffer). Having two such contexts is the typical pbuffer usage scenario. It requires a context switch from your main rendering context to your pbuffer context whenever you wish to change the destination of rendered output from, say, the visible screen to your pbuffer. This context switch is a considerable performance disadvantage to using pbuffers as compared with framebuffer objects.

Some key differences in standard OpenGL texturing must be considered when using CGLTexImagePBuffer. First, a texture ID of 0 (otherwise known as the default texture) is off limits. You must bind a non-zero texture ID, generated through use of glGenTextures, by using glBindTexture to a texture with pbuffers. Second, you must use a clean, newly generated texture ID that has not been populated (or, more accurately, "contaminated") with data from any OpenGL call that is capable of doing so. Examples are any variant of glTexImage, glCopyTexImage, glCopyTexSubImage, or glTexSubImage. You can purify a contaminated texture ID only by deleting the texture and, by chance, getting the same ID back from a call to glGenTextures.

For clarity, the sourceBuffer argument should have been implemented in the API with a type of GLenum. sourceBuffer refers to the source buffer for texturing from the pbuffer. It must correspond to a valid OpenGL buffer that was defined as part of the pixel format used to create the renderer for this pbuffer. The set of possible values for sourceBuffer is simply GL_FRONT or GL_BACK. If neither is specified, a kCGLBadValue error code will be returned.

Pbuffer contents may be read back by using a call to glGetTexImage2D when the main rendering context is current and your pbuffer is bound as the current texture, or by using a call to glReadPixels when the pbuffer's context is current.

Off-Screen Drawables

Off-screen drawables are simply a block of host memory that is used as a destination for rendering. This block of memory must be allocated by your application and submitted to CGL through a call to

```
CGLError CGLSetOffScreen(CGLContextObj ctx, long width, long height, long
rowBytes, void *buffer);
```

You must allocate a `buffer` that is at least `rowBytes * height` in size.

As you might expect, because the off-screen buffer is in host memory, off-screen rendering is the slowest kind of rendering of all the possibilities.

If you wish to retrieve the off-screen buffer (as well as its size parameters) and do some processing on the pixel data, you can do so with a call to

```
CGLError CGLGetOffscreen(CGLContextObj ctx, long *width, long *height, long
*rowBytes, void **buffer);
```

If a call is made to `CGLGetOffscreen` when the drawable associated with the context is not an off-screen buffer, all size parameters are set to 0 and the buffer pointer is set to `NULL`.

Full-Screen Drawables

Unlike pbuffers and off-screen drawables, full-screen drawables are not created as separate entities from the context. Instead, they are created implicitly by specifying `kCGLPFAFullScreen` as a parameter for the pixel format you use to create the context.

Not all renderers support full-screen rendering, with the Apple software renderer being the most notable example. You can test for full-screen support of a renderer during the pixel format selection process, as shown in Example 6-3.

Example 6-3 Testing for Full-Screen Rendering Support

```
CGLPixelFormatAttribute attribs[] =
{
    kCGLPFAFullScreen,
    kCGLPFARendererID, kCGLRendererGeForce3ID,
    0
};

CGLPixelFormatObj pixelFormat;
long matchingPixelFormatsCount;

CGLChoosePixelFormat(attribs, &pixelFormat,
    &matchingPixelFormatsCount);

// Test for matching pixel formats.
```

```
if(pixelFormat == NULL)
{
    // kCGLRendererGeForce3ID does NOT support full screen rendering
}
else
{
    // kCGLRendererGeForce3ID supports full screen rendering
}
```

Example 6-3 is rigged because we know that kCGLRendererGeForce3ID supports full-screen rendering, so this test should never fail. Of course, you could substitute your renderer of interest in this example.

Testing for support of any full-screen renderers is a simple matter of removing the kCGLPFARendererID attribute and its value kCGLRendererGeForce3ID from the attribute list. This leaves only the full-screen attribute kCGLPFAFullScreen. Assuming your context was created with a renderer that supports full-screen rendering, a call to

```
CGLError CGLSetFullScreen(CGLContextObj ctx);
```

will establish the associated full-screen drawable as the destination for rendering.

Virtual Screen Management

A virtual screen, remember, is the pairing of a hardware renderer and the physical displays that are driven by that renderer. In Mac laptop computers, for example, the graphics hardware is represented by a single renderer and drives both the built-in display of the computer and any external monitor attached to the laptop. In this scenario, there would be exactly one virtual screen. Thus, regardless of the number of physical displays attached to the computer, there is one virtual screen for each hardware device that drives them.

Now that we have the terminology defined, consider that there are two types of virtual screen changes as far as the OpenGL application programmer is concerned: implicit and explicit. An implicit virtual screen change occurs when the user of the application drags an application window used for OpenGL rendering from a display being driven by one hardware renderer to a different display being driven by a different hardware renderer. The implicit virtual screen change that occurs is the reason your application should call CGLUpdateContext whenever your application windows are moved. This behavior allows CGL to update your context with the renderer information it needs to drive the application on the new display.

Explicit virtual screen changes are done with

```
CGLError CGLSetVirtualScreen(CGLContextObj ctx, long virtualScreen);
```

Such explicit virtual screen changes are a much less common occurrence than implicit changes. Consider what happens when you force a virtual screen change in your application. First, you're changing the renderer from one hardware renderer to another without regard to the location of the application window where your drawing occurs. Consider what would happen if, in a desktop system with an ATI and NVIDIA card installed, and the OpenGL rendering window residing on a display connected to the ATI card, calls to `CGLSetVirtualScreen` change the NVIDIA renderer. Because the window location is not updated with this call, and because OpenGL commands and rasterization occur on the NVIDIA hardware, the results of rendering must be propagated by the Mac OpenGL implementation from the backing store reserved for the NVIDIA hardware (the framebuffer) to that of the ATI hardware for display. As a consequence, the rendering takes place on the NVIDIA hardware and the results are copied to the ATI hardware.

The copying of framebuffer bits from the backing store of one device to the backing store of another device will have major consequences for applications that are performance sensitive. Use care when explicitly setting the virtual screen configuration.

"If it is so costly, why would an application ever do an explicit virtual screen change?" you may ask. In the event that one renderer is more capable than another, yet you need to see the results of the more capable renderer on a less capable device, explicit setting of the virtual screen may be the way to go. A good example of this configuration is when you have one hardware device that is capable of doing hardware shaders and another device that is not. Consider an application that allows configuration of shaders in a tools window with some parameter sliders to adjust the shader. Suppose you want to render a sphere with the shader applied on the more capable renderer, yet maintain the tools window itself on a less capable virtual screen. In this example, the sphere would be updated infrequently and the size of the buffer being copied would be relatively small, thus mitigating any performance dropoff.

You can retrieve the current virtual screen of a context as follows:

```
CGLError CGLGetVirtualScreen(CGLContextObj ctx, long *virtualScreen);
```

Global CGL State Functions

CGL allows for setting and retrieving global state parameters. Unlike all other CGL API entry points, the global state functions are context independent. These values can be set at any time and affect any subsequent CGL operations.

`CGLSetOption` is used to set a global CGL option. Its function prototype is

```
CGLError CGLSetOption(CGLGlobalOption globalOption, long\break optionValue);
```

For retrieving global options, use

```
CGLError CGLGetOption(CGLGlobalOption globalOption, long optionValue);
```

The global options for CGL are as follows:

```
typedef enum _CGLGlobalOption {
    kCGLGOFormatCacheSize   = 501,
    kCGLGOClearFormatCache  = 502,
    kCGLGORetainRenderers   = 503,
    kCGLGOResetLibrary      = 504,
    kCGLGOUseErrorHandler   = 505,
    } CGLGlobalOption;
```

`kCGLGOFormatCacheSize` corresponds to the number of pixel formats CGL will maintain at any given time. The default number is 5, but it can be decreased or increased to match the number of pixel formats your application uses. Most applications use only a single pixel format, so memory-conscious applications of this general kind can set the `kCGLGOFormatCacheSize` to 1. As a point of reference, at the time of this writing, each of these pixel format data structures was approximately 60 bytes in size. This value, of course, is subject to change at any time. It is not likely that it will ever be less than its present value, however.

You may clear the CGL format cache at any time by using `kCGLGOClearFormatCache`. This will free the memory of the format cache but has no effect on future allocations. For persistent control of these allocations, use `kCGLGOFormatCacheSize`. As it is essentially an operation, rather than a parameter, `CGLGetOption` will return `false` for this constant.

`kCGLGORetainRenderers` is used to retain renderers in the Mac OpenGL engine's plug-in renderers list. Plug-in renderers maintain a reference count for all contexts that are referencing them. When the last context referencing a renderer is destroyed, the renderer is normally unloaded from the plug-in list and its memory freed. This behavior, though good in the general case, is not suitable if your application frequently creates and destroys contexts that are unique to a single renderer in the plug-in list. Setting `kCGLGORetainRenderers` will result in much less plug-in management under the scenario described. You can toggle the renderer retention mode by setting `kCGLGORetainRenderers` to either `true` or `false`.

`kCGLGOResetLibrary` is the global reset button for CGL. It restores CGL to its initial state, destroys all contexts, and releases all plug-in renderers from the list. Pixel format objects and renderer information objects are not destroyed. If it's not obvious, here's a warning: Use extreme care with this option. As this is another "action" constant, `CGLGetOption` will return `false` when queried with this option.

Using CGL Macros

With OS X, Apple engineers came up with a way to avoid the cost of determining the CGL context from the current thread. The cost of this lookup is significant because it must be done for every entry point in the OpenGL API. Cumulatively speaking, this context determination logic adds up.

CGL macros allow you, as the application developer, to provide some valuable information to OpenGL and thereby avoid the cost of this lookup—in particular, the name of the current CGL context for the thread you are in. Using such a macro requires two simple steps. First, you must include the header file `CGLMacros.h`. Second, you must stick to a convention for the variable name you use to define the current context. You may specify this context name by defining `CGL_MACRO_CONTEXT`. For example:

```
#define CGL_MACRO_CONTEXT    ctx
#include <OpenGL/CGLMacros.h>
```

Even easier, you can leave `CGL_MACRO_CONTEXT` undefined, and use the default CGL context name `cgl_ctx`.

CGL macros can make a profound difference in the performance of your application. Generally speaking, the more immediate-mode rendering you do, the bigger the improvement produced by using CGL macros. To be formulaic about it, the larger the ratio of OpenGL function calls your application makes relative to the amount of data referenced by those calls, the bigger your performance gains will be using CGL macros. This, of course, doesn't mean we're advocating the use of immediate-mode rendering for the sake of big gains with CGL macros! You're much better off keeping your data in VRAM by doing as much retained-mode rendering as you possibly can.

Summary

Whether you use CGL, AGL, or Cocoa for your OpenGL application on the Mac, having at least some knowledge of CGL will improve your understanding of the higher-level windowing system interfaces to OpenGL on OS X. CGL-derived functions, data types, and constants make many appearances in both the AGL and AppKit APIs. Therefore, if you keep in mind that this information is derived, you may be able to find the more detailed documentation you're looking for by examining the CGL analog to whatever it is you're investigating.

For example, try reading the AGL reference guide segment on `aglChoosePixelFormat` and then reading the CGL reference guide segment on `CGLChoosePixelFormat`. You may or may not find additional information on your topic, but it's a good information path to keep in mind.

We hope we've disuaded you from using either the surface texturing or pbuffer methods of rendering to textures on OS X in favor of using OpenGL framebuffer objects. Taking pbuffers out of CGL simplifies its usage to renderer selection and context management.

Popular belief says that Carbon applications are a thing of the past and that the future belongs to Cocoa applications on OS X. While we're not here to weigh in on this opinion, remember that CGL is not part of the Carbon–Cocoa equation. CGL is part of the OpenGL framework and will be supported with as much vigilance as OpenGL itself.

Chapter 7

The AGL API
for OpenGL
Configuration

Overview

OS X has both Carbon and Cocoa windowing interfaces to OpenGL. AGL, or
"Apple OpenGL" is the Carbon windowing interface to OpenGL. Like CGL and
Cocoa, the AGL interface provides a set of routines for managing pixel formats,
OpenGL contexts, and drawables (a.k.a *surfaces*).

As far as Apple technologies are concerned, AGL is overshadowed by the more
modern and objectified Cocoa. Still, AGL has its place in today's applications
and is still a first-class citizen when it comes to Apple's ongoing support of
the API.

Despite AGL being "the old way" to do things from the perspective of hard-
core Apple technology buffs, it has its advantages. Because Cocoa is defined as
an Objective C class hierarchy, there are some obvious reasons why adapting
an existing application not written in Objective-C would pose more challenges.
This is especially true if the existing application doesn't have a distinct software abstraction defining its view in the model-view-controller design pattern.
In other words, if the UI logic is not easily separated from the application logic,
it's difficult to replace the UI logic with code from a different object-based UI
library like that of Cocoa.

Another potential challenge of using Cocoa is its use of Objective-C.
Although Objective-C applications can be written as a conglomeration of C,
C++, Objective-C, and even Java, moving between the syntax and semantics of
different programming languages always imposes some overhead to the software development process.

AGL then, being defined as a simple, procedural C API, has its advantages. It
can more easily be integrated into existing C and C++ applications. Developing

89

a porting strategy from windowing interfaces of other platforms such as GLX or WGL is relatively simple.

To make the Cocoa versus AGL decision even more complex, the Carbon event model, in the humble opinion of the authors, is more complicated than the event model used by Cocoa.

One of the most redeeming aspects of AGL is its clear and apparent similarity to CGL. It has the simplicity of CGL with the additional logic and entry points required to build windowed applications.

Software Layering

The composited desktop of Mac OS X arguably provides the best user experience of any OS available. The underpinnings of such an amazing user experience are necessarily more complex than conventional windowing systems. This complexity manifests itself to some extent in the software layering of AGL and its related APIs (see Figure 7-1).

As we've said, AGL is built on top of CGL. Because of the compositing interaction of Quartz window server and drawables used as a destination for rendering in AGL applications, AGL also has dependencies on the Core Graphics API. Add the obvious interaction with OpenGL, and you have all the pieces with which AGL interacts.

The AGL API lives in either your particular SDK framework path or /System/ Library/Frameworks. As with other APIs, linking against AGL requires specification of this framework path. Similarly, compiling using headers from the AGL framework requires specification of the framework. Table 7-1 indicates the relevant locations for building and linking with the AGL framework.

AGL is an interface for Carbon applications. It is incompatible with Cocoa applications. Because AGL is built on top of CGL, you may make CGL calls from an AGL application so long as you respect the distinct data structures and types for the two APIs.

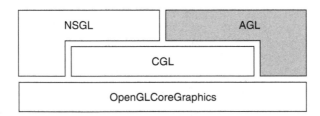

Figure 7-1 AGL Software Dependencies

Table 7-1 Locations of AGL Headers and Frameworks

Framework path	/System/Library/Frameworks/AGL.framework
Build flag	-framework AGL
Header	#include<AGL/agl.h>

With the fundamentals of AGL now described, and the locations in which to fully explore the framework identified, let's move directly into pixel format and context configuration.

Pixel Format and Context

As we've discussed in earlier chapters of this book, the layer of "glue" between your OpenGL code and the window system of your application performs two key tasks: pixel format selection and OpenGL context creation. The name for that layer, in this chapter at least, is AGL.

The pixel formats describe attributes, per pixel, of your OpenGL rendering destination, and the context binds that pixel format to your window system drawable. To review, a drawable is an object such as a window, pixel buffer, framebuffer object, or other graphics target used in OpenGL rendering. In this chapter we'll examine the APIs for basic pixel format selection and creation. We'll explain all the enumerants used to specify the pixel format and the functions necessary to configure them and create contexts using those pixel formats.

The overview of how to use AGL to create the relevant glue code for rendering should be familiar. In fact, this process, aside from the specifics of what function calls to use, remains the same as that for CGL. Specifically, you perform four simple steps:

1. Describe, create, and find a matching pixel format (AGLPixelFormat, aglChoosePixelFormat).
2. Create an OpenGL context (AGLContext, aglCreateContext), using the pixel format created in step 1.
3. Bind that context to a drawable (AGLDrawable, aglSetDrawable).
4. Initialize OpenGL, handle events, and render!

Here, we'll look at the relevant application code to create and use a windowed AGL application and a full-screen AGL application as examples of the creation and use of pixel formats and contexts. In the Cocoa chapter (Chapter 8), we'll spend time walking through how to configure and create an XCode project for that set of examples. For now, however, we'll leave it to you to create an XCode project on your own to insert these samples—Carbon event management and plumbing are well beyond our scope. But without further ado, let's begin the construction of our application.

Full-Screen Application

We will begin by creating a full-screen AGL application, so we must create a new XCode project and configure it to depend on the key libraries necessary for OpenGL and AGL on the Mac—that is, the `AGL.framework` and `OpenGL.framework` frameworks. Once it is configured, we can create a main c program. You'll next want to add code to include the OpenGL and AGL headers, as in Example 7-1.

Example 7-1 Headers for OpenGL and AGL

```
#include <OpenGL/OpenGL.h>
#include <AGL/agl.h>
```

We'll also configure a pair of standard methods we'll use in a variety of examples to initialize our OpenGL state, once we've got a context, and to draw in our main loop. With one minor exception, these methods look like other initialization and draw methods you've seen other places. Example 7-2 shows these two routines, and their resultant bodies.

Example 7-2 AGL OpenGL Initialization and Draw Functions

```
void initGLstate()
{
    glMatrixMode( GL_PROJECTION );
    glOrtho(0.0, 1.0, 0.0, 1.0, -1.0, 1.0);

    glClearColor( 0.0, 0.5, 0.8, 1.0 );
}

void draw(void)
{
    glClear( GL_COLOR_BUFFER_BIT );
    glMatrixMode( GL_MODELVIEW );
    glLoadIdentity();
    glRotatef( 5.0, 0.0, 0.0, 1.0 );
    glColor4d( 0.0, 1.0, 0.0, 1.0 );
    glRectd( 0.1, 0.1, 0.9, 0.9 );

    aglSwapBuffers(context);
}
```

The difference between this code and code you've seen before, and will see again later, is the method used to swap the implicitly double-buffered pixel format we're using. The call `aglSwapBuffers()` takes one argument, the AGL context to be swapped, which for our purposes is declared in a globally accessible variable outside this routine. We also have an externally declared pixel format that we use elsewhere, too. That's all there is to our initialization and draw methods; they're pretty much boilerplate OpenGL.

Let's now look at the entirety of our example application `main` method and see how a pixel format is declared, described, and initialized.

Example 7-3 AGL Full-Screen Application `main` Method

```
int main(int argc, char **argv)
{
    // create pixelformat
    AGLPixelFormat pixelFormat;
    GLint attribs[] =
    {
        AGL_DOUBLEBUFFER,
        AGL_ACCELERATED,
        AGL_NO_RECOVERY,
        AGL_RGBA,
        AGL_NONE
    };
    pixelFormat = aglChoosePixelFormat( NULL, 0, attribs );

    // create context & bind to full-screen
    context = aglCreateContext( pixelFormat, NULL );
    aglDestroyPixelFormat( pixelFormat );
    aglSetCurrentContext( context );
    aglSetFullScreen( context, 0, 0, 0, 0 );

    // main loop
    initGLstate();
    draw();
    sleep( 3 );

    // cleanup
    aglSetCurrentContext( NULL );
    aglDestroyContext( context );
    return 0;
}
```

In Example 7-3, we build code in a few `main` sections. The first of these methods creates and fills out an `AGLPixelFormat` structure. In it, we specify the desired attributes of our OpenGL render target—in this case, that we would like an RGBA, double-buffered, hardware-accelerated drawable. Each pixel format specification must end with the `AGL_NONE` token or you'll encounter unexpected pixel format selections at best, and crashes at worst.

Next, we issue the command to actually find a pixel format matching our criteria using `aglChoosePixelFormat`. The last argument is our attribute list, and the first two arguments are a handle to a list of graphics devices and the number of devices, respectively. Specifying `NULL` as the list indicates that all devices should be searched for matching visuals. In this example, that's what we'll do, and see what we get back. The `aglChoosePixelFormat` call will return an opaque handle that describes one or many pixel formats supported by the devices-and-attribute combination in the call. If this were production code, you'd want to ensure that the returned pixel format results were valid and, if they were not, check for other pixel formats that would better meet your needs. If a variety of pixel formats met the criteria you specified, you will want to call aglNextPixelFormat to cycle through the pixel formats in the return value, and then examine each of those options using aglDescribePixelFormat to see which characteristics each has, and if any of them are particularly well-suited to your needs.

One final note on pixel format specification and selection: A variety of AGL functions can generate verbose errors (much like OpenGL does through its glGetError mechanism). You should look at Apple's reference documentation to see which calls can generate these errors and to learn when to query them using aglGetError.

So what are all the tokens that you can specify in conjunction with aglChoose PixelFormat? There are quite a few, and the Apple documentation describes them reasonably well. We include our own descriptions of a useful selection of these tokens in Table 7-2. Among the things that can be specified are stereo or monoscopic rendering capabilities (also known as quad-buffering), stencil planes, depth- and color-buffer sizes, floating-point pixels, anti-aliasing, and even exact specification of the renderer and pixel format by ID. There's quite a lot of capability, and there are close analogs to any of the pixel format tokens exposed in Cocoa as well. Read the table, experiment some, decide which best fit your needs, and then customize your baseline code with your pixel format requirements.

The second major component of the code in Example 7-3 creates and sets the context for our rendering. We simply call aglCreateContext and clean up our pixel format using aglDestroyPixelFormat, since our context is bound to that pixel format. We then make the new context current by using aglSetCurrentContext and bind our context to a full-screen drawable by using aglSetFullScreen. As before, robust production code should check for failure at any step in this process, and subsequently use aglGetError to provide detailed error information for user feedback.

The final component of the code in Example 7-3 is a main loop, one in which you'd handle events. For purposes of our example (that is, raw simplicity), our event loop simply contains calls to initialize the OpenGL machine, draw our scene, and display the results for a few seconds. Because this is a full-screen application managed by Carbon, you'd need to create a Carbon event handler to capture mouse and keyboard events. We'll provide demo code on this book's website (www.macopenglbook.com) to show how this works and a preview in the next section here showing a windowed visual selection and event-handling loop.

Table 7-2 Pixel Format Specifiers for Use with `aglChoosePixelFormat`

Token	Description
AGL_ALL_RENDERERS	Choose from all available renderers. This can include non-OpenGL-compliant renderers. Usually better to specify.
	Type: Boolean
	n/a
	Default: n/a
	Policy: n/a
AGL_BUFFER_SIZE	Number of bits per color buffer. If AGL_RGBA is specified, this value is the sum of all components. If a color index pixel format is specified, the buffer size is the size of the color indices.
	Type: Unsigned integer
	n/a
	Default: n/a
	Policy: Greater than or equal to value.
AGL_LEVEL	Level in plane stacking. Used to specify overlay or underlay planes.
	Type: Integer
	n/a
	Default: n/a
	Policy: Exact.
AGL_RGBA	Choose an RGBA format.
	Type: Boolean
	GL_TRUE
	Default: GL_FALSE
	Policy: If GL_TRUE, search only RGBA pixel formats; else search only color index pixel formats.
AGL_DOUBLEBUFFER	Select double-buffered pixel formats.
	Type: Boolean
	GL_TRUE
	Default: GL_FALSE
	Policy: If GL_TRUE, search only among double-buffered pixel formats; else search only single-buffered pixel formats.
AGL_STEREO	Select stereo pixel formats.
	Type: Boolean
	GL_TRUE
	Default: GL_FALSE
	Policy: If GL_TRUE, search only among stereo pixel formats; else search only monoscopic pixel formats.
	(Continued)

Table 7-2 Pixel Format Specifiers for Use with `aglChoosePixelFormat` (*Continued*)

Token	Description
AGL_AUX_BUFFERS	Number of aux buffers.
	Type: Unsigned integer
	0 specifies no aux buffers.
	Default: n/a
	Policy: Greater than or equal to value.
AGL_RED_SIZE	Number of red component bits.
	Type: Unsigned integer
	0 if AGL_RGBA is GL_FALSE.
	Default: n/a
	Policy: Closest.
AGL_GREEN_SIZE	Number of green component bits.
	Type: Unsigned integer
	0 if AGL_RGBA is GL_FALSE.
	Default: n/a
	Policy: Closest.
AGL_BLUE_SIZE	Number of blue component bits.
	Type: Unsigned integer
	0 if AGL_RGBA is GL_FALSE.
	Default: n/a
	Policy: Closest.
AGL_ALPHA_SIZE	Number of alpha component bits.
	Type: Unsigned integer
	0 if AGL_RGBA is GL_FALSE.
	Default: n/a
	Policy: Closest.
AGL_DEPTH_SIZE	Number of depth bits.
	Type: Unsigned integer
	n/a
	Default: n/a
	Policy: Closest.
AGL_STENCIL_SIZE	Number of stencil bits.
	Type: Unsigned integer
	n/a
	Default: n/a
	Policy: Greater than or equal to value.
AGL_ACCUM_RED_SIZE	Number of red accum bits.
	Type: Unsigned integer
	n/a
	Default: n/a
	Policy: Closest.

Token	Description
AGL_ACCUM_GREEN_SIZE	Number of green accum bits.
	Type: Unsigned integer
	n/a
	Default: n/a
	Policy: Closest.
AGL_ACCUM_BLUE_SIZE	Number of blue accum bits.
	Type: Unsigned integer
	n/a
	Default: n/a
	Policy: Closest.
AGL_ACCUM_ALPHA_SIZE	Number of alpha accum bits.
	Type: Unsigned integer
	Value
	Default: Default
	Policy: AGL_CLOSEST_POLICY
AGL_PIXEL_SIZE	Framebuffer bits per pixel, including unused bits, ignoring alpha buffer bits.
	Type: Unsigned integer
	n/a
	Default: n/a
	Policy: n/a
AGL_MINIMUM_POLICY	Never choose smaller buffers than the type and size requested.
	Type: Boolean
	n/a
	Default: GL_FALSE
	Policy: n/a
AGL_MAXIMUM_POLICY	Choose largest buffers of type and size requested. Alters default policy for color, depth, and accumulation buffers.
	Type: Token
	n/a
	Default: n/a
	Policy: n/a
AGL_CLOSEST_POLICY	Find the pixel format most closely matching the specified size. Alters default policy and size for color buffers.
	Type: Unsigned integer
	n/a
	Default: n/a
	Policy: Closest match.
	(Continued)

Table 7-2 Pixel Format Specifiers for Use with `aglChoosePixelFormat` (*Continued*)

Token	Description
AGL_OFFSCREEN	Choose an off-screen renderer.
	Type: Token
	n/a
	Default: n/a
	Policy: Closest match.
AGL_FULLSCREEN	Choose a full-screen renderer.
	Type: Token
	n/a
	Default: n/a
	Policy: n/a
AGL_SAMPLE_BUFFERS_ARB	Number of multisample buffers.
	Type: Unsigned integer
	n/a
	Default: n/a
	Policy: n/a
AGL_SAMPLES_ARB	Number of samples per multisample buffer.
	Type: Unsigned integer
	n/a
	Default: n/a
	Policy: n/a
AGL_AUX_DEPTH_STENCIL	Specify number of depth or stencil buffers for the aux buffer.
	Type: Unsigned integer
	n/a
	Default: n/a
	Policy: n/a
AGL_COLOR_FLOAT	Select pixel buffers with color buffers that store floating-point pixels.
	Type: n/a
	n/a
	Default: n/a
	Policy: n/a
AGL_MULTISAMPLE	Select pixel formats with multisample buffers.
	Type: n/a
	n/a
	Default: n/a
	Policy: Hint: prefer.
AGL_SUPERSAMPLE	Select pixel formats with supersample buffers.
	Type: n/a
	n/a
	Default: n/a
	Policy: Hint: prefer.

Token	Description
AGL_SAMPLE_ALPHA	Request alpha filtering
	Type: n/a
	n/a
	Default: n/a
	Policy: n/a
AGL_RENDERER_ID	Choose renderer by a specific ID.
	Type: Unsigned integer
	One of AGL_RENDERER_*_ID tokens
	Default: n/a
	Policy: Exact.
AGL_SINGLE_RENDERER	Choose a single renderer for all screens.
	Type: Boolean
	GL_TRUE
	Default: n/a
	Policy: n/a
AGL_NO_RECOVERY	Disable all failure recovery systems. The OpenGL driver layer will fall back to other renderers if a drawable or surface cannot be attached, typically due to insufficient graphics memory resources. AGL would, in this failure case, usually switch to another renderer; however, specifying GL_TRUE to this option will prevent a failover to a software renderer from occurring in this instance.
	Type: Boolean
	GL_TRUE: Disable failure modes.
	GL_FALSE: Fail to alternate renderers.
	Default: n/a
	Policy: Exact.
AGL_ACCELERATED	Choose a hardware-accelerated renderer. Note that in a multiscreen system configuration, it's possible that you may not get windows that span, because a spanning window usually causes OpenGL to choose the software renderer.
	Type: Boolean
	GL_TRUE: Specify that only hardware renderers are searched.
	Default: GL_FALSE
	Policy: Exact.
	(Continued)

Table 7-2 Pixel Format Specifiers for Use with `aglChoosePixelFormat` (*Continued*)

Token	Description
`AGL_ROBUST`	Choose a renderer that doesn't have a hardware failure mode due to lack of graphics resources.
	Type: Boolean
	`GL_TRUE`: Search renderers with no hardware failure modes as described.
	Default: `GL_FALSE`
	Policy: Exact.
`AGL_BACKING_STORE`	Specify that only renderers with a back buffer that accommodates the full size of the drawable/surface object should be searched. Ensure that the back buffer is copy-swapped to the front buffer, meaning that the contents are usable after a "swap buffers" command.
	Type: Boolean
	`GL_TRUE`: Consider only renderers with this capability.
	Default: n/a
	Policy: Exact.
`AGL_WINDOW`	Can be used to render to a window.
	Type: n/a
	n/a
	Default: n/a
	Policy: n/a
`AGL_MULTISCREEN`	A single window can span multiple screens.
	Type: n/a
	n/a
	Default: n/a
	Policy: n/a
`AGL_VIRTUAL_SCREEN`	Specify a virtual screen number on which to search for pixel formats.
	Type: Integer
	n/a
	Default: n/a
	Policy: Exact.
`AGL_PBUFFER`	Choose a renderer that can be used to render to a pbuffer.
	Type: Boolean
	`GL_TRUE`: Choose a pbuffer pixel format.
	Default: n/a
	Policy: Exact.

Token	Description
AGL_REMOTE_PBUFFER	Specifies that the renderer can render to an off-line pixel buffer.
	Type: Boolean
	n/a
	Default: n/a
	Policy: n/a
AGL_NONE	Token to signal the end of the pixel format parameter array. Every pixel format attribute list for AGL must end with this token.
	Type: n/a
	n/a
	Default: n/a
	Policy: n/a

The final piece of code we perform, after our main loop has exited, is to clean up our context and return.

Using AGL can be as simple as that! If you're coding along with this example, your application should be essentially complete and ready to run. If you've followed this discussion successfully, you'll see results as in Figure 7-2, completely covering your display.

There's a lot more to discuss, so let's move on to our next example, which involves a windowed pixel format and event loop.

Windowed Application

If you're writing example code in an application like we've talked you through in the previous section, create another XCode project, and populate it with headers, initialization methods, and draw methods as seen before in Example 7-1 and Example 7-2. All of those pieces of code will remain exactly the same, and the only differences are how we choose our pixel format, bind it to the Carbon window, and process events. We'll begin by presenting the main routine seen in Example 7-4 and then we'll walk through it.

Example 7-4 AGL Windowed main Example

```
int main(int argc, char **argv)
{
    AGLPixelFormat pixelFormat;
    GDHandle display = GetMainDevice();
    Rect windowRect = { 100, 100, 100 + width, 100 + height };
```

Figure 7-2　AGL Full-Screen Example Results

```
    WindowRef window;

    GLint attribs[] =
{
        AGL_DOUBLEBUFFER,
        AGL_ACCELERATED,
        AGL_NO_RECOVERY,
        AGL_RGBA,
        AGL_NONE
};

// Context creation
pixelFormat = aglChoosePixelFormat( &display, 1, attribs );
context = aglCreateContext( pixelFormat, NULL );
aglDestroyPixelFormat( pixelFormat );
aglSetCurrentContext( context );

// Window creation
CreateNewWindow( kDocumentWindowClass,
    kWindowStandardDocumentAttributes |
    kWindowStandardHandlerAttribute |
    kWindowResizableAttribute |
    kWindowLiveResizeAttribute |
    kWindowCloseBoxAttribute,
    &windowRect,
    &window);
```

```
SetWindowTitleWithCFString( window, CFSTR( "AGL Window" ) );

ShowWindow(window);
aglSetDrawable( context, GetWindowPort( window ) );
aglUpdateContext( context );

// opengl setup and render
initGLstate();
draw();

// mainloop
while( !done )
{
    processEvent();
}
// cleanup
aglSetCurrentContext( NULL );
aglDestroyContext( context );
return( 0 );
}
```

The first section of code performs some Carbon window management, necessary later both to choose a pixel format from a specific device and then to create a window on it. This section also chooses the pixel format, looking in particular at a specific graphics device. First, we find the main graphics device and store it in a variable; we then set up a Rect defining our window size; and finally we declare a handle to our window. The next part of this code is familiar from our earlier full-screen example—that is, the declaration of an AGLPixelFormat and the population of it with our desired pixel format parameters. As a reminder, this list *must* end with the AGL_NONE token. Finally, we invoke aglChoosePixelFormat, but in a different form than in the full-screen example; instead of passing it a NULL as the first argument, we specify a particular device to be searched—in this case, our main device on the system. Excepting that one addition, the same caveats from the full-screen example apply: Check the return values for validity, and ensure that the resultant pixel format matches your needs.

The second section of the code creates the AGL context, cleans up the pixel format, creates a Carbon window, and binds the AGL context to the window, also know as an AGL drawable.[1] Creating a context is done as in our prior

---

1. It's probably useful to mention the two data types in AGL that are remapped from basic Carbon types for window and device management. When using AGL methods that interface with devices, these two types are syntactically the same GDHandle and AGLDevice. Similarly, for AGL methods referring to drawables, CGrafPtr and AGLDrawable are interchangable. In much of the code presented in this book and in Apple examples, these types are interchanged, but it's not explained why, directly. The reason they are interchangeable is that the AGL types are simply typedefs of their Carbon base types. Please note, however, that QuickDraw is deprecated in Leopard.

full-screen example. Window creation, the next step, is just the standard Carbon window creation and is beyond the scope of this book. However, the necessity of having our window setup is visible in the final step in this section, in which we bind the AGL context to the AGL drawable. In our full-screen example, we did this create-and-bind operation in a single step through `aglSetFullScreen`; here, because we're binding to an already-created `Window`, we use `aglSetDrawable`. We use the Carbon adapter `GetWindowPort` to convert our `WindowRef` into an `AGLDrawable` type. The piece in this section is to call `aglUpdateContext`. This method is an AGL required method used any time the AGL drawable changes size. As we just created and bound our window, it's prudent to ensure that the AGL context is informed of the AGL drawable's size at this point.

The final section of the code in Example 7-4 is also similar to our full-screen example. The essence of this section is to initialize OpenGL, process events, and clean up. We do this through two calls to code from our earlier example, followed by a hand-crafted main loop. As before, we won't go into detail about the guts of `processEvent` except to say that this is how, for our example application, we handle Carbon events from the mouse, keyboard, and so on. You can see this code in our code archive online.

Finally, as in our full-screen example, we unbind our context, clean it up, and exit.

If you were to compile and build that code, you'd see something that looked like Figure 7-3. Windowed AGL is essentially as simple as full-screen AGL but with a little more setup when binding the context.

Summary

So far, we've seen how to create and destroy pixel formats and contexts using AGL. We've demonstrated how to use them together to create full-screen and windowed AGL applications. With this knowledge you should be ready to create AGL-based applications if you choose to do so. However, for those of you with the opportunity to write new applications from scratch, we strongly recommend investigating the Cocoa options first.

Additional Topics

Renderers

AGL provides a few methods to access renderers directly, in addition to basic pixel format and context handling. Why might you want to access a renderer? Perhaps you're curious about the theoretical memory made available to you by your renderer of choice, or maybe you'd like to see how many overlay planes

Figure 7-3 AGL Window Example Results

your renderer supports. You can query the renderer information independently of any OpenGL context, and then you can use this discovered renderer information with your AGL pixel format to customize it to your needs. We now present some example code to search the list of renderers through AGL, and query some properties in Example 7-5.

Example 7-5 AGL Renderer Query Example

```
int main(int argc, char **argv)
{
    AGLRendererInfo ri = aglQueryRendererInfo( NULL, 0 );
    if ( ri != NULL )
    {
        unsigned int ii=0;
        while( ri != NULL )
        {
            GLint vram, tram, accel, id;
            GLint mm = 1024*1024;
            aglDescribeRenderer( ri, AGL_RENDERER_ID, &id);
            aglDescribeRenderer( ri, AGL_ACCELERATED, &accel);
            aglDescribeRenderer( ri, AGL_VIDEO_MEMORY, &vram);
            aglDescribeRenderer( ri, AGL_TEXTURE_MEMORY, &tram);
            cout << "renderer " << ii << ": "
```

```
        << "id: " << id << " "
        << "hardware: " << accel << " " << endl;
    cout << "\t"
        << "vram (Mb): " << vram/mm << " "
        << "tram (Mb): " << tram/mm << endl;
    ri = aglNextRendererInfo( ri ); ii++;
    }
}
else
{
    GLenum error = aglGetError();
    cout << "error: " << error << endl;
}

    return( 0 );
}
```

This code begins by getting the renderer information structure for all devices on this Mac, using `aglQueryRendererInfo` with `NULL` to indicate all devices, similarly to the way `aglChoosePixelFormat` operates. If we were particularly interested in a specific device, we could customize this call to just query that device, or a sublist of `AGLDevices`. This code then ensures that the result isn't `NULL`, which indicates the last of our `AGLRendererInfo` structures, and walks through the list, invoking `aglDescribeRenderer` on a few properties. The output from this example looks like the following, for the author's Intel-based iMac:

```
renderer 0: id: 137473 hardware: 1
    vram (Mb): 128 tram (Mb): 128
renderer 1: id: 132096 hardware: 0
    vram (Mb): 0 tram (Mb): 0
```

An AGL renderer query of this type, for video and texture memory, isn't the most useful, as these results indicate hardware limits (all of that memory may not necessarily be available to a running application), but it's an easy way to demonstrate the concept. Furthermore, we derive certain satisfaction from programmatically validating that the hardware actually has the capabilities listed on the marketing literature. From these results, we can see the renderer ID, determine whether it has hardware acceleration, and learn about its video and texture memory limits. This method provides an easy way of querying supported renderers on a particular platform. A complete and current list of tokens can always be found in the `AGL/agl.h` header file, and we've also documented a useful set of tokens in Table 7-3.

For the most part, querying renderers prior to their use is sometimes helpful if you have specific needs (say, pbuffers) and need to ensure that your renderer can support them. Most commonly, however, you'll want to use an `AGL_ACCELERATED` renderer, and keep within its capabilities, to have the best performance possible. On systems with multiple graphics cards, you might

Table 7-3 Tokens for Use with `aglDescribeRenderer`

Token	Description
AGL_FULLSCREEN	Supports full-screen applications
AGL_RENDERER_ID	Renderer ID value
AGL_ACCELERATED	Supports hardware acceleration
AGL_ROBUST	Has no failure mode for lack of resources
AGL_BACKING_STORE	Has copy-on-swap back buffer
AGL_WINDOW	Supports render-to-window
AGL_MULTISCREEN	Can support multiple screens with the same AGL context
AGL_COMPLIANT	Supports offline pixel-buffer rendering
AGL_PBUFFER	Supports pbuffer rendering
AGL_BUFFER_MODES	Supports bitwise OR of mono, stereo, single, and double constants from `AGL/agl.h`
AGL_MIN_LEVEL	Minimum overlay (or maximum underlay, if negative) plane value
AGL_MAX_LEVEL	Maximum overlay plane value.
AGL_COLOR_MODES	Supports bitwise OR of color mode constants from `AGL/agl.h` color buffers
AGL_ACCUM_MODES	Supports bitwise OR of color mode constants from `AGL/agl.h` for accumulation buffers
AGL_DEPTH_MODES	Supports bitwise OR of depth mode constants from `AGL/agl.h`
AGL_STENCIL_MODES	Supports bitwise OR of stencil mode constants from `AGL/agl.h`
AGL_MAX_AUX_BUFFERS	Maximum number of aux buffers supported
AGL_VIDEO_MEMORY	Maximum video memory available to renderer in bytes
AGL_TEXTURE_MEMORY	Maximum texture memory available to renderer in bytes

prefer to run on the most capable graphics card, or one with which you know your code performs particularly well.

Context Sharing

Context sharing is an essential element to high-performance, resource-friendly OpenGL applications. Context sharing allows sharable elements from one context to be used in other OpenGL contexts. There is one primary reason to share contexts: reuse of the same graphics data in two or more different windows. One very common example of this is sharing data between a full-screen version and a windowed version of the same application. There may be other reasons, such as when a number of windows are all viewing the same OpenGL data but from different views. Finally, you might want to share data among multiple rendering destinations, such as windows and pbuffers.

Context sharing is typically requested when a new OpenGL context is created, and the context with which it will be sharing has been created and its sharable resources have been initialized. The context with items you wish to access is passed to some form of initialization for your new context, usually along with a pixel format. For two contexts to be compatible, their pixel formats must be compatible as well, which is why you see these two things specified together to successfully enable sharing. So what makes pixel formats incompatible? On the Mac usually it's one thing: incompatible renderers. Thus, as a rule of thumb, if you can choose pixel formats that use the same renderers, you can share contexts created with those pixel formats.

As context sharing is a very simple feat to perform, we'll simply look at the code first and only then discuss what's going on. Example 7-6 demonstrates how we can create two contexts, the first shared with the second.

Example 7-6 Sharing One Context with Another in AGL

```
// create first context
pixelFormat = aglChoosePixelFormat( &display, 1, attribs );
context = aglCreateContext( pixelFormat, NULL );

// create second context, sharing with first
otherContext = aglCreateContext( pixelFormat, context );
aglDestroyPixelFormat( pixelFormat );
```

As you can see in Example 7-6, sharing a context is as simple as passing the context to be shared into each subsequent context creation call. If, as in our example, there are no errors, the sharable contents of the first context exist for the second. In Example 7-6, we share a display list of the rendered object between two windows. We clear each window to a different color to demonstrate that they are, in fact, separate contexts, with separate states, except for sharable items. For reference, the following items can be shared among contexts:

- Display lists
- Buffer objects (vertex buffer objects, fixer buffer objects)
- Texture objects
- Vertex and fragment programs and shaders
- Framebuffer objects

Like most windowing system interfaces to OpenGL, AGL exposes the ability to duplicate context contents. Specifically, in Example 7-6, we took pains to demonstrate that each context was different by setting a unique glClearColor for each. However, if we'd like the rest of the state to be the same between these two contexts, we'd use the AGL method aglCopyContext to specify a copy from one context to another. This routine takes arguments for the source context, the destination context, and the attribute mask describing which pieces of state to copy. Specifically, the mask and constants are the same ones that the `glPushAttrib()` call uses. For our example, we'd write code as in Example 7-7.

Example 7-7 Copying the Context State Between Two Contexts in AGL

```
aglCopyContext( context, otherContext, GL_ALL_ATTRIB_BITS );
```

One last note on shared contexts, which applies to the general concept of context sharing, not to any particular implementation: When you are using context sharing and you reach the point in your application where you need to destroy the second (sharer) context, make sure that you do *not* delete the shared contents within that context. If one context cleans up shared objects but another context continues to use those contents, it's possible that visual data corruption or, even worse, a crash of the application could occur. The solution to this problem is that, as with data shared through pointers, only one application element should be responsible for both construction and deletion of shared elements. Thus, when you are sharing data between contexts, make sure that shared objects are created once, used many times, and then deleted once, only when the last sharer of those contents has completed its usage.

Alternative Rendering Destinations

In AGL, as in CGL and Cocoa, an increasingly more popular OpenGL rendering technique is to render to a hardware-accelerated nonvisible buffer. There are numerous reasons for doing so, most commonly to create an image to use somewhere else as a texture. For example, you might create an image to represent a reflection image in service of creating nice shiny water. A variety of rendering destinations can be used to create this sort of image for reuse, or for any other purpose. In this section, we'll look at techniques to render to modern off-screen render destinations, as well as some bridge technology techniques, such as render-to-texture, used for compatibility with older hardware.

Off-Screen Surfaces

Apple refers to "off-screen" buffers as a particular form of alternative rendering destinations. In Apple's terminology, "off-screen" denotes a rendering target that is without hardware acceleration. For this reason, and because creating hardware-accelerated render targets with no on-screen footprint is so easy, you'll probably want to avoid pixel formats with "off-screen" attributes. We'll describe a few caveats of creating and managing these entities, but only for reference: If you see off-screen surfaces used in a modern application, it's probably a good time to consider refactoring to use framebuffer objects.

Creation and use of off-screen surfaces begins with specification of the GL_AGL_OFFSCREEN token when constructing a pixel format. Only an AGLContext that has been successfully created with a pixel format using this token can be used to perform true off-screen rendering. After creation of a context, the next steps are to bind this off-screen render area, to make it active for rendering, and to render. As with full-screen and windowed rendering, there is an analogous command, aglSetOffScreen, to perform this binding. The target of this binding is a memory buffer you specify in the call, rather than an existing Carbon window. The Apple documentation pages have detailed information on all the arguments these calls take. As this isn't really recommended practice, we won't describe this technique in more detail. Consult the Apple documentation for the most complete descriptions of the methods.

Pbuffers

Pixel buffers are another alternative rendering destination commonly used for off-screen rendering. However, unlike the named "off-screen" areas, pbuffers can be fully hardware accelerated. That makes them quite useful for real-time generation of textures, among other things. Pbuffers are an invention of the late 1990s (circa 1997) and, though fully functional, they contain a bit of complexity that more modern render implementations such as framebuffer objects do not. In essence, pbuffers are useful analogs to framebuffer objects, but for modern code, framebuffer objects are preferred.

Table 7-4 shows the list of functions within AGL useful for creation and use of pbuffers.

Chapter 6 showed the same procedure necessary for this task, so we'll simply summarize and show some example code here. The basic process is as before: Create a pbuffer (aglCreatePBuffer), make it active (aglSetPBuffer), and perform some rendering into it. Example 7-8 demonstrates the main loop performing the basic AGL context and AGL pbuffer context creation tasks.

Table 7-4 AGL Pbuffer Functions

Function	Description
aglCreatePBuffer	Creates an AGL pixel buffer for use with an OpenGL texture type
aglDestroyPBuffer	Destroy an AGL pixelbuffer
aglDescribePBuffer	Gather information about an AGL pixelbuffer
aglGetPBuffer	Query a context for the pixelbuffer attached to it
aglSetPBuffer	Set the pixel buffer to be the target for the specified context
aglTexImagePBuffer	Binds a pixel buffer as a texture; analogous to glTexImage2D

Example 7-8 Pbuffer and Windowed Context Creation in AGL

```
int main(int argc, char **argv)
{
    // setup the pixelformat
    GLint attribs[] =
    {
        AGL_RGBA,
        AGL_DOUBLEBUFFER,
        AGL_ACCELERATED,
        AGL_NO_RECOVERY,
        AGL_DEPTH_SIZE, 16,
        AGL_NONE
    };
    const int width = 451;
    const int height = 123;
    AGLPixelFormat pixelFormat;
    AGLPbuffer pbuffer;
    AGLContext context, pbContext;
    long virtualScreen;

    GDHandle display2 =
        CGDisplayIDToOpenGLDisplayMask( CGMainDisplayID() );
    GDHandle display = GetMainDevice();
    Rect windowRect = { 100, 100, 100 + width, 100 + height };
    WindowRef window;

    // pbuffer pixelformat and context setup and creation
    printf( "%d\n", display2 );
    pixelFormat = aglChoosePixelFormat( display2, 1, attribs );
    pbContext = aglCreateContext( pixelFormat, NULL );
    aglDestroyPixelFormat( pixelFormat );
    aglCreatePBuffer( width, height, GL_TEXTURE_2D,
        GL_RGBA, 0, &pbuffer );

    // bind pbuffer
    virtualScreen = aglGetVirtualScreen( pbContext );
    aglSetCurrentContext( pbContext );
    aglSetPBuffer( pbContext, pbuffer, 0, 0, virtualScreen );

    // draw into pbuffer
    drawPBuffer();

    // window pixelformat and context setup and creation
    pixelFormat = aglChoosePixelFormat( &display, 1, attribs );
    context = aglCreateContext( pixelFormat, NULL );
    aglDestroyPixelFormat( pixelFormat );
    aglSetCurrentContext( context );

    // window creation
    CreateNewWindow(kDocumentWindowClass,
        kWindowStandardDocumentAttributes |
        kWindowStandardHandlerAttribute,
        &windowRect, &window);
```

```
    SetWindowTitleWithCFString( window, CFSTR("AGL PBuffer Texture") );
    ActivateWindow(window, true);
    ShowWindow(window);

    // bind context to window
    aglSetDrawable( context, GetWindowPort(window) );
    aglUpdateContext( context );

    // initialize window context & draw window
    GLuint texid;
    init( context, pbuffer, &texid );
    drawWindow( context, texid );

    // stub event loop
    sleep( 4.0 );

    // cleanup and exit
    aglSetCurrentContext( NULL );
    aglDestroyContext( context );
    aglDestroyContext( pbContext );
    aglDestroyPBuffer( pbuffer );

    return( 0 );
}
```

At some point in the future, when you're ready to use this result as data, reference the contents as the image portion of a texture (`aglTexImagePBuffer`). Example 7-9 shows this process happening for our main OpenGL windowed AGL context. This method shows the key step in pbuffer usage (CGL or AGL, documented fully in Chapter 6 when generating a new texture ID.

Example 7-9 OpenGL Context Initialization, Referencing a Pbuffer as the Texture

```
void init( AGLContext context,
           AGLPbuffer pbuffer,
           GLuint * textureID )
{
    // Initialize the projection matrix
    glMatrixMode( GL_PROJECTION );
    glOrtho( -1, 1, -1, 1, -1, 1 );
    glMatrixMode( GL_MODELVIEW );

    glClearColor( 0.0f, 0.5f, 0.8f, 1.0 );
    glClear( GL_COLOR_BUFFER_BIT );

    // Generate a texture ID to allow pbuffer texturing
    glEnable( GL_TEXTURE_2D );
    glGenTextures( 1, textureID );
    glBindTexture( GL_TEXTURE_2D, textureID );

    // Set up the texturing environment
    glTexEnvi( GL_TEXTURE_ENV, GL_TEXTURE_ENV_MODE, GL_MODULATE );
```

```
glTexParameteri( GL_TEXTURE_2D, GL_TEXTURE_WRAP_S,
    GL_CLAMP_TO_EDGE );
glTexParameteri( GL_TEXTURE_2D, GL_TEXTURE_WRAP_T,
    GL_CLAMP_TO_EDGE );
glTexParameteri( GL_TEXTURE_2D, GL_TEXTURE_MIN_FILTER,
    GL_NEAREST );
glTexParameteri( GL_TEXTURE_2D, GL_TEXTURE_MAG_FILTER,
    GL_NEAREST );
// Specify the pbuffer as the source for our texture data
// This acts as a substitute for a glTexImage2D call.
aglTexImagePBuffer( context, pbuffer, GL_FRONT );
}
```

The draw methods for each of the pbuffers and the main window are as you would expect. In this case, our pbuffer clears to yellow (that's what we draw into it), and then we use that result as a texture on a GL_QUAD, drawn as shown in Figure 7-4. Many more interesting things can be done using this technique, such as rendering reflection images for glass or water scenes and rendering intermediate computations for use in GPGPU applications. However, this section deals with the infrastructure for performing the rendering and that's what we've presented here

Figure 7-4 AGL Pbuffer Example Results

Render-to/Copy-to-Texture

In this section we describe a very common and widely available technique known as render-to-texture. Render-to-texture is as simple as it sounds: You simply render your intermediate scene, copy it to a texture, and then later use that texture in your final render. The method is simple and concise, with the only downside being the "copy of pixels" phase. Of course, you must deal with some details concerning how you target the texture into which you want to render and, in some cases, how you move pixels around the system and into your final texture. Nevertheless, on the whole, this process is largely as simple as described. This technique is interesting because it is widely available and offers relatively high performance. It has some problems, too: It's not as clean as the most modern OpenGL technique of framebuffer objects, and there may be extra data copies. Overall, though, it works pretty well. Performance is pretty good, too, albeit not as consistently good as using framebuffer objects. Sometimes, you may run into problems on different cards from different vendors where this technique is actually moderately expensive. However, if you can't use framebuffer objects, this method is a good option. We'll now explore the details of this technique and look at some example code and results.

Because we're only going to render and copy into a texture, that's the extent of the information we need to keep track of throughout our methods. Because creation of textures is so universal, we present the initialization and draw code all at once, in Example 7-10. This code shows three things: the overall initialization, the draw methods for both the textured scene, and the texture itself.

Example 7-10 AGL OpenGL Initialization and Draw Functions for Copy-Texture Rendering

```
void initGLstate()
{
    glMatrixMode( GL_PROJECTION );
    glLoadIdentity();
    glOrtho(0.0, 1.0, 0.0, 1.0, -1.0, 1.0);
    glClearColor( 0.0, 0.5, 0.8, 1.0 );

    // enable, generate, and bind our texture objects
    glEnable( GL_TEXTURE_2D );
    glGenTextures( (GLsizei) 1, &textureID );
    glBindTexture( GL_TEXTURE_2D, textureID );
    const unsigned int texdim = 64;
    const unsigned int nbytes = 3;
    char data[ texdim * texdim * nbytes ];
    memset( data, 0xff, texdim * texdim * nbytes );
    unsigned int ii;
    for( ii=0; ii<texdim*texdim; ii++ )
    {
        data[ ii*nbytes + 0 ] = 0xff;
    }
```

```
        gluBuild2DMipmaps( GL_TEXTURE_2D, // 0,
                        GL_RGB, texdim, texdim, // 0,
                        GL_RGB, GL_UNSIGNED_BYTE, data );
        glTexEnvf( GL_TEXTURE_ENV, GL_TEXTURE_ENV_MODE, GL_REPLACE );
        glBindTexture( GL_TEXTURE_2D, 0 ); // unbind texture
}

void drawTexture()
{
        glClearColor( 1.0, 1.0, 0.0, 1.0 );
        glClear( GL_COLOR_BUFFER_BIT | GL_DEPTH_BUFFER_BIT );

        glBindTexture( GL_TEXTURE_2D, textureID );
        glCopyTexSubImage2D( GL_TEXTURE_2D, 0,
                        0, 0,
                        0, 0,
                        64, 64 );
}

void draw()
{
        glClearColor( 0.0, 0.5, 0.8, 1.0 );
        glClear( GL_COLOR_BUFFER_BIT );

        glMatrixMode( GL_MODELVIEW );
        glLoadIdentity();
        glRotatef( 5.0, 0.0, 0.0, 1.0 );

        glBindTexture( GL_TEXTURE_2D, textureID );
        glColor4d( 0.0, 1.0, 0.0, 1.0 );
        glRectd( 0.1, 0.1, 0.9, 0.9 );

        aglSwapBuffers( context );
}
```

We'll spend a bit more time discussing this technique, its strengths, its weaknesses, and its applicability in Chapter 8, but for now a few words on what's happening should suffice. The initialization code performs two steps: (1) as seen in our prior examples, setup of the projection matrix, and (2) a simple texture generation (all white) and load of that texture. That's all we do to prepare a texture for usage later. The drawTexture function performs our rendering into our texture, and it's as simple as it always has been, a clear to yellow transition. The last step in this function is the workhorse of this technique, and simply copies the contents of the active framebuffer read target (set through glReadBuffer) to the texture specified. We use the glTexSubImage2D flavor of texture copy because it's the most efficient way to replace some or all of a texture with updated image pixels.

Finally, we see in Example 7-10 the draw code, which does the same draw as in our earlier AGL examples. This time, however, it binds this texture before rendering the main scene. The results are seen in Figure 7-5.

Figure 7-5 AGL Render-to-Texture Example Results

One quick note: We must invoke this code in this order if we want to achieve the proper results. This is a key step, and perhaps obvious, but Example 7-11 makes clear that you must first set up the texture, then draw contents into it, and finally draw the main scene.

Example 7-11 AGL Copy-Texture Render Call Sequence

```
// opengl setup and render
initGLstate();
drawTexture();
draw();
```

There's really not much else to this technique. Essentially, you render two scenes, and copy the contents of one for use as a texture by the other. That basic idea is the premise behind all of these techniques, but rarely is there as little configuration as in Example 7.11.

We've now finished our discussion of how to perform textured renders from the contents of a texture filled by another render. The technique is very portable but carries some overhead concerning texture and window sizes, and has some performance limitations based on the underlying OpenGL operations. This technique is a capable fallback for when framebuffer objects are not available.

Framebuffer Objects

In this section we describe a modern and widely available technique for intermediate renders using framebuffer objects. The interfaces to framebuffer objects were designed to closely resemble texture objects, provide a simple enable/disable mechanism that is similar in usage to textures, and yet offer a lot of flexibility in terms of what can be rendered and how to use it later. Framebuffer objects are also similar to pbuffers in terms of their usage. We have a more detailed discussion of these objects in the Cocoa chapter (Chapter 8), so for now we'll simply say a few quick things.

First, framebuffer objects are the best thing since sliced bread, and really your best consideration for new applications. They're too easy, too familiar to texture object users, and too widely supported to not use them. In fact, framebuffer objects are an easy port from pbuffers if your application already supports those, but they will clean up some code and remove some worrying restrictions. So, without further ado, let's look at our original AGL windowed example, but extend it to use framebuffer objects.

In Example 7-12, we see code covering the main steps involved in configuring and setting up a framebuffer object. You'll notice that this example is virtually the same as the prior texture-copy example from Example 7-11. The main differences occur after texture creation and initialization. The pieces given here are the essential elements of how to create a framebuffer object. You'll notice the parallels to texture creation—specifically, that we generate a unique framebuffer object ID, bind it, construct a framebuffer object linking it with our texture, and then unbind it so we're returned to a default state. The draw method should look similar, too, except that in this case we first say where we're targeting our draw commands, much like making an OpenGL context active, using `glGenFramebuffersEXT`. We draw into that target and then again reset our state back to the default. Finally, our main draw method looks identical to that of Example 7-11. This is because we've drawn our contents directly into the framebuffer. Using the texture linked with that framebuffer now gets us the proper results, as seen in Figure 7-6.

Example 7-12   AGL Initialization and Draw for a Framebuffer Object and Main Buffer

```
void initGLstate()
{
    glMatrixMode( GL_PROJECTION );
    glLoadIdentity();
```

```
        glOrtho(0.0, 1.0, 0.0, 1.0, -1.0, 1.0);
        glClearColor( 0.0, 0.5, 0.8, 1.0 );

        // enable, generate, and bind our texture objects
        glEnable( GL_TEXTURE_2D );
        glGenTextures( (GLsizei) 1, &textureID );
        glBindTexture( GL_TEXTURE_2D, textureID );
        const unsigned int texdim = 64;
        const unsigned int nbytes = 3;
        char data[ texdim * texdim * nbytes ];
        memset( data, 0xff, texdim * texdim * nbytes );
        unsigned int ii;
        for( ii=0; ii<texdim*texdim; ii++ )
        {
            data[ ii*nbytes + 0 ] = 0xff;
        }
        gluBuild2DMipmaps( GL_TEXTURE_2D, // 0,
                        GL_RGB, texdim, texdim, // 0,
                        GL_RGB, GL_UNSIGNED_BYTE, data );
        glTexEnvf( GL_TEXTURE_ENV, GL_TEXTURE_ENV_MODE, GL_REPLACE );
        glBindTexture( GL_TEXTURE_2D, 0 ); // unbind texture


        // generate & bind our framebuffer object to our texture object
        glGenFramebuffersEXT( 1, &fboID );
        glBindFramebufferEXT( GL_FRAMEBUFFER_EXT, fboID );
        glFramebufferTexture2DEXT(  GL_FRAMEBUFFER_EXT,
                                    GL_COLOR_ATTACHMENT0_EXT,
                                    GL_TEXTURE_2D, textureID, 0 );
        glBindFramebufferEXT( GL_FRAMEBUFFER_EXT, 0 ); // unbind fbo
}

void drawFBO()
{
    glBindFramebufferEXT( GL_FRAMEBUFFER_EXT, fboID ); // bind fbo
    glClearColor( 1.0, 1.0, 0.0, 1.0 );
    glClear( GL_COLOR_BUFFER_BIT | GL_DEPTH_BUFFER_BIT );
    glBindFramebufferEXT( GL_FRAMEBUFFER_EXT, 0 ); // unbind fbo
}

void draw()
{
    glClearColor( 0.0, 0.5, 0.8, 1.0 );
    glClear( GL_COLOR_BUFFER_BIT );
    glMatrixMode( GL_MODELVIEW );
    glLoadIdentity();
    glRotatef( 5.0, 0.0, 0.0, 1.0 );

    glBindTexture( GL_TEXTURE_2D, textureID );
    glColor4d( 0.0, 1.0, 0.0, 1.0 );
    glRectd( 0.1, 0.1, 0.9, 0.9 );

    aglSwapBuffers( context );
}
```

Figure 7-6 Results of Rendering to a Framebuffer Object and Texturing a Quad with That Result in AGL

Before we leave the topic of framebuffer objects, we'd like to point out a few reasons why they are superior to other forms of indirect rendering.

First, framebuffer objects consist of memory allocated on the graphics card itself that is directly usable in its target form—for example, as a texture. This means that you avoid not only off-card copies to and from the host but also avoid on-card copies in good implementations of the extension.

Second, framebuffer objects present a consistent, platform-agnostic interface in terms of their usage. There just isn't a more simple interface to intermediate rendering than these objects, largely due to the evolutionary process by which OpenGL is developed.

Third, framebuffer objects avoid expensive context switching that can cost you a great deal of performance. A variety of intermediate target rendering APIs and implementations have been explored over the years, culminating in today's design and implementation. Framebuffer objects are the best choice for modern rendering on the Mac, regardless of whether you're using AGL, CGL, or Cocoa.

Summary

In this chapter, we explored how to create and configure AGL-based OpenGL rendering areas for on-screen and full-screen windows and for various intermediate render targets. We also saw how to create custom pixel formats, explored some of the common flags that these pixel formats take, and demonstrated how to configure and initialize contexts and pixel formats. In addition, we saw how to integrate a variety of rendering destinations into an AGL application. We learned how to share data among multiple contexts, and to configure full-screen surfaces. Now that you have explored the fundamentals of AGL OpenGL setup covered in this chapter, you should have a solid foundation from which to begin building your own Carbon and AGL OpenGL applications.

Chapter 8

The Cocoa API
for OpenGL
Configuration

Cocoa, also known as AppKit, is the Objective-C API for writing modern Mac OS X applications. Cocoa provides a high-level, object-oriented set of classes and interfaces for the OpenGL subsystem and for user–interface interaction. Cocoa is the modern successor to the NextStep API from NeXT Computer; the company's initials explain the "NS" prefix on all of the class definitions and data types. Cocoa provides a more object-oriented API than any other option on the Mac, which is useful for building UIs, handling events, and functioning as an interface to OpenGL.

We presume you're reading this chapter with a fundamental understanding of the Objective-C language and basic Cocoa, so we won't spend any time reviewing core Cocoa concepts like the Objective-C language, views, actions, outlets, Interface Builder, and so on. We also assume you've already read one of the many good books on these key background elements of Cocoa. If not, we've got a reference or two for you in Appendix D. In the following sections, we'll explore two ways of creating a Cocoa-based application: one that relies heavily on Interface Builder and one that requires more code but yields a bit more flexibility and capability. We'll also tackle some advanced OpenGL topics concerning off-screen rendering, context sharing, and more.

One final note to the reader before you read this chapter: This chapter is designed around Mac OS X 10.4, Tiger, the most current and relevant of the Mac OS versions available at the time this book was produced. However the final version of Leopard arrived late in the publishing cycle. Because of this, we were faced with a tough decision—either update this section to show how things work in Leopard, Mac OS X 10.5, and leave our Tiger 10.4 readers behind, or leave our Leopard readers without updated content. Neither of those answers satisfied us completely, so we did the next best thing.

The chapter you're reading is focused on Tiger, Mac OS X 10.4, and the images and text reflect that. Appendix C is an updated version of this chapter with new

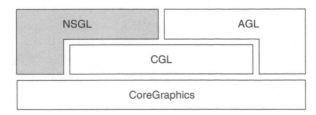

Figure 8-1 AppKit API and Framework in Overall OpenGL Infrastructure on the Mac

and relevant images, workflow, and text for Mac OS X 10.5. If you're looking for Mac OS X 10.4 content, read on, but if you're looking for the same version of this chapter, addressing Leopard-specific changes, and with a Leopard look-and-feel, please read Appendix C.

Overview

The AppKit OpenGL API is part of the overall Apple OpenGL infrastructure. It constitutes a layer above CGL but also has the ability to reach down into both CGL and lower layers. Figure 8-1 shows where the AppKit (also known as Cocoa or NSGL) API and framework reside relative to other API layers.

The AppKit framework is typically found at `/System/Library/Frameworks` but may also be in a path specific to your SDK installation. As with other APIs, linking against AppKit requires specification of this framework path (Table 8-1).

NSOpenGLView

In this section, we will create an XCode project showing how to create a custom view to handle OpenGL rendering using a Cocoa UI element. This project will be a foundation project that we will return to when we create other examples with increased functionality later in the book. We'll begin with the overall project setup and creation—so launch XCode, and we'll get started.

Create a new XCode project of type `Cocoa Application`. This action will create your project, set it to link properly against the Cocoa frameworks, and create a sample main program from which we'll begin. If you do not feel like walking through the steps or would like to see the finished product first, check out the sample code from our website (www.macopenglbook.com).

Table 8-1 AppKit Cocoa Headers, Frameworks, and Overview

Framework path	`/System/Library/Frameworks/AppKit.framework`
Build flag	`-framework AppKit`
Header	`#include<AppKit/NSOpenGL.h>`

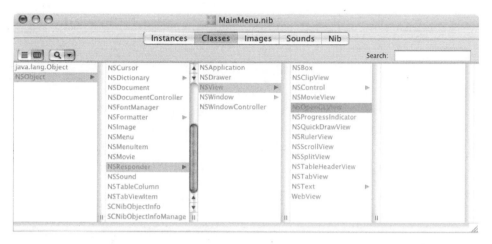

Figure 8-2   Subclassing `NSOpenGLView` in Interface Builder

Open the `Resources` folder, and double-click on the `MainMenu.nib` icon. This will open the nib file for this project in Interface Builder. Now switch to Interface Builder.

In the `MainMenu.nib` window, click on the `Classes` tab, and navigate through the three-pane system until you finally click on `NSOpenGLView`. The panes should look like Figure 8-2 when selected.

Next click on the `Classes` menu and `Subclass NSOpenGLView` item to create a new derived class based on the `NSOpenGLView` type. A new text entry field will appear, suggesting the name `MyOpenGLView`. Accept the default name by pressing the Enter key or choose something more interesting and type away. Your results should look similar to Figure 8-3.

So what did we just do? We told Interface Builder that we wanted to subclass `NSOpenGLView` for our own purposes. `NSOpenGLView` is derived from the `NSView` class. It provides the integration between OpenGL and Cocoa. By subclassing it, we become able to customize many aspects of its behavior, including pixel format selection and context sharing. But we're getting ahead of ourselves. First we've got to get `MyOpenGLView` into a form where we can write some code.

We'll now use Interface Builder to instantiate a default object when the nib file is loaded, create some sample code, and arrange our view in the window.

First, let's create an instance of our class. Return to the `MainMenu.nib` window, where you should still have `MyOpenGLView` selected. If not, navigate through the hierarchy to re-select it. With `MyOpenGLView` selected, click on the `Classes` menu and `Instantiate MyOpenGLView` item. This will create an

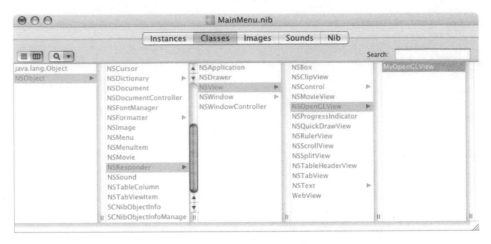

Figure 8-3 Subclassed `NSOpenGLView` in Interface Builder

instance of this class in the nib, and the interface will update to return you to the `Instances` tab in the `MainMenu.nib` window. You should see something like Figure 8-4.

Now let's create the actual headers and code. In the `MainMenu.nib` window, click on the `Classes` tab. If you're lucky, `MyOpenGLView` will still be selected, if not, navigate to it and select it. Click on the `Classes` menu and `Create Files for MyOpenGLView` item. This will prompt you to create files for both the header and the source for this view. Accept the defaults, and we'll begin laying out the view in a window.

Figure 8-4 Instantiated OpenGL View Object in Interface Builder

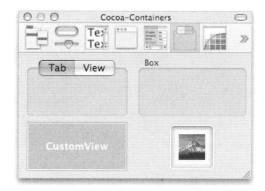

Figure 8-5 Custom View Palette in Interface Builder

At this point, we've created the necessary infrastructure, but we still have to place our view in our window. As with most Interface Builder tasks, we accomplish this by dragging and dropping and by applying a little customization. We begin by dragging a `Custom View` into the window named `Window`. Go to the `Cocoa-Interfaces` window (if it's not visible, get there by clicking the menu `Tools`, the submenu `Palettes`, and then the item `Show Palettes`) and navigate to the `Custom View` pane. This palette can be seen in Figure 8-5. Drag the `CustomView` icon from the palette into `Window` and arrange it as shown in Figure 8-6.

The final step in this setup operation is to change the `CustomView` to be your `MyOpenGLView` object. To do so, open the `Inspector` (if it's not open, click

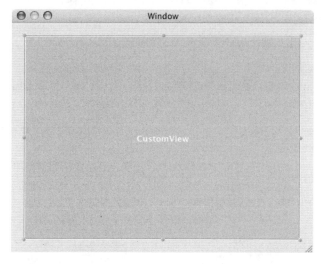

Figure 8-6 Adding a Custom View to a Window in Interface Builder

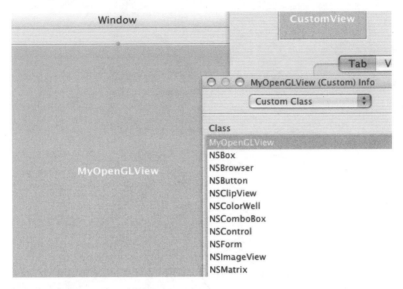

Figure 8-7 Binding a Custom View to the `NSOpenGLView` Subclass Object

the `Tools` menu and `Show Info` item) and click on the `CustomView` you just dragged into place. Choose the `Custom Class` pop-up menu entry in the `Inspector` window, and navigate and choose `MyOpenGLView` from the list. You should see results like those shown in Figure 8-7.

We could have handled all of this setup, configuration, and routing programmatically—but this book isn't about Cocoa plumbing, so we'll stay at this level for now. In a later section, we'll explore Cocoa configuration of a generic `NSView`, which allows us a bit more flexibility. For now, switch back to XCode and we'll dig into the code.

In XCode, open the file `MyOpenGLView.m`. We'll now begin adding methods to handle key elements of the OpenGL render cycle. We start by adding a method to select pixel formats. This code performs pixel format selection in three steps:

1. A structure is created containing a list of pixel format configuration parameters.
2. That structure is passed to an `NSOpenGLPixelFormat` constructor to create a new pixel format object.
3. That pixel format object is passed on to the base `NSOpenGLView` method for finishing the initialization of this view.

Either add the code yourself to your project or grab it from the sample code provided in Example 8.1. Compile and run the code, and you should have a window!

Table 8-2 Selection Policies and Behaviors

Policy	Description
Match	Choose only from the set of pixel formats that match exactly.
Closest	Choose a match closest to the size specified, but not necessarily an exact match.
Minimum	Require a match of at least this size. Can choose larger sizes.
Maximum	Require a match of at most this size. Prefers larger sizes.

"But wait," you say, "what about the rest of the key OpenGL configuration pieces: the context and the drawable or surface?" By subclassing NSOpenGLView, you're getting the last two pieces configured for you, you lucky dog—no extra work required. The base NSOpenGLView class creates a context from the pixel format you passed in, and it creates a drawable such that it can be visualized in the window we created with our CustomView back in Interface Builder. Later, however, we'll go through the process of specializing an NSView so we can do the fun bits in creating a context and a drawable, too. This step is necessary if you want to do more advanced context things, such as share data with another context. More on that in later sections.

Moving along, now that you know how to choose a pixel format, it's probably an appropriate time to discuss what the various flags mean to an NSOpenGLPixelFormat. These flags are generally well documented by Apple, but we're including a list of all the flags in one spot for handy reference here. Take a look at Tables 8-2 and 8-3, see which values make sense for your application, and try a few in the code we've just developed. Table 8-3 contains a fair bit of exposition on these flags, including what the various values mean and how you might use them—it's worth a quick read.

In particular, pixel format selection can have a profound impact on both the performance of and the video memory usage by your application. Keep in mind that choosing pixel formats with more capabilities may lead to slower performance than choosing pixel formats with fewer options and smaller buffers. For example, if you have a choice between a pixel format with a color buffer size of, say, 8 bits per color component (32 bits total) or one with a color buffer represented as a 32-bit floating-point number per component (128 bits total), it's pretty clear that writing to a single pixel in your drawable requires four times the bandwidth just for color. We'll get into these performance implications later and explore issues like this one in more detail. For now, just realize that a good rule of thumb for choosing pixel formats is to choose the one that most closely matches your application's needs.

Example 8-1 Configuration of an OpenGL View in initWithFrame

```
#include <OpenGL/gl.h>
#include <GLUT/glut.h>
```

```
#include <math.h>
#import "MyOpenGLView.h"

@implementation MyOpenGLView

- (id) initWithFrame: (NSRect) frame
{
    time = 0;
    angle = 0;

    GLuint attributes[] =
    {
        NSOpenGLPFAWindow,
        // choose among pixelformats capable of rendering to windows
        NSOpenGLPFAAccelerated,
        // require hardware-accelerated pixelformat
        NSOpenGLPFADoubleBuffer,
        // require double-buffered pixelformat
        NSOpenGLPFAColorSize, 24,
        // require 24 bits for color-channels
        NSOpenGLPFAAlphaSize, 8,
        // require an 8-bit alpha channel
        NSOpenGLPFADepthSize, 24,
        // require a 24-bit depth buffer
        NSOpenGLPFAMinimumPolicy,
        // select a pixelformat which meets or exceeds these requirements
        0
    };

    NSOpenGLPixelFormat* pixelformat =
        [ [ NSOpenGLPixelFormat alloc ] initWithAttributes:
            (NSOpenGLPixelFormatAttribute*) attributes ];

    if ( pixelformat == nil )
    {
        NSLog( @"No valid OpenGL pixel format" );
        NSLog( @"matches the attributes specified" );
        // at this point, we'd want to try different sets of
        // pixelformat attributes until we got a match, or decide
        // we couldn't create a proper graphics environment for our
        // application, and exit appropriately
    }
    // now init ourself using NSOpenGLViews
    // initWithFrame:pixelFormat message
    return self = [ super initWithFrame: frame
                        pixelFormat: [ pixelformat autorelease ] ];
}
```

We'll finish this Cocoa example by adding a few more useful methods to our code. These will allow two more key tasks—namely, context setup (that is, things you might do in an OpenGL application, such as, `glEnable` certain states and bind textures) and drawing.

Table 8-3 Common Pixel Format Qualifiers for Use with
NSOpenGLPixelFormat

Token	Description
NSOpenGLPFAAllRenderers	Look in entire set of renderers to find a match.
	Type: Boolean
	YES: Search entire set of available renderers, including those that are potentially non-OpenGL compliant.
	Default: YES
	Policy: Any
NSOpenGLPFADoubleBuffer	Double buffer requirements.
	Type: Boolean
	YES: Search only for a double-buffered pixel format. NO: Require a single-buffered pixel format.
	Default: NO
	Policy: Any
NSOpenGLPFAStereo	Stereo requirements.
	Type: Boolean
	YES: Require a stereo pixel format. NO: Require a monoscopic pixel format.
	Default: NO
	Policy: Any
NSOpenGLPFAAuxBuffers	Auxiliary buffer requirements.
	Type: Unsigned integer
	Number of auxiliary buffers required by this pixel format.
	Default: NA
	Policy: Smallest
NSOpenGLPFAColorSize	Color bits requirements.
	Type: Unsigned integer
	Number of color buffer bits required by all color components together.
	Default: If this token is not specified, a ColorSize that matches the screen is implied.
	Policy: Closest
NSOpenGLPFAAlphaSize	Unsigned integer: The value specified is the number of alpha buffer bits required.
	Default: If no value is specified, pixel formats discovered may or may not have an alpha buffer.
	Selection policy: Pixel formats that most closely match this size are preferred.
	(Continued)

Table 8-3 Common Pixel Format Qualifiers for Use with
NSOpenGLPixelFormat (*Continued*)

Token	Description
NSOpenGLPFADepthSize	Unsigned integer: The value specified is the number of depth buffer bits required.
	Default: If no value is specified, pixel formats discovered may or may not have a depth buffer.
	Selection policy: Pixel formats that most closely match this size are preferred.
NSOpenGLPFAStencilSize	Unsigned integer: The value specified is the number of stencil planes required.
	Selection policy: The smallest stencil buffer of at least the specified size is preferred.
NSOpenGLPFAAccumSize	Unsigned integer: The value specified is the number of accumulation buffer bits required.
	Selection policy: An accumulation buffer that most closely matches the specified size is preferred.
NSOpenGLPFAMinimumPolicy	YES: Change to the selection policy described.
	Selection policy: Consider only buffers greater than or equal to each specified size of the color, depth, and accumulation buffers.
NSOpenGLPFAMaximumPolicy	YES: Change to the selection policy described.
	Selection policy: For non-zero buffer specifications, prefer the largest available buffer for each of color, depth, and accumulation buffers.
NSOpenGLPFAOffScreen	YES: Consider only renderers capable of rendering to an off-screen memory area that have a buffer depth exactly equal to the specified buffer depth size. An implicit change to the selection policy is as described.
	Selection policy: NSOpenGLPFAClosestPolicy
NSOpenGLPFAFullScreen	YES: Consider only renderers capable of rendering to a full-screen drawable. Implicitly defines the NSOpenGLPFASingleRenderer attribute.
NSOpenGLPFASampleBuffers	Unsigned integer: The value specified is the number of multisample buffers required.

Token	Description
NSOpenGLPFASamples	Unsigned integer: The value specified is the number of samples for each multisample buffer required.
NSOpenGLPFAColorFloat	YES: Consider only renderers capable of using floating-point pixels. NSOpenGLPFAColorSize should also be set to 64 or 128 for half- or full-precision floating-point pixels (Mac OS 10.4).
NSOpenGLPFAMultisample	YES: Consider only renderers capable of using supersample anti-aliasing. NSOpenGLPFASampleBuffers and NSOpenGLPFASamples also need to be set (Mac OS 10.4).
NSOpenGLPFAAuxDepthStencil	If present, searches for pixel formats for each AuxBuffer that has its own depth stencil buffer.
NSOpenGLPFARendererID	Unsigned integer: ID of renderer.
	Selection policy: Prefer renderers that match the specified ID. Refer to CGLRenderers.h for possible values.
NSOpenGLPFAAccelerated	YES: Modify the selection policy to search for pixel formats only among hardware-accelerated renderers.
	NO (default): Search all renderers, but adhere to the selection policy specified.
	Selection policy: Prefer accelerated renderers.
NSOpenGLPFAClosestPolicy	YES: Modify the selection policy for the color buffer to choose the closest color buffer size preferentially. This policy will not take into account the color buffer size of the current graphics devices.
	NO (default): No modification to selection policy.
NSOpenGLPFABackingStore	YES: Constrain the search of pixel formats to consider only renderers that have a back color buffer that is both the full size of the drawable and guaranteed to be valid after a call to a buffer flush.
	NO (default): No modification to the pixel buffer search.
NSOpenGLPFAWindow	YES (default): Search only among renderers that are capable of rendering to a window.
	Note: This attribute is implied only if neither NSOpenGLPFAFullScreen nor NSOpenGLPFAOffScreen is specified.
NSOpenGLPFAPixelBuffer	YES: Rendering to a pixel buffer is enabled.

Figure 8-8 Teapot Rendered with NSOpenGLView Subclass

The first of these methods, which is named prepareOpenGL, is defined to be the first opportunity that your class will have to make some OpenGL calls. prepareOpenGL will be called once a valid pixel format, context, and drawable are all available, so you can go ahead and call anything you'd like there. Keep in mind that this method will be called only once, so from that point on, you'll have to manage your OpenGL state changes on the fly.

The second method to implement is drawRect. This method will be called every time a scene redraw is necessary; you will do the bulk of your OpenGL work there. As part of the drawRect signature, you will be handed an NSRect containing the current origin and size of the drawing area, in pixels.

With that introduction out of the way, we'll simply point you at the code (Example C-2) to add to your MyOpenGLView.m file, somewhere between the @implementation and @end tokens. Once you've added this code, recompile and run the code again, and you should see something like Figure 8-8.

Example 8-2 Cocoa drawRect Rendering Method with Sample OpenGL Content

```
- (void) drawRect: (NSRect) rect
{
    // adjust viewing parameters
    glViewport( 0, 0, (GLsizei) rect.size.width,
                      (GLsizei) rect.size.height );
```

```
    glClearColor( 0, .5, .8, 0 );
    glClear( GL_COLOR_BUFFER_BIT | GL_DEPTH_BUFFER_BIT );

    glMatrixMode( GL_MODELVIEW );
    glLoadIdentity();

    glTranslatef( 0, 0, -1 );

    GLfloat green[ 4 ] = { 0, 1, 0, 0 };
    glMaterialfv( GL_FRONT_AND_BACK,
        GL_AMBIENT_AND_DIFFUSE, green );
    glutSolidTeapot( .5 );

    [ [ self openGLContext ] flushBuffer ];
}

@end
```

If you see a teapot—success! In this section, we've explored one of the ways to configure a Cocoa OpenGL Surface, delved into the details of how to specify a pixel format, and constructed a functional application. This should serve as a starting point in your exploration of Cocoa, pixel format selection, and OpenGL rendering in these frameworks. In the next section, we'll examine how you create a custom NSView-derived class for even more flexibility.

NSView

Now that we've seen what NSOpenGLView can do for us, let's create our own NSView-based application to expose some of the functionality that NSOpenGLView performed behind the scenes. Why expose this extra complexity? You may want to take this path if your application features many OpenGL views of the same data. The technique we'll demonstrate here allows you to share data between these multiple views. But whatever your needs, this exploration will show you how to attach a context to an NSView, getting at the guts of how contexts are created, and then do some rendering. If you need precise management of a context, this is the way to do it in a Cocoa application. We'll end up exactly where we did before, with a cozy teapot on a calming blue background. We'll also begin where we did last time as well, in XCode. Launch it, and we'll get started.

We begin with the big picture—an overview of where we're going in this section. If you'd like to try to do this chunk on your own before the walkthrough, we encourage you to apply what we did in the last section to create a custom view. This time, however, we'll create our subclass based on NSView. Here are the steps:

1. Create a subclass of NSView named MyView.
2. Create the files for this class.

3. Create an instance of this class in `MainMenu.nib`.
4. Write code in XCode to create a custom pixel format and context.
5. Write code to create the teapot and handle the OpenGL initialization.

We won't say any more about how to accomplish the XCode project setup and configuration at this point, but rather will leave you to try to figure it out on your own. The walkthrough here will take you through all the details if you'd prefer to try it this way.

Create a new XCode project of type `Cocoa Application`. This action will create your project, set it to link properly against the Cocoa frameworks, and create a sample main program from which we'll begin. If you don't feel like walking through the steps or would like to see the finished product first, check out the sample code from our website (www.macopenglbook.com).

Open the `Resources` folder, and double-click on the `MainMenu.nib` icon. This will open the nib file for this project in Interface Builder. Now switch to Interface Builder.

In the `MainMenu.nib` window, click on the `Classes` tab, and navigate through the three-pane system until you finally click on `NSView`. The panes should look like Figure 8-9 when selected.

Next click on the `Classes` menu and `Subclass NSView` item to create a new derived class based on the `NSView` type. A new text entry field will appear, suggesting the name `MyView`. Accept the default name by pressing the Enter key or choose something more interesting. Your results should look similar to Figure 8-10.

As before, we must create headers and code. In the `MainMenu.nib` window, click on the `Classes` tab, navigate to `MyView`, and select it. Click on the `Classes` menu and `Create Files for MyView` item. It will prompt you to

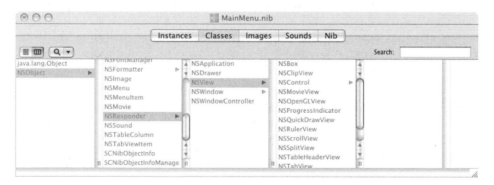

Figure 8-9 Subclassing `NSOpenGLView` in Interface Builder

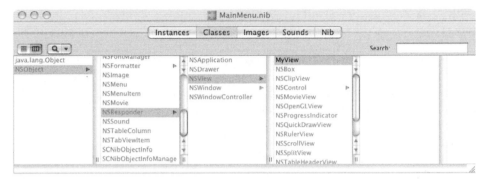

Figure 8-10 Subclassed NSOpenGLView in Interface Builder

create files for both the header and the source for this view. Accept the defaults, and we'll begin laying out the view in a window.

We now need to place our view in our window, and designate it to be our MyView object. Drag a Custom View into the window named Window. Go to the Cocoa-Interfaces window as before, and navigate to the Custom View pane. Drag one of those icons into your Window and arrange it as in Figure 8-6. Finally, modify the CustomView to be your MyView object by opening the Inspector as before. Choose the Custom Class pop-up menu entry in the Inspector window, and navigate and choose MyView from the list. You should see the results shown in Figure 8-11.

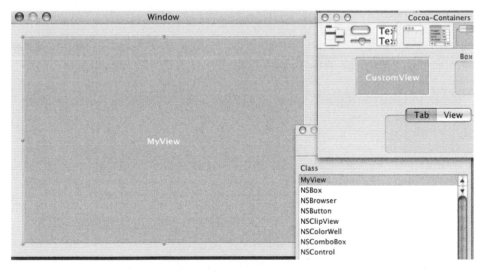

Figure 8-11 MyView Binding in Interface Builder

With that configuration out of the way, we move straight into the code phase. Save your `MainMenu.nib`, and switch to XCode. As before with the `NSOpenGLView`-derived project, we'll do many of the same things, including creating a pixel format and creating a subclassed version of `drawRect`. We'll also mimic some of the infrastructure automatically provided in `NSOpenGLView`, so you can see how it does its work. This time around, we'll present all the code in the final versions of both the header file (Example 8-3) and the source file (Example 8-4) first, and then walk you through each.

Example 8-3 `MyView.h` Final Header

```
#import <Cocoa/Cocoa.h>

@interface MyView : NSView
{
    @private
        NSOpenGLContext *_context;
        NSOpenGLPixelFormat* _pixelformat;
}

- (NSOpenGLContext*) openGLContext;
- (void) prepareOpenGL;

@end
```

We begin by looking at the `MyView.h` header. We've inserted both a few member variables and a few methods. We've also created member variables to store pointers to our context and to our pixel format; we'll create code to initialize these variables in the source file. We also declare two methods, `openGLContext` and `prepareOpenGL`, named to emulate the behavior of the Cocoa-supplied `NSOpenGLView`. `openGLContext` will be used to return the current context or to create one if none exists. `prepareOpenGL` will be used as our first call to our OpenGL context to initialize the basic OpenGL functionality, as we did before for our `MyNSOpenGLView` class.

That's all there is to do in the header, so let's look at the source, see which other methods we've overloaded from `NSView`, and see how the code behind these signatures works.

Example 8-4 `MyView.m` Final Code

```
#include <OpenGL/gl.h>
#include <GLUT/glut.h>

#import "MyView.h"

@implementation MyView

- (id)initWithFrame:(NSRect)frameRect
```

```
{
    NSLog( @"myView::initWithFrame" );
    if ((self = [super initWithFrame:frameRect]) != nil)
    {
        GLuint attributes[] =
        {
            NSOpenGLPFAWindow,
            NSOpenGLPFAAccelerated,
            NSOpenGLPFADoubleBuffer,
            NSOpenGLPFAColorSize, 24,
            NSOpenGLPFAAlphaSize, 8,
            NSOpenGLPFADepthSize, 24,
            NSOpenGLPFAMinimumPolicy,
            // select a pixelformat which meets or
            // exceeds these requirements
            0
        };
        _pixelformat = [ [ NSOpenGLPixelFormat alloc ]
            initWithAttributes:
                (NSOpenGLPixelFormatAttribute*) attributes ];

        if ( _pixelformat == nil )
        {
            NSLog( @"No valid OpenGL pixel format" );
            NSLog( @"matching attributes specified" );
        }
    }
    // init the context for later construction
    _context = nil;

    return self;
}

- (NSOpenGLContext *) openGLContext
{
    if ( _context == nil )
    {
        // if this is our first time to initialize
        _context = [ [ NSOpenGLContext alloc ]
            initWithFormat: _pixelformat shareContext: nil ];

        if ( _context == nil )
        {
            NSLog( @"No valid OpenGL context can be" );
            NSLog( @"created with that pixelformat" );
            /*
            we can fail a few ways:
                1 - bogus parameters: nil pixelformat,
                    invalid sharecontext, etc.
                2 - share context uses a different Renderer
                    than the specified pixelformat

            recovery techniques:
                1 - choose a different pixelformat
```

```
                2 -proceed without a shared context
            */
        }
    }

    return( _context );
}

- (void) lockFocus
{
    NSLog( @"myView::lockFocus" );

    // ensure we are ready to draw
    [ super lockFocus ];
    // get our context
    NSOpenGLContext *cxt = [ self openGLContext ];

    // ensure we are pointing to ourself as the Drawable
    if ( [ cxt view ] != self )
    {
        [ cxt setView: self ];
    }

    // make us the current OpenGL context
    [ cxt makeCurrentContext ];
}

- (void) prepareOpenGL
{

    NSLog( @"myView::prepareOpenGL" );

    glMatrixMode( GL_PROJECTION );
    glLoadIdentity();
    glOrtho(-1,1,-1,1,-1,100);
}

- (void) drawRect: (NSRect) rect
{
    // adjust viewing parameters
    glViewport( 0, 0,
        (GLsizei) rect.size.width, (GLsizei) rect.size.height );

    glClearColor( 0, .5, .8, 0 );
    glClear( GL_COLOR_BUFFER_BIT | GL_DEPTH_BUFFER_BIT );

    glMatrixMode( GL_MODELVIEW );
    glLoadIdentity();

    glTranslatef( 0, 0, -1 );

    GLfloat green[ 4 ] = { 0, 1, 0, 0 };
    glMaterialfv( GL_FRONT_AND_BACK, GL_AMBIENT_AND_DIFFUSE, green );
    glutSolidTeapot( .5 );
```

```
    [ [ self openGLContext ] flushBuffer ];
}
```

@end

In our MyView.m file, we start by looking at our initWithFrame overloaded method. This method is called when our object is getting constructed, with the desired layout of this particular view. As with our MyNSOpenGLView class, this method is where we set up our pixel format and prepare the rest of our class for subsequent use. In fact, the majority of the code in this method is identical to the code given earlier, with a slight inversion: We initialize the parent first and then, based on success there, create a pixel format. We end this method by initializing our _context member to nil in preparation for configuring it later.

The next method, openGLContext, is the body of what we declared in the header. This method's intent is to hand the caller a pointer to the context used by this view. It begins by checking whether the existing context is empty; if so, it creates a context using the existing pixel format we created earlier and calls the NSOpenGLContext constructor initWithFormat: NSOpenGLContext *. This constructor takes two parameters: a pixel format and either another NSOpenGLContext pointer or nil. The pixel format parameter is used by the context to configure itself with any specific information that may affect OpenGL rendering, such as anti-aliasing or stencil capability. The second parameter, a different NSOpenGLContext*, is used in the case that the context passed back by this method will be shared with the context specified. Sharing a context will be explained in further detail later. For our example here, we simply pass in nil, indicating that we want a new context that does not share any resources with any other context. In this case, the only failure mode for this routine would be if the pixel format specified were invalid or nil. This routine ends by returning a pointer to the new context.

The next method we will create is an overloaded method of NSView named lockFocus. NSView uses this method to make the current view the focus so that it's the target of whatever drawing commands follow. Quoting the Cocoa documentation, lockFocus "locks the focus on the receiver, so subsequent commands take effect in the receiver's window and coordinate system." This command essentially tells the windowing system that we will require some specific configuration to be set up and active before we render into this window.

Why do we need this? Well, every OpenGL context is essentially a snapshot of the entire OpenGL state used during rendering. Thus, if you've painstakingly configured some precise combination of OpenGL data, rendering paths, and other information, the same context in which you've done that work is likely the one in which you'd like your subsequent OpenGL commands to be executed. Put more succinctly, you want your context to be active. In context parlance, this is known as "making your context current." `lockFocus` is the place in the Cocoa framework where your view is made current, and where you can then make your context current.

If we now look at our code, we can see that we need to overload this method to do the usual `lockFocus` work when we call our superclasses `lockFocus`. We then do work to get our OpenGL context and make it current. And that, as they say, is that: We've got a context, it's current, and we're ready to finish this exercise with two methods that we've seen before.

The last two methods we implement are identical to those we've used before. The `prepareOpenGL` and `drawRect` methods contain the same code as in the prior example. As before, they perform two tasks in your context—OpenGL initialization and rendering, respectively. With their completion, you're ready to build and run the application. You should see the same teapot against a blue background as in Figure 8-8.

Additional Topics

So far, we've explored ways to render directly to the screen using Cocoa. Now we'll dig into how to render somewhere off-screen. There are many reasons why you might want to do this—for example, to create a cube map for reflection, to create shadow maps, or to create another form of dynamic texture. For off-screen rendering, we'll be building on the foundation from the Cocoa examples in previous sections, so if you've skipped to this point without reading those sections, you may want to review them to gather additional details.

Manipulating Images and Pixels in OpenGL

Before we get into specific techniques, let's talk about the various ways that an image of some sort can be moved around, rendered, and copied in OpenGL. OpenGL provides two main paths for pixel data:

- Pixel path
- Texture path

These two paths are very different in the way they're ultimately available to be rendered. The pixel path consists of two basic calls, `glDrawPixels` and `glReadPixels`, which allow for drawing and reading, respectively, of pixels from the current write and read buffers. These pixel path calls are 2D only and can read and write only screen-aligned data. By comparison, the texture path differs from the pixel path specifically in that texture data can be rendered in 3D. Because the texture path can also be used to render screen-aligned images as well, it is ultimately the more flexible of the two paths, so we'll focus on the texture path here. The *Red Book* [22] has lots of details on the imaging pipeline, if you'd like more information on that.

Any pixel data that you might want to render in an OpenGL scene, you can handle through textures. To do so, you would download that image as a texture using `glTexImage[123]D` calls. Let's provide an overview of this process and then translate it into code:

1. Create and configure a texture (`glGenTextures`, `glBindTexture`, `glTexImage2D`, `glTexEnv`, `glTexParameter`).
2. Bind that texture (`glBindTexture`).
3. Draw using that texture (`glBegin ... glTexCoord2f ... glEnd`).

This book isn't meant to teach you fundamental OpenGL rendering techniques, but the preceding sequence is essential to understand for two key reasons. First, texturing is the primary means by which you'll access the data you render to off-screen surfaces and the primary way by which you'll re-render those data in another form. Second, textures are chunks of data that are intimately bound to OpenGL contexts, and we'll need to know how to share data among contexts if we want to use textures rendered in one context in another context. Essentially, this section is a segue into sharing contexts, which is the topic we explore next.

Context Sharing

A key concept in many aspects of OpenGL rendering—on the Mac or otherwise—is what lives in an OpenGL context and how to efficiently use that data for multiple purposes. Essentially, a context contains all OpenGL state data associated with rendering, such as the viewport dimensions, active color, and rendering modes. A context also includes much heavier-weight items, such as texture objects and vertex objects.

Large objects consume nontrivial amounts of memory on a graphics card, so the designers of OpenGL anticipated the need to avoid duplicating resources among multiple rendering areas. This anti-redundancy capability is exposed at the window-system level as a feature called *context sharing*. This capability is typically requested when a new OpenGL context is created, after the first rendering context has been created and used. The context with items you wish to access is passed into some form of initialization for your new context, usually along with a pixel format. For two contexts to be compatible, their pixel formats must be compatible, which is why you see these two things specified together to successfully enable sharing.

What makes pixel formats incompatible? On the Mac, usually it's one thing—incompatible renderers. As a rule of thumb, if you can choose pixel formats that use the same renderers, you can share contexts created with those pixel formats.

So we've covered the how and why of sharing a context, but what, exactly, is shared when context sharing is enabled? Interestingly enough, most OpenGL objects are shared, but the overall context state is not. That's not entirely intuitive, but it correlates well with what people usually want to do. You save valuable card memory by reusing heavyweight objects in multiple spots, but still preserve the ability to customize each OpenGL view as needed. Specifically, the following entities are shared:

- Display lists
- Vertex array objects (VAOs)
- Buffer objects (VBOs, PBOs)
- Texture objects
- Vertex and fragment programs and shaders
- Frame buffer objects (FBOs)

Now that we have an overview of how context sharing works, let's walk through some code. For purposes of this example, we will build a two-windowed version of our earlier Cocoa example in which we created a custom context. In this case we'll modify the example to share the context between the two views and surfaces, render some shared data (a display list), and visualize the data in two views, each with a different-color background color. The plan is to demonstrate what is and what isn't shared in context sharing.

We begin by setting up a new project as we did for the simple Cocoa context example. The exact process isn't described here, except to say that you duplicate the steps from before but add a new window in your MainMenu.nib and create two custom NSOpenGL-derived views. Your results should look like Figure 8-12.

Working in XCode, add an OpenGL framework dependency, and ensure that your frameworks and classes appear as shown in Figure 8-13. Try building and running this application, knowing that we've not yet connected up the drawing or context sharing. On the off-chance that you see only one window, make sure you've added the "Visible at Launch" flag to your Interface Builder properties, as in Figure 8-14.

Finally, let's look at the code necessary for context sharing. There are a number of techniques for deciding which context to share, but one approach that is particularly nice, from an architectural perspective, is to use an "external" context provider. In this model, we configure and create a context in a separate class, and then share it with any OpenGL view that needs to render using its shared objects. In our example, we'll use the pattern of a singleton—that is, an object-based wrapper around a static object. This code is very straightforward, so we'll

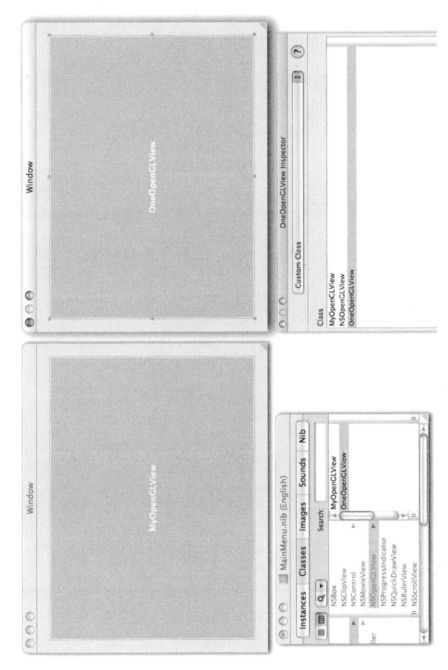

Figure 8-12 Context Sharing: Two Windows and Two Custom NSOpenGLViews in Interface Builder

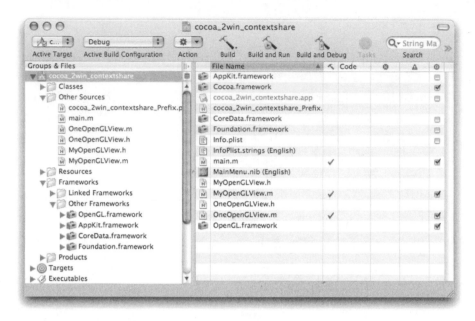

Figure 8-13 Context Sharing: Two Custom `NSOpenGLViews` in XCode

present it here and then discuss a bit more after presentation. The header code
lives in Example C-5 and the source code is found in Example C-6.

Example 8-5 Singleton Class Declaration for Managing a Shared Context

```
#import <Cocoa/Cocoa.h>
@interface SharedContext : NSObject
{

    NSOpenGLPixelFormat* _pixelformat;
    NSOpenGLContext * _context;
}

- (NSOpenGLPixelFormat *) pixelFormat;
- (NSOpenGLContext *) context;
+ (SharedContext *) instance;

@end
```

Example 8-6 Singleton Class Implementation for Managing a Shared Context

```
#import <AppKit/NSOpenGL.h>
#import <OpenGL/gl.h>

#import "SharedContext.h"

SharedContext *_sharedContext = nil;
```

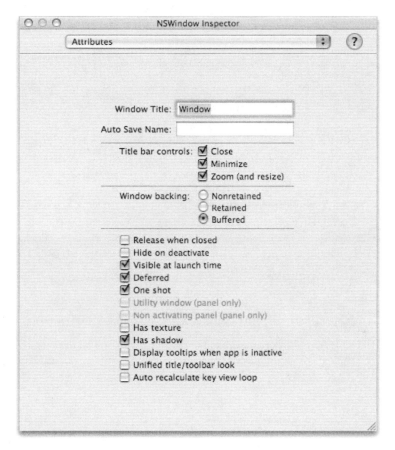

Figure 8-14   Context Sharing: Set Visible on Launch for Second Window

```
@implementation SharedContext

- (id) init
{
    if (self = [super init])
    {
        _pixelformat = nil;
        _context = nil;

        GLuint attributes[] =
        {
            NSOpenGLPFAWindow,          // windowed pixelformats
            NSOpenGLPFAAccelerated,     // hw-accel pixelformat
            NSOpenGLPFADoubleBuffer,    // double-buffered pixelformat
            NSOpenGLPFAColorSize, 24,   // 24 bits for color-channels
            NSOpenGLPFAAlphaSize, 8,    // 8-bit alpha channel
            NSOpenGLPFADepthSize, 24,   // 24-bit depth buffer
```

```
            NSOpenGLPFAMinimumPolicy,    // meets or exceed reqs
            0
        };
        _pixelformat = [ [ NSOpenGLPixelFormat alloc ]
            initWithAttributes:
                (NSOpenGLPixelFormatAttribute*) attributes ];

        if ( _pixelformat == nil )
        {
            NSLog( @"SharedContext: No valid OpenGL pixel" \
                @"format matching attributes specified" );
            // at this point, we'd want to try different
            // sets of pixelformat attributes until we
            // got a match, or decided we couldn't create
            // a proper working environment for our
            // application
        }
        else
        {
            _context = [ [ NSOpenGLContext alloc ]
                initWithFormat: _pixelformat shareContext: nil ];
        }
    }
    return self;
}

- (NSOpenGLPixelFormat *) pixelFormat
{
    return( _pixelformat );
}

- (NSOpenGLContext *) context
{
    return( _context );
}

+ (SharedContext *) instance
{
    if ( _sharedContext == nil )
    {
        _sharedContext = [ [ SharedContext alloc ] init ];
    }
    return _sharedContext;
}

@end
```

If you're familiar with the singleton pattern, the `instance` method and idea should be familiar to you. If not, consult the classic *Design Patterns* book by the notorious Gang of Four [16]. Essentially, `instance` provides a handle to our static context manager object. Upon its creation, this object allocates a pixel format and a context based on that pixel format. This code should look familiar, as we've written code similar to it earlier in this book. The only caveat when writing context-sharing code of your own is to keep in mind that any context that is meant to be shared must be compatible with the other contexts. Compatibility implies many things, but chiefly that the destination pixel depth, color depth, and other factors are similar. We work around that problem in this example by first exposing a common pixel format through the `pixelFormat` method, and then using that method to construct our pixel format and context for each window's view.

Let's revisit the code we used for our custom OpenGL view example for initialization and setup. This code, with one minor twist, does everything we need and is presented in Example C-7.

Example 8-7   Initialization of an OpenGL View with a Shared Context

```
@implementation MyView

- (id)initWithFrame:(NSRect)frameRect
{
    NSLog( @"MyView::initWithFrame" );

    if ((self = [super initWithFrame:frameRect]) != nil)
    {
        _pixelformat = [ [ SharedContext instance ] pixelFormat ];

        if ( _pixelformat == nil )
        {
            NSLog( @"No valid OpenGL pixel format" \
                "matching attributes specified" );
            // at this point, we'd want to try different
            // sets of pixelformat attributes until we
            // got a match, or decided we couldn't create
            // a proper working environment for our
            // application
        }
    }

    // init the context for later construction
    _context = nil;

    return self;
}

- (NSOpenGLContext *) openGLContext
{
    if ( _context == nil ) // only if uninitialized
    {
        // if this is our first time to initialize
        _context = [ [ NSOpenGLContext alloc ]
            initWithFormat: _pixelformat
                shareContext: [ [ SharedContext instance ] context ] ];
```

```
    if ( _context == nil )
    {
        NSLog( @"No valid OpenGL context can be" \
                "created with that pixelformat" );
        /*
        we can fail a few ways:
        1 - bogus parameters: nil pixelformat, invalid
            sharecontext, etc.
        2 - share context uses a different Renderer
            than the specified pixelformat

        recovery techniques:
        1 - choose a different pixelformat
        2 - proceed without a shared context
        */
    }
}

    return( _context );
}
```

As you can see in Example 8-7, the only changes we made from our original custom view example are to use the [[SharedContext instance] pixelFormat] accessor to create a pixel format for this view and then, similarly, to use the [[SharedContext instance] context] accessor when constructing our context. We should always, of course, confirm that all pixel formats and contexts are successfully created for our production code as well. So, add code like this to your existing code and then make one last change—specifically, change the clear color in one of your custom View drawRect methods. If everything works as planned, your application should produce results like these shown in Figure 8-15.

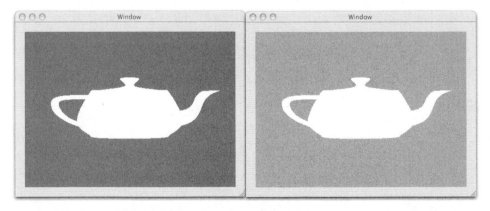

Figure 8-15 Context Sharing: Two Windows Demonstrating Common Shared Data and Unshared (Clear Color) Context Data

Remember that the OS X OpenGL implementation follows the conventions established in the GLX specification. Applications are responsible for synchronizing the state of objects between contexts. This implies that multithreaded applications with shared context establish mutex locks between the threads, use `glFlush` to flush pending commands that modify object state, and call `glBind` to realize changes to shared objects in other contexts. These may seem like a lot of steps, but they are usually worth the resulting resource conservation and performance gains.

In this section, we've seen how to configure context sharing in Cocoa, how to use it with a custom OpenGL view, and under which circumstances you'd want to share contexts. We've provided examples of how this sharing mechanism works in Cocoa, and we'll revisit this topic for AGL and CGL later. Context sharing is a key principle we'll use for a variety of on- or off-screen rendering techniques, so you'll likely revisit this section from time to time for hints when performing full-screen and off-screen rendering.

Full-Screen Surfaces

Every now and again, you might want to put your Cocoa OpenGL application into full-screen mode. There are lots of reasons why you might want to do this, and Apple often uses this approach for many of its applications. Apple software examples include QuickTime full-screen movie presentation, iPhoto/Finder slideshows, DVD playback, and FrontRow set-top display. The most common example of this technique in user software is found in games, usually where a game takes over the display for a complete and unobstructed experience of slaying dragons, flying through canyons at Mach 0.8, or conquering the galaxy. A rule of thumb to decide when full-screen rendering is needed is this: Any time you want to present a completely custom user interface, full-screen applications are one way to go. In this section we'll first tackle some plumbing details necessary to render full-screen OpenGL surfaces and then demonstrate how to create and use a full-screen OpenGL area.

Display Capture

One major reason for using a full-screen area is to coherently display some content without the distraction of other UI elements. A key element of this experience would be blocking interruption by other applications while in this mode. Apple provides hooks to allow an application to essentially take over the display, preventing other applications from presenting their content over the top. This behavior is known as *display capture*. Display capture exists at the Core-Graphics level of graphics, typically a 2D layer, and is not part of our discussion in this book. Nonetheless, the ability to capture the display is a useful—albeit not required—element of a full-screen application, even in Cocoa. Performing display capture is a very easy task, but entails strict ordering of the tasks. Essentially, the process proceeds as follows:

1. Capture the display.
2. Configure and display a full-screen window.
3. Handle events.
4. Release the display.

It's important to ensure that both event handling and teardown (or display release) occur. If they do not, you'll probably get into a deadlock of some sort—one in which either you can't do anything with your application or other applications move to the foreground, respectively. You're almost guaranteed to experience this problem once unless you're really listening to me here, and you'll never repeat the mistake—rebooting in the middle of your development cycle is a pretty good deterrent. The specifics of display capture and release are sketched out, in Example C-8. Please read Apple's developer documentation on the methods described here for additional information. Because these methods are so fundamentally simple, we will just show you the code and have you use it without further discussion.

Example 8-8   Capturing and Releasing the Display

```
/*!
    Captures all displays, returning true/false for
    success/failure.
 */
bool capturedDisplaysLoop()
{
    bool error = false;
    CGDisplayErr err = CGCaptureAllDisplays();
    if (err != CGDisplayNoErr)
    {
        // failure - maybe another application is already
        // fullscreen
        error = true;
    }
    else
    {
        // your code here: open fullscreen window

        // your code here: event handler loop.

        // stay here until no longer in fullscreen mode.
        // upon exit, we transition back to windowed mode, and
        // release the display

        CGReleaseAllDisplays();
    }
    return( error );
}
```

For simplicity, we use the global form of display capture—that is, the form in which all displays are captured. You may have a need or a preference to control which display you capture more precisely. For those circumstances, Apple provides `CGDisplayCapture` and `CGDisplayRelease` to specify a particular display. And that's really all there is for display capture as it relates to OpenGL, except for the event-handling part, which we'll discuss next.

Event Handling

One key caveat to full-screen windows, regardless of the amount of OpenGL window-system integration, relates to event handling: Who's handling the events now that your window-system and UI elements are hidden? Yes, Virginia, this is another headache of full-screen windows, but you've got to do it. Otherwise, nothing will be handling events, making it very difficult to even quit your application. So what's an application to do, especially in Cocoa? As we do a number of times throughout the book, we will not go into the details of this operation, as numerous Cocoa books deal with this topic. Here we simply present Example 8-9, in which code modeled closely on an Apple source example shows what you might do with events while you're in a full-screen mode.

Example 8-9 Custom Controller Event-Handling Loop in a Full-Screen Context

```
stayInFullScreenMode = YES;
while ( stayInFullScreenMode )
{
    NSAutoreleasePool *pool =
        [ [ NSAutoreleasePool alloc ] init ];

    // Check for and process input events.
    NSEvent *event;
    while ( event =
        [ NSApp nextEventMatchingMask: NSAnyEventMask
                            untilDate: [ NSDate distantPast ]
                               inMode: NSDefaultRunLoopMode
                              dequeue: YES ] )
    {
        switch ([event type])
        {
            case NSLeftMouseDown:
                [ self mouseDown:event ];
            break;

            case NSLeftMouseUp:
                [ self mouseUp:event ];
            break;

            case NSLeftMouseDragged:
                [ self mouseDragged:event ];
            break;
```

```
            case NSKeyDown:
            {
                unichar cc =
                    [ [ event charactersIgnoringModifiers ]
                        characterAtIndex:0 ];
                switch ( cc )
                {
                    case 27: // escape key
                        stayInFullScreenMode = NO;
                    break;
                    default:
                    break;
                }
            }
            break;

            default:
            break;
        }
    }
```

The basic idea is that while in full-screen mode, no external UI controls (Cocoa or other) exist that have natural event-handling mechanisms, so you need to do whatever your application requires when an event occurs. This includes mouse handling, key handling, and external device (e.g., joystick, tablet) handling. Example 8-9 does nothing more than simply handle the Escape key, quit the render loop, and return to windowed mode. The example deals specifically with key events, handling the Escape key by quitting full-screen mode, and calling out to other methods (not shown) for handling mouse events.

This structure and code should be enough of a basis for you to get started. If you need more detail, we provide a more comprehensive example on our website (www.macopenglbook.com).

Alternative Rendering Destinations

In the following sections we'll explore what it takes to render an intermediate image for use later in your application. You'll probably already know if this is something you're interested in. If not, let's discuss a case or two in which you might need to render intermediate results.

One example in which intermediate rendering results are useful is for rendering of reflections. Suppose you've got a scene with some watery bits and some shiny bits in it. Picture a rainy street scene with puddles and a car: The puddles would reflect the buildings across the street, and those shiny rims would reflect the buildings behind the viewer. To reflect something on those wheels and puddles, we have two options. One is to use a fake scene to create the reflections, and the other is to use the real scene. Obviously the real scene is the better option, so we'll need to generate a view of the scene that contains the images to be reflected. This would be the image that we'd render in our intermediate buffer.

In another example, we might want to render the same view of the street scene, but perhaps after the viewer hit his or her head on something—a painful simulation, to be sure! Perhaps your character was jogging and ran into a signpost. We want to render the scene slightly blurred and wavy regardless of the method of cranial impact. In this case, our intermediate scene would be the original street scene rendering. We would then take that image and run it through our `BluntTrauma.frag` shader.

Our example code will render scenes of similar complexity, or at least a teapot, to demonstrate this process, but the idea remains the same. The basic path for performing this render is as follows:

1. Render to an alternative destination.
2. Configure those results for use in the final scene render.
3. Render the final scene.

The following sections describe the various techniques available on the Mac for alternative destination rendering and subsequent reuse of those data. We'll prioritize these strategies in terms of their modernity, encouraging you to use the most modern of these, framebuffer objects, whenever possible. For a variety of reasons (not least of which are simplicity and performance), framebuffer objects are the best choice when your hardware supports them. However, as always with more advanced OpenGL features, the most modern features are not always supported on the hardware your customers have, so choosing fallbacks for those cases may require you to implement some of the other techniques. We cover the basics of each below. Dive in.

Framebuffer Objects

In this section we describe a modern and widely available technique for intermediate renders using framebuffer objects (FBOs). Rendering to FBOs is a technique born out of frustrations with the complexity of many of the other intermediate rendering techniques. FBOs were designed to provide a simple enable/disable mechanism that is familiar in usage to textures, and yet provide a great deal of flexibility in terms of what can be rendered and how to use it later. FBOs are an evolution from earlier extensions—namely, `GL_ARB_render_texture`. However, they are a vast improvement over the older techniques, as you'll hear shortly. FBOs are really the only choice for new applications, as they offer high performance, are flexible, and are easy to use.

That's our perspective on the matter, but for reference, you should defer to the extension specification as the authority. The specification declares:

Previous extensions that enabled rendering to a texture have been much more complicated. One example is the combination of GL_ARB_pbuffer and GL_ARB_render_texture, both of which are window-system extensions. This combination requires calling glxMakeCurrent, an expensive operation used to switch between the window and the pbuffer drawables. An application must create one pbuffer per renderable texture in order to portably use GL_ARB_render_texture. An application must maintain at least one GL context per texture format, because each context can operate on only a single pixel format or FBConfig. All of these characteristics make GL_ARB_render_texture both inefficient and cumbersome to use.

GL_EXT_framebuffer_object, on the other hand, is both simpler to use and more efficient than GL_ARB_render_texture. The GL_EXT_framebuffer_object API is contained wholly within the GL API and has no (non-portable) window-system components. Under GL_EXT_framebuffer_object, it is not necessary to create a second GL context when rendering to a texture image whose format differs from that of the window. Finally, unlike the pbuffers of GL_ARB_render_texture, by changing color attachments, a single framebuffer object can facilitate rendering to an unlimited number of texture objects.

We believe that this extension is the best way to render to texture and authoritatively settles the question of what to use when performing a render-to-texture operation. Without further ado, let's walk through how to use FBOs for intermediate rendering and look at code to do so as well.

The overall algorithm for using FBOs is straightforward:

1. Build and initialize the target object to be used with this FBO. This object is typically a texture.
2. Build and initialize the FBO by attaching the target objects.
3. Bind the FBO and render the FBO contents.
4. Unbind the FBO and render the final scene using the target object.

We'll begin by revisiting our old standby Cocoa example and extending it to configure and render to an FBO. We will then use those results on our final rendered object. Example 8-10 shows our custom view header, which indicates where we'll store our texture object and FBO IDs.

Example 8-10 Custom View Header for FBO Example Code

```
#import <Cocoa/Cocoa.h>
#import <OpenGL/OpenGL.h>

@interface MyOpenGLView : NSOpenGLView
```

```
{
    GLuint fboID;
    GLuint textureID;
    float time;
    float angle;
}

- (void) angleUpdate: (NSTimer*) tt;
- (void) reshape;

@end
```

We next look at the code in our `prepareOpenGL` method. As before, this is the place where we create and initialize things that we need to set up once per context. We look at the entire `prepareOpenGL` method in Example 8-11, so essentially we see the first two phases of our outlined FBO usage: build and initialization for both our target texture and our FBO. We begin by creating and initializing a texture object, which we'll both bind to our FBO and use in our final rendering. We then create an FBO and bind it to that texture for color rendering. Finally, after configuration, we unbind our current FBO (by binding the FBO ID of 0).

Example 8-11   OpenGL Setup for FBO Rendering

```
- (void) prepareOpenGL
{
    glMatrixMode( GL_PROJECTION );
    glLoadIdentity();
    glOrtho(-1,1,-1,1,-1,100);

    // enable, generate, and bind our texture objects
    glEnable( GL_TEXTURE_2D );
    glGenTextures( (GLsizei) 1, &textureID );
    glBindTexture( GL_TEXTURE_2D, textureID );
    const unsigned int texdim = 64;
    const unsigned int nbytes = 3;
    char data[ texdim * texdim * nbytes ];
    memset( data, 0xff, texdim * texdim * nbytes );
    unsigned int ii;
    for( ii=0; ii<texdim*texdim; ii++ )
    {
        data[ ii*nbytes + 0 ] = 0xff;
    }
    gluBuild2DMipmaps( GL_TEXTURE_2D, // 0,
                    GL_RGB, texdim, texdim, // 0,
                    GL_RGB, GL_UNSIGNED_BYTE, data );
    glTexEnvi( GL_TEXTURE_ENV, GL_TEXTURE_ENV_MODE, GL_REPLACE );


    // generate & bind our framebuffer object to our texture object
    glGenFramebuffersEXT( 1, &fboID );
```

```
glBindFramebufferEXT( GL_FRAMEBUFFER_EXT, fboID );
glFramebufferTexture2DEXT( GL_FRAMEBUFFER_EXT,
                           GL_COLOR_ATTACHMENT0_EXT,
                           GL_TEXTURE_2D, textureID, 0 );
glTexEnvi( GL_TEXTURE_ENV, GL_TEXTURE_ENV_MODE, GL_DECAL );
glBindFramebufferEXT( GL_FRAMEBUFFER_EXT, 0 ); // unbind fbo

// add a timer to oscillate the modelview
NSTimeInterval ti = .1;
[ NSTimer scheduledTimerWithTimeInterval: ti
                                 target: self
                               selector: @selector(angleUpdate:)
                               userInfo: nil
                                repeats: YES ];
}
```

The OpenGL designers did a pretty good job of keeping the design clean and consistent with that of other objects in the OpenGL system. Specifically, note the parallels in the setup and configuration of FBOs and texture objects. In essence, you simply bind the FBO, do some rendering, and unbind the FBO. At that point, the texture bound to that FBO is ready to be used. We'll demonstrate this usage of the FBO next, even though we've really covered it all in the setup. It couldn't be much simpler. Example 8-12 shows our `drawRect` routine.

Example 8-12 Cocoa `drawRect` Routine for FBOs

```
- (void) drawRect: (NSRect) rect
{
    // render to offscreen
    glBindFramebufferEXT( GL_FRAMEBUFFER_EXT, fboID );
    [ self drawIntermediateContents ];
    glBindFramebufferEXT( GL_FRAMEBUFFER_EXT, 0 );

    // render to final
    [ self drawFinalContents ];

    // complete rendering & swap
    glFlush();
    [ [ self openGLContext ] flushBuffer ];
}
```

Finally, for interest, we present the code we actually draw with in those routines in Example 8-13.

Example 8-13 Cocoa Draw Methods for Contents of the FBO and the Final Render

```
- (void) drawIntermediateContents
{
    glClearColor( 1, 1, 0, 1 );
    glClear( GL_COLOR_BUFFER_BIT | GL_DEPTH_BUFFER_BIT );
    glMatrixMode( GL_MODELVIEW );
```

```
        glLoadIdentity();
        glTranslatef( 0, 0, 1 );
        glColor3f( 0, 1, 1 );
        glBegin( GL_QUADS );
        float ww = .9;
        float hh = .9;
        float zz = 0.0;
        glDisable( GL_TEXTURE_2D );
        glVertex3f( -ww, -hh, zz );
        glVertex3f( ww, -hh, zz );
        glVertex3f( ww, hh, zz );
        glVertex3f( -ww, hh, zz );
        glEnd();
}

- (void) drawFinalContents
{
        glClearColor( 0, .5, .8, 1 );
        glClear( GL_COLOR_BUFFER_BIT | GL_DEPTH_BUFFER_BIT );

        glMatrixMode( GL_MODELVIEW );
        glLoadIdentity();
        glRotatef( angle, 0, 0, 1 );

        glTranslatef( 0, 0, 1 );
        glColor3f( 0, 1, 0 );
        glBindTexture( GL_TEXTURE_2D, textureID );
        glEnable( GL_TEXTURE_2D );
        glBegin( GL_QUADS );
        float ww = .9;
        float hh = .9;
        float zz = 0.0;
        glTexCoord2f( 0, 0 );
        glVertex3f( -ww, -hh, zz );
        glTexCoord2f( 1, 0 );
        glVertex3f( ww, -hh, zz );
        glTexCoord2f( 1, 1 );
        glVertex3f( ww, hh, zz );
        glTexCoord2f( 0, 1 );
        glVertex3f( -ww, hh, zz );
        glEnd();
}
```

So what does our example do? Our goal is to render a textured quad to the screen, where the texture represents an intermediate rendered result. We begin by configuring our FBO and texture so that they refer to each other. In the render loop, we make the FBO active, clear to yellow, and then unbind the FBO. Because of the magic of FBOs, those results are now usable as a texture, so we render a textured quad to the screen. When we set up the texture environment parameters for texturing, we specified GL_REPLACE to wholly replace any color on the quad with the texture image. If everything works as we've described (and it does), we should see the final rendered image as shown in Figure 8-16.

Figure 8-16 Results of Rendering to an FBO and Texturing a Quad with That Result (Texture Courtesy of NASA's Earth Observatory)

You can do a lot more with FBOs, including capturing other rendering results such as depth, stencil, and other render targets, but this kind of advanced usage is beyond the scope of this book. We refer you to the OpenGL framebuffer object extension for complete details.

Before we leave the topic of FBOs, we'd like to point out a few more reasons why FBOs are superior to other forms of off-screen rendering. First, FBOs consist of memory allocated on the graphics card itself that is directly usable in its target form—for example, as a texture. As a consequence, you avoid any off-card copies to and from the host: You can even avoid on-card copies in good implementations of the extension. Second, FBOs present a consistent, platform-agnostic interface. There just isn't a simpler interface to intermediate rendering than FBO, largely due to the evolutionary process by which OpenGL is developed. A variety of intermediate target rendering APIs and implementations were explored over the years, culminating in the design and implementation that exists today. FBOs are the best choice for modern rendering on the Mac. Third, FBOs avoid expensive context switching that can cost you a great deal of performance.

Copy-to-Texture

In this section we describe a very common and widely available technique known as render-to-texture. Render-to-texture is as simple as it sounds:

You simply render your intermediate scene, copy it to a texture, and then use that texture in your final render. Elegant, simple, and concise. There are, of course, details to deal with concerning how you target the texture into which you want to render and, in some cases, how you move pixels around the system into your final texture. Nevertheless, the process is largely as simple as described. Render-to-texture is interesting because it's a widely available technique and offers relatively high performance. There are problems with it, too: It's not as clean as the most modern OpenGL technique of FBOs, and there may be extra data copies. Overall, however, it works pretty well. Performance is pretty good, though not as consistently good as using FBOs. Even so, you may sometimes run into problems when using cards from different vendors on which this technique is actually moderately expensive. But if you can't use FBOs, and this is the best alternative available, you gotta do what you gotta do.

The essence of the render-to-texture technique is actually a bit simpler than the FBO example presented earlier. The code is virtually the same, but we omit the pieces of the rendering that relate to the FBO. We begin by looking at the header for our custom view (Example 8-14).

Example 8-14 Custom View Header for Copy-to-Texture Example Code

```
#import <AppKit/NSOpenGL.h>

#import <Cocoa/Cocoa.h>

@interface MyOpenGLView : NSOpenGLView
{
    GLuint textureID;

    float time;
    float angle;
}

- (void) angleUpdate: (NSTimer*) tt;
- (void) reshape;

@end
```

Because we're only going to render and copy into a texture, that's the extent of the information we need to keep track of throughout our view class. We then look at the initialization code, which is again very similar to the FBO example, but now without the FBO configuration (Example 8-15).

Example 8-15 OpenGL Setup for Copy-to-Texture Rendering

```
- (void) prepareOpenGL
{
    glMatrixMode( GL_PROJECTION );
    glLoadIdentity();
```

```
glOrtho(-1,1,-1,1,-1,100);
glMatrixMode( GL_MODELVIEW );

// enable, generate, and bind our texture objects
glEnable( GL_TEXTURE_2D );
glGenTextures( (GLsizei) 1, &textureID );
glBindTexture( GL_TEXTURE_2D, textureID );
const unsigned int texdim = 64;
const unsigned int nbytes = 3;
unsigned char data[ texdim * texdim * nbytes ];
memset( data, 0, texdim * texdim * nbytes );
unsigned int ii;
for( ii=0; ii<texdim*texdim; ii++ )
{
    data[ ii*nbytes + 0 ] = 0xff;
}
gluBuild2DMipmaps( GL_TEXTURE_2D, // 0,
            GL_RGB, texdim, texdim, // 0,
            GL_RGB, GL_UNSIGNED_BYTE, data );
glTexEnvf( GL_TEXTURE_ENV, GL_TEXTURE_ENV_MODE, GL_REPLACE );

// add a timer to oscillate the modelview
NSTimeInterval ti = .1;
[ NSTimer scheduledTimerWithTimeInterval: ti
                                  target: self
                                selector: @selector(angleUpdate:)
                                userInfo: nil
                                 repeats: YES ];
}
```

As before, our main `drawRect` routine does the bulk of the work—but here is where the code differs from the FBO version. Let's look at it now in Example 8-16 and talk about the differences and caveats to this technique.

Example 8-16 Cocoa `drawRect` Routine for Copy-to-Texture Rendering

```
- (void) drawRect: (NSRect) rect
{
    // setup and render the scene
    [ self drawIntermediateContents ];

    // copy it to a texture
    glBindTexture( GL_TEXTURE_2D, textureID );
    glCopyTexSubImage2D( GL_TEXTURE_2D, 0,
                    0, 0,
                    0, 0,
                    64, 64 );

    // render final scene
    [ self drawFinalContents ];

    // complete rendering & swap
    glFlush();
```

```
    [ [ self openGLContext ] flushBuffer ];
}
```

Notice two things in Example 8-16. First, our draw routines are the same as the FBO example, so we won't present them again. The first method draws the stuff to be used as a texture, and the second draws the scene using the texture generated from the first method. Second, there is no binding or other redirection of where this routine renders. Instead, we do all of the rendering in the back buffer, and then copy it to a texture. This approach has one important implication: This technique really works only for double-buffered visuals.

Another consequence of the way this technique works is that we're actually copying the contents of the back buffer to a texture, so performance may be less than that in the FBO case. Specifically, we perform this copy between each of the `[ self draw* ]` methods. Thus performance is likely to be slower than in the FBO case, but there's a lot of bandwidth available in modern graphics hardware, so if you can spare it, this technique will be pretty efficient. But the reason we're explaining this method at all is that the hardware on which you run potentially might not support a real off-screen technique like FBO, so a technique like render-to-texture may be required.

And that brings us to the final point: This technique is window-dependent. You'll notice that we're copying only a fixed area of pixels from within our drawing surface in our example. If we wanted to capture the entire area, we'd have to monitor the size of the drawable area (using the reshape routine) and ensure that the width and height of the copy call were updated accordingly. Another way of looking at this problem is to consider texture resolution: You'll need a window at least as big as the texture size you want to use, because you're directly copying pixels from within it. Thus, if your user wants a window smaller than this texture size, either you have to fall back to a smaller-sized texture or you have to limit the window minimum size. At any rate, the hairy details of the bookkeeping surrounding pixel sizes are not the most fun part of this technique, and constitute another way in which FBOs are a better solution.

In this section, we've covered how to perform textured renders from the contents of a texture filled by another render. The technique is very portable, but carries some overhead concerning texture and window sizes, and has some performance limitations based on the underlying OpenGL operations. This technique is a capable fallback for when FBOs are not available.

Pbuffer, Off-Screen, and Other Intermediate Targets

There exist a variety of other ways of writing intermediate rendering results for reuse in later final renderings in your OpenGL application. Among these are pbuffers, off-screen render areas, and a variety of extensions for directly rendering into textures. Though many other choices are possible, we faced a difficult decision when writing this book—either to cover them all or to cover only a subset.

To free up some weekends, we chose the latter option. To be fair, since we began this project, the FBO extension has really come of age, and we would recommend it without hesitation for those cases when you need intermediate rendering. The other techniques that we do not cover here are all genealogical predecessors to the FBO extension and, in many ways, are inferior to it. Specifically, off-screen render areas, regardless of the interface (CGL, AGL, or Cocoa) are software renderers and so have only nominal performance. They should be avoided for interactive or real-time applications. Pbuffers are complex and unwieldy to implement. Although they often perform at native hardware speeds, the complexity of managing the interface is not worth the headache if you can write to a modern render target like an FBO instead.

The pure simplicity, flexibility and generality, and raw performance of what can be accomplished via FBO are unmatched by these alternative techniques. If you've got older code that uses one of these approaches, a move to FBOs will likely both simplify and accelerate your code. Take the leap.

Summary

In this chapter, we explored how to create and configure Cocoa-based OpenGL rendering areas for on-screen windows and for various intermediate render targets. We saw how to create custom pixel formats, examined some of the flags that these pixel formats take, and demonstrated how to configure and initialize pixel formats. We also saw how to customize NSViews and NSOpenGLViews to use custom pixel formats and create contexts. We considered how to share data among multiple contexts, and we learned how to configure full-screen surfaces. Now that you know the fundamentals of OpenGL and Cocoa setup, you have a solid foundation from which to begin building your own Cocoa OpenGL applications.

Chapter 9

The GLUT API
for OpenGL
Configuration

GLUT is an older, tried-and-true, cross-platform API for quick and dirty access to OpenGL application infrastructure. GLUT provides a very simple and straightforward CAPI to create windows, manage device input, monitor windowing events, handle a run loop, and so on. It also provides low-level primitive construction elements such as Spheres, Cubes, and Torii. This API is not unique to the Mac: in fact, you'll find it on most every platform. GLUT allows you to quickly prototype some OpenGL code in such a way that you can test it on every platform on which you must deploy. Although not really a good infrastructure for more complex applications, it's a great way to get started. In this chapter, we'll provide only a cursory examination of the API on the Mac because, with only one or two extremely minor exceptions, GLUT on the Mac is the same as GLUT on any platform.

GLUT first arrived in November 1994, as a creation of Mark Kilgard of SGI. It was created as a basic infrastructure for quickly and simply bringing up a window for OpenGL rendering. Over the years, GLUT evolved into a cross-platform API, providing support through its same basic interface to bring windows up for OpenGL rendering on most Unix systems, including Linux, and eventually adding Windows and Mac support. GLUT evolved in scope, too, as it grew beyond its windowing roots to provide a variety of other wrapper functions. These wrapper functions focus on tasks such as device handling, from keyboard and mouse, to SpaceBall, joysticks, and more. There are also wrapper functions for quick and easy creation of objects such as spheres, cones, and cubes. In addition, font handling, video resize functions, render-to-texture capabilities, and basic dynamic function binding are all features that GLUT has acquired over the years.

Although GLUT has evolved to have a lot of capability, the core of what GLUT is remains unchanged: It is a simple and uniform way of bringing up an OpenGL application in a platform-independent way.

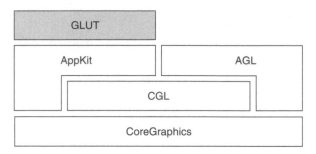

Figure 9-1 GLUT API and Framework in the Overall OpenGL Infrastructure on the Mac

Overview

The GLUT API is part of the overall Apple OpenGL infrastructure. It leverages AppKit for its windowing and event requirements. Figure 9-1 shows where the GLUT API and framework reside relative to other API layers.

The GLUT API lives in your particular SDK framework path or in `/System/Library/Frameworks/GLUT.Framework`. As with other APIs, linking against GLUT requires specification of this framework path (in our code examples, specifying the variable `SDKROOT`). Compiling using headers from the GLUT framework will also require specification of the framework. The relevant locations for building and linking with the GLUT framework are found in Table 9-1.

GLUT is an interface for complete, stand-alone applications that provides a comprehensive set of windowing, event management, device input, OpenGL setup, OpenGL configuration, and a few other miscellaneous functions. If for whatever reason you can't find the interface you need within GLUT, you're best off investigating one layer beneath it, such as Cocoa or CGL. For the most part, GLUT provides a rich feature set that can be used to meet all of your full-screen, windowed, and accelerated off-screen needs. With the fundamentals of GLUT described, and armed with the locations in which to fully explore the framework, let's move directly into GLUT configuration.

Table 9-1 GLUT Headers, Frameworks, and Overview

Framework path	`/System/Library/Frameworks/GLUT.framework`
Build flag	`-framework GLUT`
Header	`#include<GLUT/glut.h>`

Configuration and Setup

Configuring and using GLUT is pretty straightforward, and given what we've covered in prior chapters, it should all feel somewhat familiar. We'll waste no time in this section; we'll just jump right into a code example and cover the only Mac-specific change you'll need to be aware of for GLUT applications on the Mac.

Begin by going to XCode and creating a new project, of type C++ tool, as seen in Figure 9-2. We're choosing a C++ project just because we feel like it and prefer some C++ idioms, rather than because GLUT requires C++. In fact, as mentioned earlier, GLUT is a C-API.

In Figure 9-2, we create a new project; in Figure 9-3, we add the GLUT framework; and in Figure 9-4, we see what the resultant framework should look like. Specifically, in Figure 9-3, navigate to /System/Library/Frameworks/ and select GLUT.framework to add to the project.

Now that we've got a project, we must address the first Mac-specific element—linking against the library. We do that as seen in Figure 9-3, with the result shown in Figure 9-4. This specifies that we will use the GLUT framework to resolve include files and link libraries. The only other Mac-specific element is the way in which we include the headers, as seen in Figure 9-3. On other platforms, the GLUT headers may live in different directories (in fact, they usually

Figure 9-2 New Project Creation for GLUT Application

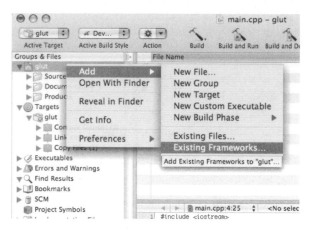

Figure 9-3   Adding a Framework to This Project

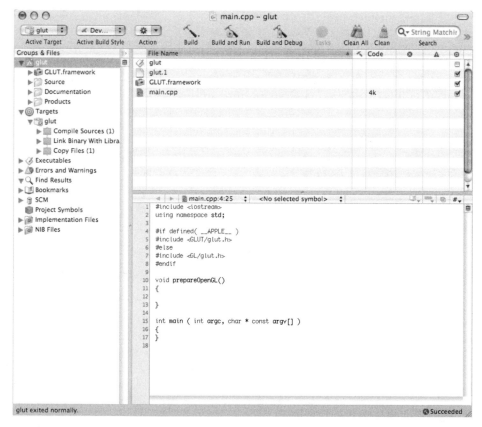

Figure 9-4   Resultant GLUT Project Showing Framework and Sample Code

live in the GL directory), so some wrangling is necessary to ensure that your compiler can find the header file. The code in Example 9-1 performs this operation to include the glut.h header using a preprocessor check to determine whether we're building on the Mac and, if so, to adjust where we find GLUT to use the framework-resolved path. Those are really the only two unique elements to using GLUT on the Mac.

Simple enough. Now let's look at fleshing out this code.

Example 9-1 GLUT Header Inclusion on the Mac

```
#if defined( __APPLE__ )
#include <GLUT/glut.h>
#else
#include <GL/glut.h>
#endif
```

Pixel Format

We'll now look at a complete application, from window creation to GL initialization through swap buffers. This code is presented here for your edification, but not because we plan to explain it in painstaking detail. As we've said before, GLUT is GLUT is GLUT. You'll find that the code we write here will function on many platforms, and the GLUT examples on the Mac are a great way to learn more about how to use the API. In fact, Apple ships a complete set of GLUT examples with its developer tools; you'll find them in /Developer/ Examples/OpenGL/GLUT/. Now, let's move on to our code. It renders a

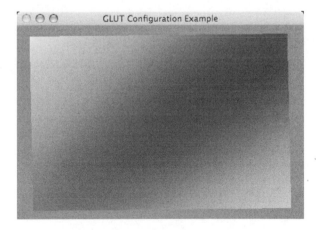

Figure 9-5 GLUT Project Results Showing Visual Selection and Rendered Object

simple animated shape, but doesn't do much else. The results of Example 9-2 are seen in Figure 9-5.

Example 9-2   Basic GLUT Sample Application

```
void prepareOpenGL()
{
    myAngle = 0;
    myTime = 0;
}

void draw()
{

    glClearColor( 0, .5, .8, 1 );
    glClear( GL_COLOR_BUFFER_BIT | GL_DEPTH_BUFFER_BIT );

    glMatrixMode( GL_MODELVIEW );
    glLoadIdentity();
    glRotatef( myAngle, 0, 0, 1 );

    glTranslatef( 0, 0, 1 );
    glColor3f( 0, 1, 0 );
    glBegin( GL_QUADS );
    float ww = .9;
    float hh = .9;
    glTexCoord2f( 0, 0 );
    glVertex3f( -ww, -hh, 0 );
    glTexCoord2f( 1, 0 );
    glVertex3f( ww, -hh, 0 );
    glTexCoord2f( 1, 1 );
    glVertex3f( ww, hh, 0 );
    glTexCoord2f( 0, 1 );
    glVertex3f( -ww, hh, 0 );
    glEnd();

    glutSwapBuffers();
}

void angleUpdate( int delay )
{
    float twopi = 2*M_PI;
    myTime = (myTime>twopi)?0:myTime+.03;
    myAngle = sinf(twopi*myTime);
    glutTimerFunc( delay, angleUpdate, delay );
    glutPostRedisplay();
}

int main ( int argc, char * argv[] )
{
    glutInit( &argc, argv );

    // choose a visual and create a window
    glutInitDisplayString( "stencil>=2 rgb8 double depth>=16" );
```

```
    // this is comparable to glutInitDisplayMode with the
    // tokens below, and achieves a similar effect
    // glutInitDisplayMode( GLUT_RGB | GLUT_DOUBLE | GLUT_DEPTH );

    glutInitWindowSize( 450, 300 );
    glutCreateWindow( "GLUT Configuration Example" );

    // initialize our opengl (context is now valid)
    prepareOpenGL();

    // register callback functions
    int delay = 50;
    glutTimerFunc( delay, angleUpdate, delay );
    glutDisplayFunc( draw );
    glutMainLoop();
}
```

GLUT is a good way to bring up a rendering window quickly and efficiently. It also provides a fair degree of specificity for window management. You can use the glutInitDisplayMode, as shown in Example 9-2, to specify a variety of flags to set the visual that is used. For example, you can use any combination of the bit flags as described in Table 9-2 to customize which visual you use. These bit fields are described in complete detail in the glutInitDisplayMode manual page, and we present only a few in Table 9-2. A simplified version of the use of this visual specification was presented in Example 9-2. This function, along with its bit field settings, allows you a coarse degree of control in the visual qualities of your application.

As we've seen in other chapters, selecting a visual can be a very detailed process, and one that your application needs to specify fully. GLUT provides

Table 9-2 glutInitDisplayMode Bit Field Tokens

Token	Description
GLUT_RGBA / GLUT_RGB	Synonymous tokens to select a visual with RGBA pixel formats. The default if no other format is specified.
GLUT_SINGLE	Single-buffered visual token. The default if neither GLUT_DOUBLE nor GLUT_SINGLE is present.
GLUT_DOUBLE	Double-buffered visual token. Has priority if GLUT_SINGLE is also present.
GLUT_ACCUM	Token for accumulation buffer visuals.
GLUT_ALPHA	Token to choose alpha channel visuals.
GLUT_DEPTH	Token to select a depth-buffered visual.
GLUT_STENCIL	Token to select a stencil-buffered visual.
GLUT_MULTISAMPLE	Token to select a multisample visual. Automatically degrades to another visual if multisampling is not available.
GLUT_STEREO	Token to select a visual with stereo abilities.

a limited form of this capability through a complementary function called `glutInitDisplayString`. In no way is the GLUT process nearly as complete as the CGL, AGL, or Cocoa methods, but it does allow you to exert a fair degree of control. Among the capabilities exposed through this method, a caller can specify the number of bits in various color or depth channels, the number of samples in multisample visuals, and the policy regarding how to select which visual matches. We present a selection of states that can be specified through such a call in Table 9-3, and a complete description of these flags and their defaults can be found at the manual page: `man glutInitDisplayString`.

So how are these flags used to specify a visual? The tokens in Table 9-3 specify the individual visual elements to be specified. With each, we can also attach an optional policy. The code for doing so requires the use of a standard set of operators with meanings equivalent to those operators' meanings in C code. For example, to specify a visual with all buffer bits, including alpha, of depth 8 or greater, we would write `rgba>=8` as part of our overall string. For other specifications, such as to consider visuals of other constraints, we would use any one of `<`, `>`, `<=`, `>=`, `=`, or `!=`. A final syntax element, the character, is used to specify a match that is greater than or equal to the number specified, but preferring fewer bits rather than more. This is a good way of getting close to your literal specification, but with some fail-over capability, preferring visuals of better quality.

For a complete example of how this specification works, we'll examine a replacement for the call `glutInitDisplayString` in our previous example but now modify it to use this form of visual selection instead. Example 9-3 is set up to try to find a visual with at least 2 bits of stencil precision, double buffered, with an RGBA visual of 8 or greater bits, as closely matching 8 as possible, a 16-bit or greater depth, and multisample anti-aliasing. The results of this change

Table 9-3 `glutInitDisplayString` Policy and Capability Strings

Label	Description
alpha	Bits of alpha channel color buffer precision
red	Bits of red channel color buffer precision
green	Bits of green channel color buffer precision
blue	Bits of blue channel color buffer precision
rgba	Bits of red, green, blue, and alpha channels color buffer precision
acca	Bits of RGBA channels accumulation buffer precision
depth	Bits of depth channel buffer precision
stencil	Bits of depth channel buffer precision
single	Boolean enabling single buffer mode
double	Boolean enabling double buffer mode
stereo	Boolean enabling quad buffer stereo mode
samples	Number of multisamples to use

Figure 9-6 GLUT Project Results Showing Visual Selection and Rendered Object for Anti-Aliased Pixel Format

to Example 9-2 are subtle, because the only differences involve the addition of the stencil and anti-aliasing. The results of the anti-aliasing are visible in Figure 9-6.

For a much more verbose description of these flags, ways to use this initialization call, and more, check the manual page for this call using man glutInitDisplayString.

Example 9-3 Initializing a GLUT Visual Using a String

```
glutInitDisplayString("stencil>=2 rgb~8 double depth>=16 samples");
```

Summary

In this chapter, we saw how GLUT works on the Mac, and pointed out the key configuration differences from other platforms. GLUT is useful for rapid prototyping, in that it lets you portably and efficiently bring up a window, configure the visual with a fair degree of specificity, and draw. In essence, this API gets you rendering quickly, although, it doesn't mesh particularly well with the more native ways of integrating OpenGL drawing into a window, especially for the Mac. We devoted the majority of our discussion in this chapter to the minor differences between the Mac and other platforms—specifically, how to include and build with GLUT. This concludes our coverage of GLUT on Mac OS X. We now return you to your regularly scheduled Mac OS X OpenGL programming.

Chapter 10

API Interoperability

Overview

This chapter will cover a variety of topics related to using some of the powerful (and cool) APIs on the Mac with your OpenGL application. You might be wondering what we really mean when we say "interoperability" in the chapter title. Perhaps a better term might be "interfacing." We're going to explore how you get data from other APIs, other subsystems, and other data formats you have and use into your OpenGL application on the Mac.

That description, though general, is vague, so let's consider a concrete example of how this might be useful: You want to play a video in a scene. So how do you play a video? It's conceptually simple—you open a sequence of images and draw them as textures on an object. But how do you open images? How do you ensure that, regardless of the frame rate used, you still see your movie in real time?

This example is probably not wholly unfamiliar to anyone in computing, as we've all walked down that path from time to time. And as we get older and ideally wiser, it becomes more apparent that using someone else's expertise and API in these subjects makes a lot of sense. Here we'll focus on using Apple's expertise in image loading, media handling, and, in general, APIs to manage this external data and exchange and use it in our OpenGL applications.

One of the mantras that we return to repeatedly when discussing the Mac is this: "It just works." That mantra is true with many Mac APIs as well. Of course, not all of them are simple (or sometimes even sensible) in the way they seem to work, but they do just work. In this chapter we'll explore some of the more modern APIs for graphics data, such as Cocoa's `NSImage`, a class allowing arbitrary image loading and manipulation, and QuickTime, an API for playback of a wide variety of time-based media. While in previous chapters we've taken great pains to demonstrate all of the possible APIs and techniques for interacting with

OpenGL, in this chapter we'll focus solely on the most actively developed and most modern of Apple's APIs: Cocoa. All examples will be in Cocoa, and we won't be shy about using Cocoa to its fullest benefit to get our job done with the least amount of extra coding.

We begin by looking at images in Cocoa and considering how to populate and use them with OpenGL.

Cocoa Image: NSImage

A fundamental way of interacting with 2D images in Cocoa is the class NSImage. An NSImage is an object representing an image and is a fundamental data type used in interacting with a variety of Cocoa classes that perform image manipulation. We'll look at how images are represented in the NSImage class and provide example methods for extracting data from and importing data into NSImages. We'll begin with an overview of how NSImage functions and demonstrate a few common ways of using it in an application.

Basic NSImage

NSImage is an abstract representation of an image, but it also contains and can create concrete instantiations of images. A concrete instantiation of an NSImage is known as an NSImageRep, and any given NSImage may contain several instantiations. For the purpose of interoperating with OpenGL, the most common flavor of NSImageRep we'll use will be the NSBitmapImageRep. An NSBitmapImageRep contains the actual image pixels we'll need to use in OpenGL at lower levels. Let's back up a step for now, and look at a few useful ways to create NSImages.

NSImage contains a variety of helper methods to create images from common sources. A few choices to get us started are found in Example 10-1.

Example 10-1 Two Sample NSImage Initialization Methods

```
%
- (id)initWithContentsOfFile:(NSString *)filename
- (id)initWithContentsOfURL:(NSURL *)aURL
```

Let's look at these methods in a more complete example, using our old standby cocoa_simple example as a foundation. Our goal will be to extend the example code so that we texture a quad using the contents of an NSImage. The process we'll follow will begin by instantiating objects of each of these types in our prepareOpenGL method. As before, prepareOpenGL is where we should do anything we want to do once per context, but not more often. Downloading textures is a good example of an operation that should not be performed per frame, so it fits well in `prepareOpenGL`. Let's add two `NSImages`, one based on a URL and another based on a file (Example 10-2).

Example 10-2   Initialize `NSImage`s

```
- (void) prepareOpenGL
{
    glMatrixMode( GL_PROJECTION );
    glLoadIdentity();
    glOrtho(-1,1,-1,1,-1,100);

    NSURL *url =
        [ NSURL URLWithString:
            @"http://www.yosemite.org/vryos/turtleback1.jpg" ];
    NSImage *url_image = [ [ NSImage alloc ]
        initWithContentsOfURL: url ];

    NSImage *file_image =
        [ [ NSImage alloc ] initWithContentsOfFile:
        @"/System/Library/Screen Savers/Cosmos.slideSaver/" \
        @"Contents/Resources/Cosmos07.jpg" ];

    // resize our image to a power of 2
    NSImage *file_image_resized =
        [ self transformImage: url_image
                        toSize: NSMakeSize( 512, 512 ) ];

    // download an image as a texture
    [ self downloadImageAsTexture: file_image_resized ];

    // configure texture environment
    glTexEnvf( GL_TEXTURE_ENV, GL_TEXTURE_ENV_MODE, GL_REPLACE );
    glEnable( GL_TEXTURE_2D );

    // add a timer to oscillate the modelview
    NSTimeInterval ti = .1;
    [ NSTimer
        scheduledTimerWithTimeInterval: ti
                                target: self
                              selector: @selector(angleUpdate:)
                              userInfo: nil
                               repeats: YES ];
}
```

There's really not much to this phase of the example, and everything works as expected. We should, however, take pains to validate that the results of each of these alloc/init pairs succeeds. Each `init*` method will return `nil` if it fails to find or acquire the resource specified, either a file or a URL. A third technique commonly used to create an `NSImage` is `initWithData`—but we'll explore it later. For now, let's move on to extracting the data from our `NSImage` and using it with OpenGL.

NSImage to OpenGL

Assuming we've got a valid NSImage from some source—either from initializing one from a file or URL, or from another Cocoa API somewhere—we potentially need to do some data massaging and conversion to transform the image data into a form that is compatible with OpenGL. The major phases of this process are as follows:

1. Determine the basic NSImage parameters such as format, data size, and image size.
2. Ensure that the NSImage is sized for use with OpenGL.
3. Extract the pixel data.
4. Download the pixel data as a texture.

We'll begin by looking at what's necessary to use any formatted image data with OpenGL. We assume that you have a basic familiarity with the basics of OpenGL texturing and refer other questions to [22]. As a quick refresher, recall that unextended OpenGL (that is, any OpenGL version prior to 2.0 without non-power-of-two extensions) requires textures to be sized as a power of two. If your input image is not a power of two initially, and your OpenGL implementation requires power-of-two data, several options are available to you:

- You can resize the image data to be a power of two, per side.
- You can create the next power-of-two size texture larger than the data, subload the data, and use appropriate texture coordinates when texturing.
- You can check for and use the GL_ARB_non_power_of_two extension to load non-power-of-two data.

By far the most flexible of these solutions, especially with respect to preserving your data's original quality and integrity, and minimizing the impact on your hardware resources (by minimizing the texture size downloaded to the hardware), is using the GL_ARB_non_power_of_two extension. This extension isn't available on all graphics hardware, on all Mac computers, or on all renderers, so a cautious approach is necessary. Be sure to query for the extension before you attempt to use it. Aside from ensuring its existence, however, using GL_ARB_non_power_of_two is as simple as downloading your data into a texture.

The second most effective technique with respect to preserving your data's integrity is to create a larger texture and subload your full image data into it. This technique does waste precious texture resources, because you're creating an image that contains empty or unused pixels, which nevertheless require space in the texture cache. Your image will be represented at full fidelity, however, and there may be applications for which this requirement is paramount.

The final technique—resizing the data to be a power of two—is the most space-efficient in terms of the hardware, but at the cost of some image quality loss. However, this technique is the one most easily implemented, so we'll explain it here.

Resizing an NSImage to a Power of Two

Our goal in this section is to take an arbitrarily sized NSImage and resize it to a power-of-two-sized NSImage. We'll do so by exploiting the functionality of an NSImage—specifically, its ability to paint itself in different ways. The code to do this is fairly simple, so we'll look at it in Example 10-3 and explain it after its presentation.

Example 10-3 Resizing an NSImage to a Power of Two

```
- (NSImage *) transformImage: (NSImage *) image toSize: (NSSize) size
{
    // get a new image, the same size as this one
    // isFlipped - override to return YES to get
    // coord sys in upper left
    NSImage *newImage = [ [ NSImage alloc ] initWithSize: size ];
    [ newImage setFlipped: YES ];

    // Draw on the new Image.
    [ newImage lockFocus ]; // create a draw context
    [ image drawInRect: NSMakeRect( 0, 0, size.width, size.height )
            fromRect: NSMakeRect( 0, 0,
                          [ image size ].width, [ image size ].height )
           operation: NSCompositeSourceOver
            fraction: 1.0];
    [ newImage unlockFocus ]; // release the draw context

    // return it
    return newImage;
}
```

This code takes an input NSImage and a target NSSize and creates a new image by simply rendering the current image in the current Quartz render area. We begin by creating a new NSImage, sized to our target size. We next take this image and call its setFlipped method. This method causes coordinate system wrangling. It performs a vertical flip, so that the Y=0 axis becomes the bottom of the image, rather than the top, as is the default. Try commenting this line out and recompiling your code to demonstrate the effect of not flipping the image. Figure 10-1 shows what happens in both cases. In OpenGL, textures have their bottom at the T=0 parameter so that (S,T)=(0,0) is the lower-left corner of the image, and (S,T)=(1,1) is the upper-right corner.

Now that we've got a new image into which we can draw new contents, we make this new image become an active target for rendering by using the

Figure 10-1 `NSImage` Rendered Before `setFlipped` (left), and After `setFlipped` (right).

`lockFocus` method. `lockFocus` (and its counterpart `unlockFocus`) are elements of how Quartz rendering works, and not really something we'll explore in detail. The Apple documentation has lots of details on Quartz rendering, so check there if you are interested in other things you can do with Quartz.

We then tell the current image to draw itself at the new size into the current Quartz target that is our existing `newImage`. Finally, we deactivate `newImage` as a render target and return that image.

Now that we've computed a flipped image, we need to get the pixel data from `NSImage` and download it to the hardware.

Extracting Pixel Data from an `NSImage`

OpenGL requires access to a raw array of pixels to download those data as either texture or images to the hardware. For that reason, we must extract our data from an `NSImage` and then use the resultant transformed version to pass data down to the hardware. In Cocoa, a form of image data that allows direct access to pixel data is `NSBitmapImageRep` and its subclasses. Specifically, an `NSBitmapImageRep` has a variety of methods for determining the size and extent of its contents, as seen in Table 10-1.

An `NSBitmapImageRep` can contain a lot more information, especially if its originating data source is something like an animated GIF. We will assume the use of a simple image in our examples here, but you can search the Apple reference pages for lots of details on all the stuff you can do in `NSBitmapImageRep`. Given our simple image and the accessors in Table 10-1 for a bitmap image, how do we go about getting an `NSBitmapImageRep`? Transforming our `NSImage` into a bitmap is suprisingly simple, as we see in Example 10-4.

Table 10-1 `NSBitmapImageRep` Accessors for OpenGL Texture Data

Accessor	Description
`- (int)bitsPerPixel`	Number of bits per image pixel
`- (int)bytesPerPlane`	Number of bytes in each image plane (R, G, B, A, etc.)
`- (int)bytesPerRow`	Number of bytes in an image pixel row
`- (unsigned char *)bitmapData`	Pointer to contiguous buffer containing all pixel data

Example 10-4 Extracting a Bitmap from an `NSImage`

```
NSBitmapImageRep *bitmap = [ NSBitmapImageRep alloc ]
        initWithData : [ image TIFFRepresentation ] ];
```

This function takes our existing `image` and requests that a TIFF representation be generated. From that result we create, using the familiar Cocoa alloc/init paradigm, a new `NSBitmapImageRep`. As you can see, the conversion process is fairly heavyweight—first converting to a `TIFFRepresentation`, and then creating a new `NSBitmapImageRep` from that data. A few copies later, and we're there.

Done. Our next, and final, step is to put all these pieces together in a code example.

Downloading an `NSImage` as a Texture

In prior sections we've performed individual pieces of `NSImage` manipulation—first creating them, then discussing and performing resizing options, and finally converting the `NSImage` into an `NSImageBitmapRep` so that bitmap data can be fed into OpenGL. Let's review our `prepareOpenGL` code from a few sections back, and add a conversion and a method that downloads an image to the hardware. We begin by creating an `NSImage` (Example 10-5).

Example 10-5 Initialization and Creation of an `NSImage`

```
- (void) prepareOpenGL
{
    glMatrixMode( GL_PROJECTION );
    glLoadIdentity();
    glOrtho(-1,1,-1,1,-1,100);

    NSURL *url =
        [ NSURL URLWithString:
            @"http://www.yosemite.org/vryos/turtleback1.jpg" ];
    NSImage *url_image = [ [ NSImage alloc ]
        initWithContentsOfURL: url ];
```

```
NSImage *file_image =
    [ [ NSImage alloc ] initWithContentsOfFile:
      @"/System/Library/Screen Savers/Cosmos.slideSaver/" \
      @"Contents/Resources/Cosmos07.jpg" ];

// resize our image to a power of 2
NSImage *file_image_resized =
    [ self transformImage: url_image
                    toSize: NSMakeSize( 512, 512 ) ];

// download an image as a texture
[ self downloadImageAsTexture: file_image_resized ];

// configure texture environment
glTexEnvf( GL_TEXTURE_ENV, GL_TEXTURE_ENV_MODE, GL_REPLACE );
glEnable( GL_TEXTURE_2D );

// add a timer to oscillate the modelview
NSTimeInterval ti = .1;
[ NSTimer
    scheduledTimerWithTimeInterval: ti
                            target: self
                          selector: @selector(angleUpdate:)
                          userInfo: nil
                           repeats: YES ];
}
```

We've extended the initial example to accomplish three further tasks. The first task is resizing the image using the method we developed earlier. The second task is downloading the resultant scaled NSImage. We'll develop the body of that method in a moment. The final task is configuration of texturing in our OpenGL context to enable it and to have the texture color replace the color of the object to which it's applied. The real meat of this section deals with what it takes to download an image to the hardware, so let's present that method in Example 10-6 and walk through it.

Example 10-6 Downloading an NSImage as an OpenGL Texture

```
- (unsigned int) downloadImageAsTexture: (NSImage *) image
{
    unsigned int tid = 0;
    int texformat = GL_RGB;

    // convert our NSImage to a NSBitmapImageRep
    NSBitmapImageRep * imgBitmap =
        [ [ NSBitmapImageRep alloc ]
            initWithData: [ image TIFFRepresentation ] ];
    [ imgBitmap retain ];

    // examine & remap format
    switch( [ imgBitmap samplesPerPixel ] )
```

```
{
    case 4:
        texformat = GL_RGBA;
        break;
    case 3:
        texformat = GL_RGB;
        break;
    case 2:
        texformat = GL_LUMINANCE_ALPHA;
        break;
    case 1:
        texformat = GL_LUMINANCE;
        break;
    default:
        break;
}

// generate a texture object
glGenTextures( 1, (GLuint*)&tid );
glBindTexture( GL_TEXTURE_2D, tid );

// download the pixels
gluBuild2DMipmaps( GL_TEXTURE_2D, GL_RGBA,
                    [ imgBitmap pixelsWide ],
                    [ imgBitmap pixelsHigh ],
                    texformat,
                    GL_UNSIGNED_BYTE,
                    [ imgBitmap bitmapData ] );

// unregister interest in the bitmap - OpenGL has
// already downloaded the image
[ imgBitmap release ];

return( tid );
}
```

While there's a bit of code here, it's mostly focused on extracting data from our NSBitmapImageRep object and formatting it into the traditional glTex Image2D style. We begin by extracting a bitmap image representation from our NSImage as we demonstrated in earlier sections. We then choose our pixel data format enumerator based on the number of bytes per pixel in this bitmap. The code from this point on is pretty standard OpenGL texture object manipulation. We generate a new texture object for our use and then build mipmaps using the ever-useful GL utility library function glBuild2DMipmaps. Finally, we relinquish our interest in this new bitmap and return our texture object ID.

In this section we've seen an end-to-end process for converting an NSImage to an OpenGL texture. We've demonstrated a few techniques to generate NSImages from common sources and then taken those images and created code to allow for flexible manipulation and downloading of an NSImage to the graphics hardware. These fundamental techniques will be used again and again as we look at other methods of manipulating images and video on the Mac.

OpenGL to `NSImage`

In the previous section, we saw how to create an OpenGL downloadable object from an incoming `NSImage`. Of course, you might want to do the converse as well. That is, you might want to extract an image from the graphics hardware for later use elsewhere. The techniques demonstrated in this section are primarily designed to cross from graphics hardware back to main-memory. As a consequence, they're not at all the right thing to do if you're trying to use an image already in hardware for another rendering pass or for another graphics-hardware purpose. This caveat is important primarily because of the issues we discussed regarding bandwidth to and from the graphics hardware back in Chapter 3. For the purposes of our discussions here, we assume that you do have a good reason for dragging pixels from the graphics hardware to main memory.

That said, the major phases of this process are as follows:

1. Read the pixel data from OpenGL.
2. Create an `NSBitmapImageRep` from that data.
3. Create an `NSImage` from the `NSBitmapImageRep`.

In fact, in the space it took to describe these steps, we practically could have coded the entire process. So, without further ado, let's look at some code. The code in Example 10-7 does all three of the previously described steps and provides a physical validation of the process by writing the data to a file.

Example 10-7 Capturing OpenGL Data as an `NSImage`.

```
- (NSImage *) captureGraphicsAsImage: (NSRect) imageArea
{
    // create a bitmap image rep with allocated
    // space to contain our pixels
    NSBitmapImageRep *bitmap =
        [ [ NSBitmapImageRep alloc ]
            initWithBitmapDataPlanes: NULL
                          pixelsWide: imageArea.size.width
                          pixelsHigh: imageArea.size.height
                       bitsPerSample: 8
                     samplesPerPixel: 3
                            hasAlpha: NO
                            isPlanar: NO // NO==interleaved
                      colorSpaceName: NSDeviceRGBColorSpace
                         bytesPerRow: 0
                        bitsPerPixel: 0 ];
```

```
    // ask the gl for the pixels, storing them in our bitmap image
    glPixelStorei( GL_UNPACK_ALIGNMENT, 1 );
    unsigned char *bmdata = [ bitmap bitmapData ];
    NSLog( @"bmd: %d %d\n",
        imageArea.size.width, imageArea.size.height );

    glReadPixels( 0, 0, imageArea.size.width, imageArea.size.height,
        GL_RGB, GL_UNSIGNED_BYTE, bmdata );

    [ self writeBitmapImageRep: bitmap
                        toFile: @"/tmp/test_bitmap.png" ];

    return( [ self convertBitmapImageRepToImage: bitmap ] );
}
```

The most complex call here is the one made to initialize our NSBitmapImageRep. In initWithBitmapDataPlanes, we set the image width, height, bits per component, components per pixel, interleaved data, and image representation, but we don't fill in the data contents. The call in this format (with the data component set to NULL) makes the representation allocate space but not fill it in. To fill in the data, we use the traditional formulation of glReadPixels. We call this method with the same parameters (size, components, bits per pixel) with which we configured our NSBitmapImageRep, allowing us to read directly into the bitmap data store, pointed to by [bitmap bitmapData]. Next, we convert our bitmap into an NSImage using another function we'll present in Example 10-8.

Example 10-8 Converting a Bitmap to an NSImage

```
- (NSImage *) convertBitmapImageRepToImage:
                    (NSBitmapImageRep*) bitmap
{
    // Create a new Image and draw the bitmap into it.
    NSSize size = [ bitmap size ];
    NSImage *newImage = [ [ NSImage alloc ] initWithSize: size ];
    [ newImage setFlipped: YES ];
    [ newImage lockFocus ]; // create a draw context
    [ bitmap drawInRect: NSMakeRect( 0, 0,
                            size.width, size.height ) ];
    [ newImage unlockFocus ]; // release the draw context

    return( newImage );
}
```

This method simply renders our bitmap into an NSImage and returns this new image. As in our prior example transformImage, we use Quartz to do the rendering and use the lockFocus, unlockFocus pair to direct Quartz rendering appropriately. Also as before, we use the setFlipped method to take care to get the orientation of the image in native OpenGL coordinates. After those two manipulations, we end up with a lovely `NSImage` that we can use in another part of a Cocoa application that takes an image.

QuickTime

In this section we'll explore another way of integrating native Mac technology with your OpenGL application. Specifically, we'll look at how to integrate video content using the QuickTime API. Although there are lots of image-based techniques for performing video rendering, using Apple's QuickTime API provides a number of benefits. Chief among these is the wide variety of codecs available for easy reading and writing of a variety of video formats. Quick-Time, provides a number of other nice features as well, including time management, audio playback, and a full complement of easy video navigation controls. Integration of QuickTime with OpenGL is a little tricky, but once you get it working, the results include reliable, high-performance, seamless video playback as an OpenGL texture.

Overview

QuickTime was first introduced in late 1991. At the time, it represented a great leap forward for multimedia not just on personal computers in general, but for the Mac in particular. The architecture of QuickTime data is quite comprehensive, including a variety of features that were designed in from the start, including multiple tracks of audio and video content, and extensibility throughout. This extensibility will eventually allow QuickTime to evolve to support modern compressors, such as AAC and MPEG4. In 1994, Apple introduced QuickTime version 2.0 first for the Mac, and then later the same year for Windows. This was both a clear shot across Microsoft's media bow (if we may clumsily use a nautical metaphor) and the first sign that Apple was serious about making QuickTime into a real standard. Although QuickTime has always been fighting an uphill battle in Microsoft's backyard, it was very clear then, and is still clear today, that the format, operation, and general standard that is QuickTime are just flat-out better, regardless of the platform on which it is used.

In the years since then, QuickTime has continued to evolve, supporting more advanced formats for audio, video, and images; parallel processing capabilities; and better developer interfaces. Most recently, Apple introduced QuickTime 7, which extended the QuickTime API to natively support Apple's flagship API set, Cocoa. QuickTime 7 continues to support the fundamental Movie Toolbox for accessing time-based content but also introduced the Cocoa QTKit, which will be our focus in this portion of the book.

QuickTime has evolved much since its early days, but it retains the good design that set the foundation for the API that lies at the heart of Apple's multimedia engines.

QuickTime to OpenGL

As with other interoperability topics, we'll try to focus on the most modern techniques and the highest-level languages available to developers in our present discussion. In this case, we'll focus on Cocoa, but because of QuickTime's history, we'll make a brief diversion to explore how the legacy QuickTime routines behave, too. This section will unfold similarly to earlier sections, demonstrating interoperability by showing examples of how to get QuickTime content into your OpenGL application through code, and offering an examination of how that code works and how you can tweak it.

As mentioned earlier, QuickTime 7 introduced a native Cocoa interface for accessing QuickTime content through the QTKit framework. This framework modernized and simplified the API for use with Cocoa and is a logical successor to the Movie Toolbox API provided in all prior and current versions of QuickTime. It's also the logical successor to the existing wrappers provided in Cocoa, NSMovie and NSMovieView. We'll explore the QTKit API, the Movie Toolbox, and the existing Cocoa NSMovie API here, starting with the core Cocoa functionality for movie manipulation.

NSMovie is the Cocoa representation of a movie as managed by the Quick-Time engine. NSMovieView is the visual representation, or view, of that NSMovie QuickTime data. Both are legacy classes and, for new applications, are not the best way of approaching the QuickTime rendering problem. They are sufficient if you want to put video in a portion of a Cocoa application, but these classes don't have the depth and complexity necessary to get your data into OpenGL (okay, it's possible, but we don't really want to encourage you to follow this path). As another disincentive to use these classes, Apple has publicly stated that it intends to deprecate them, so using these classes now would be something of a poor choice. We won't really focus on NSMovie and NSMovieView any further, other than to say that they exist and that there's a lot of information available in the Apple developer documentation and website if you really must know more. However, the modern way of doing this stuff is the new QTKit, so we will focus on it for the central element of this section.

QTKit is Apple's replacement for its other Cocoa NSMovie APIs. It supports all of what was possible before with NSMovie APIs but adds numerous editing and movie manipulation capabilities. QTKit became available with Quick-Time 7 and is part of Tiger (10.4) by default, but it is also available for Panther (10.3) through installation of QuickTime 7 and the associated SDK. QTKit is a very comprehensive and powerful API, and it simplifies the process of using QuickTime by removing a lot of legacy Movie Toolbox data types, so that a new programmer can simply focus on the Cocoa techniques. However, QTKit is still a big API with lots of dark corners and complexity. In this section we'll try to remove as much of that complexity as possible and provide an example that accomplishes our goal of rendering to OpenGL as efficiently as possible in terms of both performance and overall amount of code.

Our plan of attack to integrate your QuickTime content in OpenGL is simple. We'll use similar baseline code as we included in our NSImage example but take advantage of the fancy media-handling capabilities within QuickTime to decide which frame we need to play and when to download it to the graphics. The overall process is this:

1. Initialize OpenGL.
2. Create a Movie object with content.
3. Configure the Movie.
4. Grab the current display and use it as the texture.[1]
5. Render the OpenGL data using that texture.

It's actually not that much more complex to do this in code, so let's dive in! We'll begin by looking at a snippet of code to initialize our OpenGL buffer and the QTMovie. We add code to our existing prepareOpenGL method, replacing the NSImage initialization code from our prior interoperability example with QTMovie initialization code. First the code (see Example 10-9), and then a discussion:

Example 10-9 Initialize QTMovie

```
- (void) prepareOpenGL
{
    glMatrixMode( GL_PROJECTION );
    glLoadIdentity();
    glOrtho(-1,1,-1,1,-1,100);

    // open and configure our movie
    movie =
        [ QTMovie movieWithFile: @"/tmp/Sample.mov" error: nil ];
    NSLog( @"%d\n", movie );
    if ( movie != nil )
    {
        [ movie retain ];
        [ movie play ];
    }

    // configure texture environment
```

---

1. We've said it before and we'll say it again. This is *not* the optimal technique for high-performance movie playback in OpenGL on the Mac. There are other specialized APIs that enable full-rate playback of movies as textures within OpenGL. It just so happens that they're pretty complex to set up and get running, but at the end of the day the usage in your actual run loop is pretty similar. That's what we are trying to demonstrate here. If you are interested in the highest performance techniques, see CoreVideo in Apple's documentation, or check our website (www.macopenglbook.com) for updates.

```
glTexEnvf( GL_TEXTURE_ENV, GL_TEXTURE_ENV_MODE, GL_REPLACE );
glEnable( CL_TEXTURE_2D );

// add a timer to oscillate the modelview
NSTimeInterval ti = .1;
[ NSTimer scheduledTimerWithTimeInterval: ti
                          target: self
                        selector: @selector(angleUpdate:)
                        userInfo: nil
                         repeats: YES ];
}
```

QTMovie is an API with a lot of entry points. There are dozens of ways to use this API. Consider yourself lucky, however, as this number is down from the more than 2500 entry points to the original QuickTime Movie Toolbox! At any rate, our code for creating our movie is pretty simple and uses only a few methods.

First, we create a movie using the class initializer methods. Next—and this is important—we retain that movie because it's allocated using an autorelease pool, which means it may go out of scope at the end of the method and cause you headaches later. As an aside, whenever you see weird memory issues (usually caused by a lack of documentation about how some method has allocated and returned an object), think about the retain/release cycle, and start digging into FAQs, message boards, and other sources.

At this point, we specify a method that can be used to set almost any parameter of a movie—in our case, to keep the movie playing. Finally, we provide a method to launch the movie playback.

And that's all there is to loading and playing a movie with QTKit. Now we'll look at how we take this playing movie (playing off in the background somewhere) and bind its graphics content to OpenGL.

The reason we introduced the NSImage accessor methods first in this chapter was because we planned to revisit these techniques throughout the Cocoa API. This reuse is also one of the reasons why Cocoa is so powerful for application development: You learn a technique once and continue to apply it frequently. We'll do the same thing here. In our NSImage example, we created an image and downloaded it once. In our current code, we're obviously looking at a stream of images, so we'll need to continuously download images. There's no real way around this download step, and we'll look at that in a bit more detail after exploring Example 10-10.

Example 10-10 Draw Rectangle Method Applying Movie Frames

```
- (void) drawRect: (NSRect) rect
{
    glClearColor( 0, .5, .8, 1 );
    glClear( GL_COLOR_BUFFER_BIT | GL_DEPTH_BUFFER_BIT );
```

```
// flip texture
glMatrixMode( GL_TEXTURE );
glLoadIdentity();
glScalef( 1, -1, 1 );

// grab the next frame from the movie
// and download it as a texture
if ( movie != nil )
{
    [movie play];
    [ self downloadImageAsTexture: [ movie currentFrameImage ] ];
}

// configure the view matrix and draw a textured quad
glMatrixMode( GL_MODELVIEW );
glLoadIdentity();
glRotatef( angle, 0, 0, 1 );

glTranslatef( 0, 0, 1 );
glColor3f( 0, 1, 0 );
glBegin( GL_QUADS );
float ww = .9;
float hh = .9;
glTexCoord2f( 0, 0 );
glVertex3f( -ww, -hh, 0 );
glTexCoord2f( 1, 0 );
glVertex3f( ww, -hh, 0 );
glTexCoord2f( 1, 1 );
glVertex3f( ww, hh, 0 );
glTexCoord2f( 0, 1 );
glVertex3f( -ww, hh, 0 );
glEnd();

glFlush();
[ [ self openGLContext ] flushBuffer ];
}
```

What do we see here? It's the same draw method that we used in earlier examples, with one entry point to QTMovie, the currentFrame method. The rest of the code massages the image returned so that it's readily texturable. That's really all there is to using the new QTKit to get a movie ready and rendered by OpenGL.

But what about performance? We use the same helper method we used for our NSImage example, a method to download image data as a texture named downloadImageAsTexture. That method does a variety of things, including allocating a texture ID (also known as a texture name to old-school OpenGL geeks), binding that name, and creating a texture and a stack of mipmaps. That's a lot of work, and something we do for every frame. Based on some things we know about movies—for example, that their size doesn't change—

Figure 10-2 First Frame of the Movie

we can improve this program's performance significantly, but we'll save that for Chapter 11. Check there for all the optimizations we can make to streamline this streaming media download. For now, we're focusing on functionality, not trying to prematurely optimize the application.

What do we see if we replace our `prepareOpenGL` and `drawRect` routines in our earlier examples with the code in Example 10-10? With any luck, you see something like Figures 10-2, 10-3, and 10-4.

If you don't see those images, likely culprits are that the baked-in movie doesn't exist, couldn't be found, or uses a codec the QuickTime doesn't understand. We've included a statement to log whether QuickTime thinks it can open this particular file, and all subsequent usage of the loaded movie is enabled or disabled by successful or unsuccessful loads, respectively. It's probably a good thing to check in your own applications, too, before going through the effort of creating textures and loading movies.

Earlier, we mentioned NSMovie and explained why using it is undesirable, but what about the Movie Toolbox? The Movie Toolbox has existed since the very early 1990s. For those of you who are old enough to remember the early 1990s, it was a very different coding world in general: C was prevalent, C++ wasn't yet a huge thing, and Objective-C hadn't made its debut on the Mac in a big way.

Figure 10-3 Subsequent Frames of the Movie

NeXT was cranking away on Objective-C[2] and a lot of really interesting ideas for user interface libraries, which would (much later) become the Cocoa API for Mac OS X. However, the mainline Mac world was still focused on Pascal and, in some measure, C. At that time the Mac was known for many things but none of them was ease of coding.

The QuickTime Movie Toolbox matches that expectation to this day. Though it is possible to use the movie Toolbox with OpenGL, and we've done projects for clients using it, we won't discuss it here. The main reason for avoiding it at this point is simplicity: We're not writing this book so that you can learn esoteric corners of general Mac APIs but so you can get work done efficiently. The QuickTime 7 QTKit API is a much cleaner way of doing all the Movie Toolbox work and are the best way to work with media on the Mac.

So what have we accomplished here? We now have a technique to open any QuickTime-accessible movie, to manipulate and play it, and to render the frames as an OpenGL texture. We don't have all the kinks worked out yet, however. There was a fair bit of wrangling necessary with our final image, and we paid a performance penalty for that effort, but there are ways to avoid that work, too. For now, we've got function. We will have more to say on ways to improve the download later, in Chapter 11, but for now we've achieved our basic objectives.

---

2. The "NS" in all the Cocoa API names, such as `NSMovie`, stands for NextStep.

Figure 10-4 Final Frame of the Movie

OpenGL to QuickTime

In the previous section we learned how to integrate a movie into an OpenGL application as a texture, which is then usable with any object. Now we'll learn how to take our rendered OpenGL data and configure it into a movie. Although this task has little to do with OpenGL per se, it does build on our prior NSImage experience in an earlier section, and it nicely rounds out the various Cocoa API discussed in Chapter 8. Knowing how to write a movie from an OpenGL application is a useful feature for lots of applications and not overly difficult to accomplish.

QTMovie allows reading and writing of movie data. Earlier we were able to export our data from our movie using an accessor returning an NSImage, and now we'll do a symmetric operation: We'll fill a new movie using NSImages gathered from our application. The steps are relatively simple, and we'll outline them here first, focusing solely on the image snap and Movie pieces:

1. Create an empty Movie object.
2. Read a frame from OpenGL.
3. Add a frame to the Movie.
4. When complete, write the results to disk.

The idea here is very basic: attach a bunch of image frames together to create a Movie. QTKit, working through QTMovie, exposes a lot of capabilities with which you can create movies using various codecs. At their core, however, the contents of a movie are a simple sequence of images. We already know how to read a frame from OpenGL into an `NSImage`, so we're almost completely done even before we've looked at the code. Let's update that list with the code fragments to do the actual work, and we'll leave it as an exercise for you to assemble and insert these bits and pieces in the proper places in your code. So that you're not flying completely blind, look at the earlier example that read data from OpenGL into an `NSImage`, and then flesh out the following pseudocode in the appropriate places:

```
myMovie = [ [ QTMovie alloc ] init ]; } }
myImage = [ myView captureGraphicsAsImage: (NSRect) imageArea ];
[ myMovie addImage: myImage
        forDuration: duration
    withAttributes: attr ];
[ myMovie writeToFile: @"filename.mov" withAttributes: attr];
```

This pseudocode is all we'll provide in the book. The technique is really just as simple as we've described here, and we're confident that you've got what you need to proceed. If you'd like to see, build, and compile a complete example of this technique, please check our website (www.macopenglbook.com) for an up-to-date example.

High-Performance QuickTime in OpenGL

This chapter has described how to get the contents of a movie to play and be read by OpenGL. A quick running of this example will make it clear that the image data path is not the most optimized, however. In fact, it's downright slow. We've chosen to follow the `NSImage` path because it's so nicely symmetric across a variety of Mac OS X APIs. Unfortunately, it's not the most performance oriented and it's not suitable, at this point, for real-time use. So what's a developer to do? Apple provides an excellent instructive example on its website in the QTCoreVideo101 example [10].

The short version of this demo's action is pretty simple: Let Core Video handle the entire process, from loading and playing the movie to downloading those images as textures. This may sound like delegating a lot to an API. In reality, underneath all the fancy UI goodness that the Mac provides, it's *all* OpenGL already, so doing this does not present any extra work for the API. In fact, it simplifies your life substantially, because you don't have to care about the fastest way to read and subload images from a movie. Please download and examine this example for details. It's a little bit complex to set up, but once the infrastructure is in place, it's fast and easy.

Summary

In this chapter, we saw how to read and write QuickTime movies, interfacing their content with OpenGL. To do so, we relied on previously introduced techniques for downloading textures, manipulating NSImages, and performing basic OpenGL configuration. You should now have a solid idea about how to use any form of video content accessible via QuickTime with your OpenGL application.

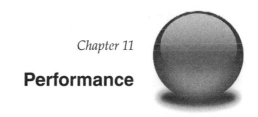

Chapter 11

Performance

Overview

Performance-tuning your OpenGL application for OS X may well be the most satisfying part of your project. No other platform can compare with OS X's great set of performance tools, especially for OpenGL-based applications. Because OpenGL is a first-class citizen on OS X, the implementation and tools have been given years of scrutiny and improvements to make your optimization process, dare we say, enjoyable.

Because the implementers of OpenGL—and, indeed, other 3D graphics APIs—face the same performance challenges, the strategy for writing an application that performs well using those APIs is often the same or at very least similar. When it comes down to it, you are trying to get vertices and pixels from the address space of your application to the screen for display. Moving that data through the enormous state machine that is OpenGL may seem daunting at first, but it's simply a matter of staying on the paths most traveled.

The good thing about the most traveled paths is that like any good freeway, they have the best pavement and get the most attention from the road crew. In this case, our road crew is the Apple's OpenGL engineering team plus the driver engineers from the graphics vendors. The performance of your application is one of their top priorities.

This chapter looks at some of the best practices to avoid common performance pitfalls of OpenGL application programming on Mac OS X.

Axioms for Designing High-Performance OpenGL Applications

Before describing the individual "blessed" logical paths in OpenGL, we thought it best to put down, in black and white, some mantras you may want to repeat to keep yourself on the straight and narrow. Wandering into the weeds can cost you a lot of frame rate.

For any of these performance awareness axioms, you may find it best to think to yourself, "If I were implementing OpenGL, which performance considerations would I have to take into account when implementing this feature of the API?" Put bluntly, OpenGL system software developers are just software developers and computer hardware is, well, just computer hardware. Both can be clever, but there is no real magic here. If your application must make a million calls into OpenGL with every frame, it's going to be slower than if it makes a thousand calls with every frame while submitting the same amount of data. This may seem to go without saying, but because it is such a common problem with applications we thought it worth mentioning explicitly.

Let's move on to those golden rules we keep talking about.

Minimize State Changes

The OpenGL ARB works hard to reduce the number of state dependencies in the specification, especially when it comes to error handling. The engineers building the Mac OS OpenGL implementation work hard to reduce the overhead of state changes in the system. Despite all of these efforts, the system is very large and there is always a cost associated with thrashing the state.

OpenGL is a state machine. In code-speak, this means the implementation has many data structures and branches that keep track of a lot of information. Each time your application makes a state change, such as changing the current color, turning lighting off, or binding a new texture, that change needs to be reflected in all of those state data structures. Besides the obvious cost of reading and writing to those data structures, these state changes effectively cool down your caches, because whenever you touch different pieces of memory in the system it has potential to evict cache lines (both instruction and data caches in this case). Keeping caches hot is paramount to high-performance streaming of data through the system.

The other undesirable artifact of making these state changes is that you always affect two pieces of hardware when you make such changes. Both the CPU and the GPU, and their respective memories, are affected. When the data structures inside OpenGL are altered, those changes inevitably have to be communicated to the GPU. This communication means more graphics bus traffic in the system and all the synchronization overhead inherent in bringing this state up-to-date.

Consider also that deferral of updates is often a good strategy for any synchronization task in a system. You may, therefore, be introducing costs into the equation that are realized at a later—and sometimes unpredictable—time. For example, often the cost of a state change is not realized until a drawing command is called that relies on that state. Textures are a good example. Defining a new texture with a `glTexImage2D()` call sets up the texturing state on the currently bound texture object, but the data passed into this function—the actual pixels making up this texture—are not uploaded to the graphics adapter until the application draws using this texture. Thus, the first time you draw with that texture bound, you could experience a much longer than usual draw time, as the data is transferred to VRAM. For game developers, this performance hiccup could show up as a sudden drop in frame rate, causing the faithful customer to get picked off by the rail gun of his or her arch nemisis!

Wherever possible, you should attempt to group your state changes and establish a rendering "mode." Once this mode, or grouping of related states, is established, draw with as much data as possible before changing modes. This means drawing with like primitives, like colors, like textures, and so on, in as large a chunk as possible, before you make state changes.

Object-Oriented Programming and State Management

While we're on the subject of minimizing state changes, we'd like to point out a common conflict of design interest between OpenGL and object-oriented programming (OOP) methodology. We believe strongly in the power of object-oriented design for applications, but unless it is applied to OpenGL programming judiciously, you can run into trouble.

Consider the primary goal of any OOP methodology—encapsulation. That is, the goal is to put data and the operations that operate on that data in a common locale and to restrict the interface to data so as to avoid debugging hassles.

Keeping this goal in mind, let's consider an example. We've decided to write an application for landscape design. For our landscape design program, suppose we have an object defined for trees and another object defined for leaves. Our leaf class knows how to draw a single oak leaf consisting of 10 vertices. The method looks something like this:

```
void Leaves:draw()
{
int i;
float v[] = { 1.0f, 1.5f, 2.1f, 2.4f, 2.0f, .... };

glColor3f(0.0f, 0.5f, 0.0f);
```

```
glBegin(GL_POLYGONS);
for(i = 0; i < 10; i++)
    glVertex2fv(v + i * 2);
glEnd();
}
```

Now consider the OpenGL efficiency of instantiating this leaf class 1000 times for a small oak tree in your scene. First, it calls `glColor3f()` 1000 times, when it needed to be called only once. Second, this code submits 10 vertices at a time, when it could have submitted 10,000.

As contrived as this example may seem, it is far and away the most common OpenGL performance programming problem: a large OOP class hierarchy that was designed with objects that fit the model of the domain. The ignorance these class instances have of one another has drastic state management consequences for OpenGL applications. The moral of the story is that you should design your application object hierarchy with an efficient scene graph that batches like state elements and can be traversed at draw time, along with all that is required to represent the objects in your problem domain.

Retained Mode versus Immediate Mode Rendering

Immediate mode rendering is the oldest and correspondingly most outdated way to render graphics in OpenGL. We don't mean to completely bash immediate mode rendering, because it is definitely the easiest approach to getting an application up and running and has its uses when you are submitting limited amounts of data to OpenGL. Generally speaking, though, with a combined 25 years of looking at this stuff, your authors have definitely seen egregious overuse of this capability within OpenGL, and it definitely leads to slow applications.

The simplicity of this mode of rendering is in that data are submitted through OpenGL commands at the precise moment they are needed for rendering—hence the "immediate" in immediate mode. Because of this, and knowing that commands are executed in order in OpenGL, following this sort of OpenGL logic is easiest. You do not need to keep any timing tables in your head, nor do you need to worry about any asynchronicity between the CPU and the GPU.

Because of this simplicity, as you probably well know, immediate mode rendering is the first thing taught to developers who are new to OpenGL. Our guess is that the pervasive use of this style of code may be simply a matter of habit. At some point, to prevent abuses and save all our companies a lot of money, immediate mode rendering may even be removed from OpenGL entirely, or perhaps relinquished to some layered API just to give it a scarlet letter.

With immediate mode rendering, data are downloaded from host memory to VRAM for every frame of rendering, whether its vertices between a `glBegin()`–`glEnd()` pair, textures, images, or shaders. This redundant data transfer limits your potential rendering performance to the bandwidth of the graphics bus and, in some cases, the performance of the CPU and the host memory system, as it manages state changes and state synchronization with the graphics device.

We do advocate one habit—namely, retained mode rendering. Retained mode rendering refers to any rendering that depends on a state that was established at some time and then referenced for rendering at some time in the future. The first retained mode rendering in OpenGL consisted of display lists, but additional modes of this style of rendering have been added to OpenGL with nearly every major release since display lists were introduced.

A big part of the "retention" in retained mode rendering for modern computers is in keeping data and state resident on the graphics adapter. This residency avoids all the travel time, by bus, between the computer's CPU and the GPU of the graphics adapter.

Here are the primary mechanisms for retained mode rendering in OpenGL:

- Display lists
- Texture objects
- Buffer objects (vertex and pixel)
- Shader objects
- Pixel buffer objects
- Framebuffer objects

The advantage of using retained mode rendering is that it allows you to get as close as possible to the theoretical bandwidth limits between the GPU and VRAM, eliminating as much correspondence with the CPU as possible. If you've seen the theoretical bandwidth numbers for today's modern graphics chipsets, you know that these numbers are quite staggering. Typically, these numbers are an order of magnitude greater than the graphics bus bandwidth that feeds the chips. Correspondingly, it's not unusual to see a 10 times performance gain when moving an application from immediate mode rendering to retained mode rendering.

In short, specify your data up front with one of the retained mode mechanisms and reference it later while drawing to reap grand performance rewards.

Unidirectional Data Flow

Once you have your rendering modes established, your objective should be to stream data (e.g., vertices, indices, textures/pixels) from the host system to the graphics device as close to the theoretical bandwidth as is achievable. To keep this stream of data flowing and going in one direction, it is important not to issue any unnecessary queries or reads from the OpenGL implementation. The rule of thumb here is that any OpenGL call that has a return value will likely stall the rendering pipeline.

You may be wondering why said stalls would occur. To optimize throughput, nearly any command or packet processing system—OpenGL included—will buffer the information into batches and submit the batches simultaneously. This strategy allows the best amortization of protocol overhead by having a relatively large amount of data per quantum of protocol information. Now further consider the state dependencies involved with any kind of query to OpenGL that returns information, such as a glGet(). If the OpenGL implementation has buffered 10 drawing commands and the eleventh command is a glGet(), the implementation is forced to process and validate the previous 10 drawing commands immediately with no further buffering allowed, because one of those prior 10 OpenGL commands could change the value of the state being requested in the eleventh command. Implementers of OpenGL have to decide how much drawing command data is buffered. If that decision was, say, 500, and an application forces that command buffer to be flushed every 10 commands, the overall throughput will be terrible.

Optimally performing applications keep track of their own rendering state. This behavior allows them to avoid using OpenGL as a ledger that they query when they need to determine what the current state is. In essence, it avoids glGet() calls, glPopAttrib() calls, or any other OpenGL commands that return state data to the implementation.

Related to state retrieval, in that all prior commands need to be completed, glReadPixels() or any of the glCopy() operations that source a framebuffer may also flush the command stream to some extent, because those prior commands may modify the framebuffer that is being sourced.

Use Shaders Where Possible

Programmable hardware offers a myriad of possibilities for increasing the frame rate. Many visual effects that were formerly achieved through multiple passes through fixed-function hardware and very costly read-backs can now be done simply in different shaders.

There are two shader types in OpenGL, fragment and vertex. Obviously, there are typically far more fragments in a scene that there are vertices. In many cases, a visual effect can be achieved using a vertex program, yet a fragment program is used instead. Successfully using a vertex program to replace a fragment program effect can have a profound impact on your application's performance.

Shader Instruction Limits

At present, we're still relatively early in the shader evolutionary chain. Much of the graphics hardware in circulation places limits on the number of shader instructions supported. If those limits are exceeded, your application could very unpleasantly find itself on a software rendering path.

Mac OS X has CGL parameters available to allow you to query this unfortunate condition, as shown in Example 11-1.

Example 11-1 Querying Shader Limits

```
GLint gpuVertexProcessing, gpuFragmentProcessing;

CGLGetParameter(CGLGetCurrentContext(),
    kCGLCPGPUVertexProcessing, &gpuVertexProcessing);

CGLGetParameter(CGLGetCurrentContext(),
    kCGLCPGPUFragmentProcessing, &gpuFragmentProcessing);
```

Remember that when setting up your pixel format at OpenGL context creation time, you can set kCGLPFANoRecovery (or its Cocoa and AGL analogs) to avoid falling back to software paths. This would obviate the need to check for hardware shader support but also has a small problem—your application may simply not launch on some systems!

There is no mechanism, at present, to allow querying for the number of instructions supported by a given GPU. The general rule of thumb is that if you're targeting lower-end GPUs for your application, write your shaders with instruction count conservation in mind and use the methods in Example 11-1 to empirically test your application on specific configurations.

OpenGL for Mac OS X Rules of Thumb for Performance

With the disclaimer that some of the ideas presented in this section may be applicable to any platform, we'll proceed with some Mac-based rules of thumb. The OS X OpenGL implementation has some distinguishing features relative to other platforms. Taking advantage of some of these features will likely make a profound difference in the performance of your application.

Minimize Data Copies

To maintain compliance with the OpenGL specification, OpenGL implementations often need to make copies of submitted vertex and pixel data, and OpenGL on OS X is no exception. This necessity arises from needing to return control to an OpenGL application after data has been submitted, yet not needing to yet submit that data for rendering. Consider, as a simple example, what happens when `glVertex3f()` is called between a `glBegin()`–`glEnd()` pair. Until `glEnd()` is called, the vertex data must be retained by OpenGL until needed for rendering.

This simple example can be extended to textures as well. Thus, if you consider how large textures can be and how many vertices you typically submit, it's easy to see how much of a performance problem the copying of this data can be.

The OpenGL Multithreaded Engine

As mentioned earlier, the OS X OpenGL implementation has some unique features that distinguish it from other implementations. One detail worth noting is its long history of running on multiprocessor systems. This means if you thread your application today, you'll immediately have a sizable audience that will benefit from your application.

A major benefit of threading an OpenGL application, aside from the obvious gains from having additional processing power, is the possibility of finer-grained control over processing tasks. By having two or more threads, you can limit the blocking that occurs when the GPU is waiting for the CPU, and vice versa. The recommended approach for threading OpenGL applications is to have all drawing commands originate from a single thread. Other threads can then be used for handling application tasks such as culling and scene management, processing of audio samples, or perhaps physics and collision detection.

The more CPU processing your application needs to do—whether it's to prepare data for drawing or to carry out other, unrelated tasks—the bigger your gains from threading will be. Gains in performance of 50 percent for properly threaded applications are not unusual.

When threading your OpenGL application on Mac OS X, you must remember to use the `CGLLockContext()` and `CGLUnlockContext()` calls to bracket your OpenGL calls for each thread. This guarantees that you will not experience state change collisions and bizarre unanticipated behavior when rendering with multiple threads.

To relieve application developers of the burden and complexity of threading their applications, the Apple OpenGL, engineering team decided to thread OpenGL, with the first release being on the Mac Pro system and its initial installed software (10.4.8). The complete form of the threaded engine will be released with Mac OS 10.5 (Leopard). Threading done within OpenGL itself effectively achieves the same goal as threading your application—namely, rapid return of control to the application after a function call into the OpenGL API.

By minimizing the time needed to return control to the application, the threaded OpenGL engine in the Mac OS allows more processing cycles for the application logic.

The threaded OpenGL engine fundamentally does more work than the standard serial engine. It relies on an additional processor to handle this extra work. The good news is that you don't have to detect the number of processors on the system to use it. If you attempt to enable the threaded OpenGL engine on a single-processor system, it will automatically fail to enable, thus no logical provisions need to be made by your application for uniprocessor Macs.

The other implication of the additional work imposed by the multithreaded engine is that if your application, by way of the GL commands it submits, forces the internal OpenGL threads to serialize with each other, you may find your application actually running slower and using more memory than if you hadn't enabled the threaded OpenGL engine at all! Read on for details about whether the threaded OpenGL engine is right for your application.

As in the threaded application case, using the threaded OpenGL engine is most effective for applications that are CPU processing bound, which most applications are. Along with being CPU bounded, your application needs to be "well written" to leverage the advantages offered by the multithreaded GL engine. "Well written" means that the application infrequently stalls the graphics pipeline; that is, it makes minimal calls to `glFlush()`, `glFinish()`, or any type of `glGet()`. Furthermore, it means that your application uses retained mode rendering wherever possible. Display lists, vertex buffer objects, pixel buffer objects, and framebuffer objects are good examples of retained mode rendering constructs.

Obviously, using some immediate mode calls in your application is acceptable. If your application predominantly uses `glBegin()`, `glEnd()` pairs calling individual vertices in between, however, you will see less benefit, or worse, your application may be slightly slower when using the threaded engine.

If your application, rather than being CPU bound, is entirely GPU limited (say, from fill constraints as in a volume rendering application), you will see little if any benefit from the threaded engine. The simple litmus test for these conditions is to run a typical scene or model through your OpenGL application and watch the graph from Apple's CPU monitoring application `Activity Monitor`. If the CPUs are busy when rendering this scene, chances are very good that your application might benefit from enabling the multiprocessor-capable OpenGL engine.

The threaded OpenGL engine can be dynamically enabled per context from CGL, AGL, or Cocoa applications. The enabling is dynamic in the sense that you don't have to specify a parameter at context creation time to enable it. Rather, you can turn the threaded engine on and off as often as you wish.

That said, turning the multithreaded engine on or off should be done judiciously. Consider all of the state management, thread management, and mutex management that accompanies a switch from rendering on a single-threaded basis to rendering with two threads. In short, it's expensive, performance-wise, to turn the threaded engine on or off. We recommended you switch it on (or off) once at initialization time using the code in Example 11-2.

Example 11-2 Enabling or Disabling the Multithreaded GL Engine

```
// Turn on the MT GL Engine
CGLEnable(CGLGetCurrentContext(), kCGLCEMPEngine);

// Turn off the MT GL Engine
CGLDisable(CGLGetCurrentContext(), kCGLCEMPEngine);
```

In short, use all the CPU hardware at your disposal—your users will thank you for it. Besides, it's fun to watch those CPU cores you paid for busily working away!

Minimizing Function Call Overhead

When OpenGL calls are made, a small cost is associated with detecting the current context from the current thread. Multiply this small cost by enough OpenGL calls, and it becomes a big cost.

You can avoid this overhead by using the macros provided in `CGLMacro.h` and maintaining your own current context. These macros bypass the top-level framework layer entry points and go directly into the OpenGL engine. For stand-alone tests that simply pound on the OpenGL API, we've observed 20 percent performance gains using CGL macros. You'll find more information about using CGL macros in Chapter 6.

Minimize CPU and GPU Idle Time by Using Asynchronous Calls

Asynchronous CPU and GPU operation is definitely the crown jewel when it comes to getting the most performance out of the Mac OS X OpenGL implementation. Asynchronous features of the implementation minimize extremely costly stalls between the CPU and the GPU. Nearly every application that keeps an eye on the frame rate can benefit greatly from these interfaces and the methods to use them.

At a higher level, asynchronous operations put more control in the hands of your application and bring a bit more peril. The peril lies in the fact that asynchronous programming is a bit more difficult because data doesn't move in the system without you telling it to do so. The pattern is this: modify some data, do some other stuff, check whether the data is ready for use, and then use the data.

The flipside of this peril is that this additional control allows your application to apply "smarts" about how its data are to be handled. Picking up the asynchronous pen and putting down the synchronous club is essential in obtaining peak overall system bandwidth.

Here's a list of the asynchronous extensions and features of the Mac OS X OpenGL API:

- Multithreaded OpenGL Engine
- Apple Texture Range
- Apple Vertex Array Range
- Apple Flush Buffer Range
- Apple Fence

The ultimate expression of asynchronicity of OpenGL on Mac OS X is the Multithreaded OpenGL Engine. Let's move on to the "Range" extensions.

The Range Extensions

The Apple Texture Range and the Apple Vertex Array Range extensions are both aggregation methods. They allow you to specify large chunks of memory in which all of your texture or vertex data are aggregated so as to more efficiently map the memory. This more efficient mapping improves direct memory access (DMA) performance.

The other key aspect of Apple Texture Range, Apple Vertex Array Range, and Apple Flush Buffer Range is the ability to update a subset within a block of data and to flush only the modified data across the bus to the graphics device. This partial update mechanism saves a tremendous amount of bus traffic. Without these interfaces, updates to a portion of a texture, a vertex array, or, in the case of Apple Flush Buffer Range, a vertex buffer object would set a flag indicating that the entire contents of the object were stale. The GPU would then be forced to transfer all of the data for the object over the bus.

The introduction of buffer objects to OpenGL, combined with the introduction of Apple's Flush Buffer Range extension, has effectively replaced the Apple Texture Range and Apple Vertex Array Range Extensions. Buffer objects for both vertices and pixels and the Apple Flush Buffer Range extension provide a consistent mechanism to perform partial updates and flushes between the two. Buffer objects are easier to use, have better cross-platform compatibility, and have a brighter future than the older mechanisms.

Here's an example of using Apple Flush Buffer Range to do partial flushing on a buffer object. In Example 11-3, we arbitrarily chose to work with pixel buffer objects. Vertex buffer objects work in exactly the same manner, albeit with some simple substitutions of the type of data created and the target parameter of the buffer object OpenGL calls (i.e., GL_ARRAY_BUFFER or GL_ELEMENT_ARRAY_BUFFER instead of GL_PIXEL_PACK_BUFFER).

Example 11-3 Partial Buffer Object Flushing

```
GLuint pboID;
GLint width, height, channels;
GLubyte *textureData;

// 2048x2048 image - GL_RGBA
width = 2048; height = 2048; channels = 4;
textureData = (GLubyte *) malloc(width * height * channels);

// Generate ID for PBO
glGenBuffers(1, &pboID);

// Bind PBO, dimension it, and supply it data.
glBindBuffer(GL_PIXEL_PACK_BUFFER, pboID);
glBufferData(GL_PIXEL_PACK_BUFFER,
    width * height * channels,
    textureData,
    GL_DYNAMIC_DRAW);

// Tell GL we want to do partial flushing on this object.
// Setting GL_BUFFER_FLUSHING_UNMAP_APPLE to false tells
// OpenGL not to flush the contents of the PBO to VRAM
// when the PBO is unmapped.
glBufferParameteriAPPLE(GL_PIXEL_PACK_BUFFER,
    GL_BUFFER_FLUSHING_UNMAP_APPLE, GL_FALSE);

// We're done with the PBO for now so unbind it.
glBindBuffer(GL_PIXEL_PACK_BUFFER, 0);

// Don't need to keep the malloc'd texture data buffer
// around now that the PBO has it.
free(textureData);

// ... later, modify the texture stored in the PBO ...

GLubyte *texturePtr;

glBindBuffer(GL_PIXEL_PACK_BUFFER, pboID);
texturePtr = glMapBuffer(GL_PIXEL_PACK_BUFFER,
    GL_READ_WRITE);

// ... Use texturePtr to modify a portion of the texture ...
```

```
// Flush the modified region to VRAM
glFlushMappedBufferRangeAPPLE(GL_PIXEL_PACK_BUFFER, 0,
    width * height);

// Unmap and unbind
glUnmapBuffer(GL_PIXEL_PACK_BUFFER);
glBindBuffer(GL_PIXEL_PACK_BUFFER, 0);
```

Apple Fence Extension

Fences are tokens in the OpenGL command stream that act like tracer bullets; they tell you where you are. Fencing is a key concept because it bridges the world of the synchronous and the asynchronous. That is, it's great to be as asynchronous as possible, but ultimately drawing operations still need to be done in order. If your GPU and CPU get too far out of whack with their asynchronicity, fences serve to bring them back in line with each other.

Please see the section entitled Vertex Array Range later in this chapter for more information and an example of using fences.

Share Data Across Contexts When Possible

If you have multiple contexts and all of them can use the same OpenGL resources, be sure to share them across contexts to eliminate redundant copies of the data. See Chapter 5 for more information.

Metrics

The overview introduced the idea of considering your application performance from a variety of perspectives, including the perspective of the user as well as the perspective of the system. Regardless of whether you have the same application style as the one described in the overview, or something more demanding, such as a visual flight or driving simulator, or game, you ultimately need to measure performance. Defining a few metrics for performance is an essential first step.

Frame Rate

The first metric useful in performance analysis is the frame rate. The frame rate measures the number of frames per second your application displays. Unlike most performance metrics, the frame rate is a discrete measurement. You cannot, for instance, have a frame rate of 12.5 frames per second (FPS).

Table 11-1 Pixel Format Buffer Selection Mode

API	Double Buffer	Single Buffer
CGL	kCGLPFADoubleBuffer, GL_TRUE	kCGLPFADoubleBuffer, GL_FALSE
AGL	AGL_DOUBLEBUFFER, GL_TRUE	AGL_DOUBLEBUFFER, GL_FALSE
Cocoa	NSOpenGLPFADoubleBuffer, YES	NSOpenGLPFADoubleBuffer, NO
GLUT	GLUT_DOUBLE	GLUT_SINGLE

Further, if your application is vertical blank synchronized your frame rate will be quantized by the refresh rate of the display device you are using. For example, a monitor can update its contents only at a fixed rate—say, 60Hz for a particular monitor. If your application is attempting to display results on a monitor as fast as possible, your application will never display more than 60 distinct frames per second. Let's look at frame rate and monitor refresh rates in more detail. See information on KCGLSwapInternal in Chapter 6 for more details on configuring your Mac OS X application to be vertical blank synchronized (vbl-sync'd).

There are two basic ways of building a pixel format and ultimately choosing a drawable or surface on which to render. Depending on whether you're using CGL, AGL, or Cocoa, you'll specify a particular token indicating your interest in using a single-buffered or a double-buffered pixel format, as seen in Table 11-1. Typically, if you're displaying data on screen, the only high-quality way to do so is with double-buffered pixel formats. The primary reason for choosing double-buffered drawing is to ensure that the user of your application doesn't see image "tearing," a visual artifact that stems from the fact that your application drew two partial images to the framebuffer as it was displayed. If your application isn't displaying data directly to the user, perhaps it is rendering graphics frames in a nonvisible buffer, so a single-buffered pixel format may be the way to go.

Double-buffered, vertical blank synchronized applications can achieve a maximum frame rate that matches the refresh rate of the monitor on which the application windows are displayed. This is a very important metric to be aware of, because it means that even in the best case, you'll still get only 60Hz on a monitor with that refresh rate. Another consequence of this limitation when using a double-buffered pixel format is that if your application takes one femtosecond longer than a single frame (16.67 ms/frame) to draw, that frame will not appear until the next swap boundary. Thus your application will be waiting for almost a full frame for the swap to return. This effect is known as *frame rate quantization*.

Throughput

Throughput is another metric of performance that is related to frame rate but is not dependent upon it. Throughput measures the data transfer rate that your application achieves for a particular form of data. It is limited by the bandwidth of the bus through which the data transfers. Some baseline transfer rates for the main memory to graphics card path were described earlier in Chapter 2.

The best way to evaluate your application performance is to use the existing Apple-written OpenGL throughput applications as benchmarks. These applications, which were written by Apple OpenGL engineers, will achieve maximum throughput, provide a number of switches and knobs that allow you to experiment with different formats, and offer a benchmark with which you can compare your application. The list of these applications available from Apple's developer website [4] is always evolving but two are particularly relevant. The Texture Range sample application [7] is useful for examining and comparing, as is the Vertex Performance Test application [8]. These two applications not only provide realistic estimates of performance rates but also are available as source code. They provide examples of optimal coding techniques and show you how to choose different techniques for rendering the same data.

Efficient Data Management Using Mac OpenGL

There are some commonalities between efficient handling of all kinds of data for the Mac OpenGL implementation, whether the data is for vertices, pixels, or texels. As mentioned earlier, the OpenGL specification allows for a lot of flexibility for data and state management. At any time, an OpenGL application can query the OpenGL server for a current state or data. From an application writer's perspective, having this "data and state on tap" is convenient and relaxes the strict need for the application to maintain its current graphics state. From an OpenGL implementer's perspective, however, this design imposes a great deal of overhead because that data will likely need to be copied to make it readily available to applications.

Another consideration along these lines is that for OpenGL entry points that submit data to the drivers, the specification naturally requires that the implementation is finished accessing the data by the time the function returns control to the application. Take `glTexImage2D()`, for instance; by the time control is returned to the application, OpenGL must have completed reading the texels provided through this interface from the application address space. So if it needs to comply with the specification, where does it put the texels? Does it make a copy in host memory? Does it go to the kernel and ask for AGP space? Does it just directly put the data into VRAM?

The answer to each of these questions is "It depends." But the important common thread is that a copy of the data is made. In many cases, if it makes sense, multiple copies of the data are made. There may be a copy in the OpenGL framework, one in the driver, and one in VRAM. All told, that's four potential copies of large data buffers.

The moral to this story can be summarized as follows: Efficient data handling on the Mac means efficient use of memory by providing a clear usage model of the memory to OpenGL using the available interfaces of both OpenGL and Apple extensions.

Efficient Handling of Vertex Data

A Brief History of the Evolution of Submitting Vertices in OpenGL

The number of different ways to submit vertex information provided via the OpenGL API through version 2.1 of the specification is staggering. From a performance perspective, most of these methods are outdated. From a convenience perspective, things are a bit more debatable.

Regardless of the outcome of the debate, the OpenGL ARB is convinced that fewer "performance nooses" need to be present in the API. Over time, older idioms will be purged from the API, leaving only the best practices intact.

Let's start with the most primitive form of submitting vertex data in OpenGL: use of immediate mode, as illustrated in Example 11-4.

Example 11-4 Immediate Mode Vertex Submission: Begin/End

```
// OpenGL context setup

glBegin(GL_TRIANGLES);
glVertex2i(0, 0);
glVertex2i(2, 0);
glVertex2i(1, 1);

// More batches of three vertices to follow for each
// triangle drawn ...

glEnd();

glFlush();
```

Taking this example apart, we can see its limitations. First, there is not only an entire OpenGL function call to delimit the batch of triangles drawn but also a function call for every vertex of those triangles! Furthermore, if this batch of triangles represents a triangle mesh, all shared vertices are specified twice. This immediate mode pattern typically is used for small batches of triangles such that the cost of handling the begin/end tokens in the OpenGL command stream is relatively high when compared to the few triangles drawn to amortize that cost.

A simple improvement in efficiency for this example is to replace the primitive type GL_TRIANGLES with the type GL_TRIANGLE_STRIP. This eliminates a great deal of the submission of redundant shared vertices.

Even with triangle strips, there is a great deal of headroom for improvement. To absorb the enormous function call overhead associated with the code in Example 11-5, batch submission of vertices was added to the OpenGL interface. This batching, which is known as vertex arrays, is shown in Example 11-5.

Example 11-5 Immediate Mode Vertex Submission: Vertex Arrays

```
// OpenGL context setup

// Preprocess vertex data as triangle strips into
// vertex buffer
glEnableClientState(GL_VERTEX_ARRAY);
glVertexPointer(3, GL_FLOAT, 0, vertex buffer);

// Draw triangle strip using 'n' vertices of vertex Buffer
// starting at index 0
glDrawArrays(GL_TRIANGLE_STRIP, 0, n);

glFlush();
```

In both of the immediate mode examples, to draw the same data over again, as with a static model, you must continually and redundantly send vertex data over the bus or wire to the graphics device. Display lists were added to OpenGL to allow reuse of data that was already submitted to a GPU and stored in VRAM. Once the list has been specified, you can simply refer to the list by ID to redraw it rather than resubmitting all of its often voluminous contents. Display lists were the earliest form of retained mode rendering. Here's an example:

```
// OpenGL context setup

listID = glGenLists(1);

glNewList(GL_COMPILE, listID);

glBegin(GL_TRIANGLE_STRIP);
glVertex2i(0, 0);
glVertex2i(2, 0);
glVertex2i(1, 1);

// More batches of two vertices to follow for each
// triangle drawn ...
```

```
glEnd();

glEndList();

// Now, as often as you wish, draw the list
glCallList(listID);

glFlush();
```

For static models, display lists yield an enormous performance gain because they effectively eliminate the transfer of data between the host CPU and the GPU. They also eliminate all of the internal copies and data management required for immediate mode vertex submission. Their drawbacks include the space required to store the display list drawing commands in VRAM and the inability to change the list contents if the data is dynamic.

Notice that the glBegin/glEnd method of specifying polygonal data was used in this example rather than the vertex array method cited earlier. Vertex arrays, along with any other OpenGL client state, may not be used in display lists. As a consequence, an OpenGL client application may reside in the address space of one machine while the OpenGL server exists in the address space of another. If a client address pointer showed up in a display list, the OpenGL server on another system wouldn't know how to resolve it.

Finally, we come to the latest and most general mechanism for submitting vertices: vertex buffer objects (VBOs). VBOs are more sophisticated than other retained mode or immediate mode rendering methods in that they provide the performance benefits of display lists, yet support the dynamism of simple immediate mode rendering.

When VBOs are created, they are initialized with parameters that characterize their anticipated pattern of use, which in turn allows the OpenGL implementation to allocate the most effective resources and choose the most effective rendering paths for the data in the VBOs. Example 11-6 shows how to use VBOs.

Example 11-6 Immediate Mode Vertex Submission: Vertex Buffer Objects

```
// OpenGL context setup

// Preprocess vertex data as triangle strips into
// vertex buffer

// Create and bind a VBO ID
glGenBuffers(1, &bufID);
glBindBuffer(GL_ARRAY_BUFFER, bufID);

// Supply data to the VBO
```

```
glBufferData(GL_ARRAY_BUFFER, VERTEX_CT, vertexBuffer,
    GL_STATIC_DRAW);

glEnableClientState(GL_VERTEX_ARRAY);
glVertexPointer(3, GL_FLOAT, 0, (char *) NULL);

...

// Now the VBO is initialized, when we're ready to draw
// Bind the VBO for drawing
glBindBuffer(GL_ARRAY_BUFFER, bufID);

// Draw triangle strip using 'n' vertices from the VBO
// starting at index 0
glDrawArrays(GL_TRIANGLE_STRIP, 0, n);

glFlush();
```

Notice that the `glBufferData()` call specifies GL_STATIC_DRAW to characterize the usage of the VBO in Example 11-6. Notice, too, that the vertex array nomenclature is used to characterize the memory layout of the VBO in the same manner that it was used for vertex arrays. In this case, however, `glVertexPointer()` is used not to specify the vertex data but rather to specify an offset into the VBO data. For VBO usage in this example, we're simply specifying a zero offset and relying on the offsets implicit in the `glDrawArrays()` call to access and draw the data of interest.

Modifying data in a VBO (it's VBOs' biggest advantage over display lists) is done using one of three methods: `glMap/UnmapBuffer()`, `glBufferData()`, or `glBufferSubData()`. In the case of `glMap/UnmapBuffer()`, when the buffer is mapped, it may be modified by the OpenGL application without concern for the state of drawing on that buffer. Similarly, `glBufferData()` and `glBufferSubData()` can be used to directly modify a VBO's contents in much the same way that a call to `glTexImage2D()` or `glTexSubImage2D()` would be used to modify a texture.

Which Methods Should You Use to Submit Vertices for Drawing?

As of OpenGL 2.0, you should consider methods of vertex submission other than VBOs to be "syntactic sugar." If you're drawing 10 triangles on the screen once, by all means use immediate mode rendering without vertex arrays. For the rest of your applications, leverage VBOs and exploit their versatility and performance. This approach will continue to pay dividends if you end up using the buffer object extension—the heart of VBOs—for pixel buffer objects as well.

Apple's Methods of Vertex Submission, Past and Present

If you're starting a new application, or if you're porting a relatively modern and well-written OpenGL application, there's a good chance that you can just learn the nuances of good VBO etiquette and forget about the now fairly complex history of submitting vertices using Apple's OpenGL implementation.

You may have noticed some limitations in the previous section with methods prior to VBOs for submitting vertices in OpenGL. Apple noticed them, too, and responded with many of its own extensions to OpenGL. Thankfully, most of these extensions are also recognized as necessary by the OpenGL ARB and have been adopted into the specification core either directly or in some other form.

If you wish to see an implementation of all methods Apple for submitting vertices in the Mac OS, check out Apple's VertexPerformanceTest application (see `http://developer.apple.com`). This application provides a comprehensive overview of different methods of submitting vertex data. Try not to get too distracted by all the possibilities. Just use VBOs.

Vertex Array Objects

Vertex arrays are designed to accommodate a number of different types of vertices, such as positional information, colors, texture coordinates, and normals. Often it's natural and, from an OpenGL perspective, efficient to group the states associated with these arrays together. Consider a model that includes positional information, texture coordinates, and normals. It's not very efficient to have to specify each of these pointers of these arrays to OpenGL anew every time you draw a different model. We show this case in Example 11-7.

Example 11-7 Inefficiencies of Not Using Vertex Array Objects

```
// Draw tortoise model
glVertexPointer();
glNormalPointer();
glTexCoordPointer();
glDrawArrays();

// Draw hare model
glVertexPointer();
glNormalPointer();
glTexCoordPointer();
glDrawArrays();
```

To remedy all of this redundant pointer setting, Apple introduced the Vertex Array Object (VAO) extension. VAOs encapsulate all of the current vertex array state such that it can be simply recalled when needed to draw various objects in a scene, as in Example 11-8.

Example 11-8 Using Vertex Array Objects

```
//  Create and bind your VAO
glGenVertexArraysAPPLE(1, &tortoiseVAO_ID);
glBindVertexArrayAPPLE(tortoiseVAO_ID);
// Set up tortoise pointers
glVertexPointer();
glNormalPointer();
glTexCoordPointer();

// Do the same init sequence for the hare model ...

// Other stuff ...

// Now when you want to draw the tortoise
glBindVertexArrayAPPLE(tortoiseVAO_ID);
glDrawArrays(GL_TRIANGLE_STRIP, 0, n);
```

VAOs will likely evolve into the OpenGL core specification in some form or another and are a good complement to using VBAs.

Vertex Array Range

Prior to VBOs, Apple introduced the Vertex Array Range (VAR) extension. VAR has two key aspects that benefit the performance of vertex submission. First, this aggregating extension improves the efficiency of mapping regions of memory dedicated to holding your vertex data. Second, VAR allows you to make piecewise modifications to vertex arrays and to subsequently flush those specific changes up to the GPU. Suppose you have a vertex array with 10MB of data that contains the vertex information for 10 different models in a scene. If a user of your application modifies one of the 10 models, ideally your application should modify the corresponding vertices of that single model and then send the changes for that model over to the GPU. Without VAR, the vertex array is treated atomically with regard to flushing the data to the GPU, leading to a great deal of unnecessary bus traffic.

It's somewhat ironic that this extension's name does not generally denote its most powerful feature. Along with the ability to modify and flush subregions of a vertex array, the VAR extension allows you to characterize the usage of vertex data, much as VBOs do, allowing the OpenGL driver to avoid making unnecessary copies of your vertex array data. For instance, if the data in a vertex array is static, it's best to cache it in VRAM and eliminate any other copies the driver may otherwise need to maintain. Example 11-9 demonstrates how we might draw static vertex array data.

Example 11-9 Using Vertex Array Range

```
// Standard vertex array setup
glEnableClientState(GL_VERTEX_ARRAY);
glVertexPointer(3, GL_FLOAT, stride, vertexBuffer);

// Tell OpenGL data is mostly static so hang on to it in VRAM
glVertexArrayParameteriAPPLE(
    GL_VERTEX_ARRAY_STORAGE_HINT_APPLE,
    GL_STORAGE_CACHED_APPLE );

// Set up the VAR
glVertexArrayRangeApple(arrayLength, vertexBuffer);

// Tell OpenGL the data has changed so it knows it needs
// to upload it to the card
glFlushVertexArrayRangeAPPLE(arrayLength, vertexBuffer );
```

Notice that `glVertexArrayParameteriAPPLE()` is the key to characterizing the vertex array memory and avoids unnecessary data transfers and copies. For dynamic data, you can use the parameter `GL_STORAGE_SHARED_APPLE` rather than `GL_STORAGE_CACHED_APPLE`. This powerful configuration instructs the GPU to fetch vertex data directly from your application, making no intermediate copies along the way.

In any case, using VAR requires more smarts that regular vertex array semantics. The VAR extension requires that you tell OpenGL when you're modifying data and when you're finished with it. Unlike `glFlush()`, `glFlushVertexArrayRangeAPPLE()` simply marks a region of memory as modified (or "dirty" in driver-speak). To guarantee coherency of the data, you must use either the Apple Fence extension (which will likely work its way into the OpenGL core in the future) or a more heavy, club-handed way of guaranteeing coherency by calling `glFinish()`.

Using Apple Fence is quite simple. Example 11-10 shows the use of fences with Apple Vertex Array Range.

Example 11-10 Apple Fence Extension

```
GLuint drawCompleteFence;

void init()
{
    glEnableClientState(GL_VERTEX_ARRAY);
    glEnableClientState(GL_VERTEX_ARRAY_RANGE_APPLE);
    glVertexArrayRangeAPPLE(allocSize, vtxCoordArray);
    glGenFencesAPPLE(1, &drawCompleteFence);
}

void draw()
{
```

```
        for(i = 0; i < vtxCt; i += stripCt)
            glDrawArrays(GL_TRIANGLE_STRIP, i, stripCt);

        // Set a fence here so that when we modify the
        // data later, we can verify that drawing with this
        // data has completed.
        glSetFenceAPPLE(drawCompleteFence);
}

void modifyData()
{
    glFinishFenceAPPLE(drawCompleteFence);

        // Modify all or some portion of the data knowing
        // that there are no pending drawing commands for
        // the previous contents of that data.
        glFlushVertexArrayRangeAPPLE(vtxCoordCt * sizeof(GL_FLOAT),
            vtxCoordArray);
}

void main()
{
    init();

    while(!done)
    {
        draw();
        modifyData();
    }
}
```

In Example 11-10, glFinishFenceAPPLE() will block all operation until all drawing has completed on the vertex array. In short, the VAR extension allows more asynchronous behavior between CPU and GPU, permitting them to be concurrently busy more often with less blocking, and effectively getting more work done.

Historically, if you were an attendee at Apple's WWDC Conference, or if you have been an Apple Developer Connection member for some time, you may have seen OpenGL performance talks that advocated the double buffering of vertex data using the VAR extension. This method relies on VAR to provide the asynchronous behavior needed to modify one copy of the data while drawing with another. Example 11-11 shows the steps and stages involved to employ this double-buffering technique with the APPLE_vertex_array_range extension.

Example 11-11 Double-Buffering Vertex Data Using the APPLE_vertex_array_range Extension

```
// Specify a number of VERTICES that will by 4 KB
// page aligned.  We're using 4 byte floats for
// the vertices below so we will be page aligned.
```

```
#define VERTICES 1024

// Define number of bytes for vertex data in our
// hypothetical model.
//
// GLint MODEL_BYTES = vertex_count * 3 (one for x, y, & z) *
//                          sizeof(GLfloat);
#define MODEL_BYTES (VERTICES * 3 * sizeof(GLfloat));

// Pointer to our vertex data buffer
GLfloat *vertexData;


// Drawing fence for coherency
GLuint drawingFence1, drawingFence2;

//  Typical init routine for setting up double buffering VAR
void InitVAR()
{
    // Multiply MODEL_BYTES by 2 to double buffer.
    GLint totalBytes = MODEL_BYTES * 2;

    // Create 2 duplicate sets of vertex data arranged
    // sequentially in memory.  We'll have both copies of our
    // model stored in this one buffer.
    vertexData = (GLfloat *) malloc(totalBytes);

    // InitModelData is a hypothetical routine to initialize our
    // model data
    // Initialize first copy of vertex data
    InitModelData(MODEL_BYTES, vertexData);

    // Initialize second copy of vertex data
    // (offset 1/2 way into the vertexData buffer)
    InitModelData(MODEL_BYTES,
        vertexData + MODEL_BYTES / sizeof(GLfloat));

    // Our data is dynamic, so specify the memory is SHARED
    // (AGP mapped)
    glVertexArrayParameteriAPPLE(
        GL_VERTEX_ARRAY_STORAGE_HINT_APPLE,
        GL_STORAGE_SHARED_APPLE );

    // Configure the VAR
    glEnableClientState(GL_VERTEX_ARRAY);
    glEnableClientState(GL_VERTEX_ARRAY_RANGE_APPLE);
    glVertexPointer(3, GL_FLOAT, 0, vertexData);
    glVertexArrayRangeAPPLE(totalBytes, vertexData);
    glFlushVertexArrayRangeAPPLE(totalBytes, vertexData);

    // Create drawing fence
    glGenFencesAPPLE(1, &drawingFence);
}

// Update routine for animating vertices in buffer
```

```
void UpdateBuffer(GLuint fence, GLint first, GLint length,
    GLfloat *currentVertexBuffer)
{
    int i;

    // Insure that we're through drawing with the memory holding
    // the vertices we're about to update.
    glFinishFenceAPPLE(fence);

    for(i = 0; i < length; i++)
        // Modify contents of currentVertexBuffer here

    // Mark our updated region as modified so OpenGL knows how to
    // establish coherency for drawing.
    glFlushVertexArrayRangeAPPLE(length,
        currentVertexBuffer + first * 3);
}

// Typical draw routine for setting up double buffering VAR
void Draw()
{
    static unsigned int currentBuffer = 0;

    if(!currentBuffer)
    {
        glDrawArrays(GL_QUADS, 0, VERTICES / 2);
        glSetFenceAPPLE(drawingFence1);

        // The first half of the buffer is now drawing so update
        // the second half.
        UpdateBuffer(drawingFence2, VERTICES / 2, VERTICES / 2,
            vertexData);
    }
    else
    {
        glDrawArrays(GL_QUADS, VERTICES / 2, VERTICES / 2);
        glSetFenceAPPLE(drawingFence2);

        // The second half of the buffer is now drawing so update
        // the first half.
        UpdateBuffer(drawingFence1, 0, VERTICES / 2, vertexData);
    }

    currentBuffer = ~currentBuffer;
}

// Typical clean-up / state reset routine for a VAR
// implementation.
void CleanUp()
{
    glVertexArrayRangeAPPLE(0, NULL);
    glDisableClientState(GL_VERTEX_ARRAY_RANGE_APPLE);
    free(vertexData);
}
```

This example shows a natural usage of the VAR extension. We've written pseudocode for this example because, like many of the other snippets, it describes the way things used to be done on OS X. With the introduction of VBOs and the APPLE_flush_buffer_range extension, this same strategy can be employed using the more modern and OpenGL standard VBO interface.

Using VBOs on OS X

As stated earlier, VBOs are the way to go for modern OpenGL applications. They have been designed with all the flexibility and all of the performance benefits associated with previous methods of vertex submission in OpenGL. We will not go into details on using VBOs; these points are well covered in the OpenGL specification and supporting documentation. We will highlight a few things about them here, however.

Aside from the characterization of usage for VBOs when you initialize them, you may notice that some of the relatively complex methods employed to obtain top-notch performance on OS X become quite simple using VBOs. For instance, the vertex double-buffering scheme described earlier is nearly free of charge: You simply use two VBOs, each of which holds a copy of the same data. You update the first copy of the data in the first VBO with glBufferData() and then draw with it. You do the same thing with the second copy of the data in the second VBO. As you switch between the two VBOs to modify and draw your vertex data, in time you will get similar results as with double-buffered vertex data using VARs.

Using two VBOs in this way relies on some implicit behavior of OpenGL to achieve the same asynchronous gains that you would enjoy using VAR. Notice that using this method you'll encounter some copying overhead when you call glBufferSubData() to update the buffers as you march along. To avoid this copy, and to precisely mirror the VAR double-buffer method using VBOs, you can use the APPLE_flush_buffer_range extension. This extension gives you the most fine-grained control over your double-buffering strategy. Double buffering with APPLE_flush_buffer_range entails using a single vertex buffer object with a usage value of GL_DYNAMIC_DRAW that is passed into glBufferData(). Specifying GL_DYNAMIC_DRAW is equivalent to specifying a vertex array storage hint of GL_STORAGE_SHARED_APPLE. It maps your VBO into AGP space, allowing the GPU to fetch vertex information directly from your application-allocated buffer and thereby avoiding the copy described in the two-VBO approach.

As with the VAR double-buffer approach, the APPLE_flush_buffer_range extension allows you to independently flush (mark as modified) the two halves of your VBO, each of which contains a copy of your model's vertex data.

Again, this doubling-up strategy increases the asynchronicity between the CPU modifying vertex data and the GPU drawing it.

We've prepared an extensive example that you can use to experiment with some of the different modalities of updating and drawing with VBOs in our source examples folder. Unlike most of the examples included with this book, the vertex_submission example contains a relatively large application to cover the various possibilities in submitting vertices efficiently. It allows you to switch between a single large VBO for double buffering or two small ones. When using a single large VBO, you may also turn on the APPLE_flush_buffer_range extension.

The vertex_submission example allows you to increase the complexity of the model to load your system differently as well. NSSlider widgets permit you to modify the width and height of the model, which, as you can see in the logic, will increase the demand of the CPU to compute updated color vertices. You may also increase the depth value of the cube. This parameter essentially controls how many planes of GL_QUADS are drawn. By increasing the depth parameter, you force the GPU to fill more polygons, thereby shifting the performance bottleneck away from the CPU and toward the GPU.

You should have fun playing with and modifying the vertex_submission example and watching the CPU history on OS X's Activity Monitor application, which is found in the /Applications/Utilities folder. Try increasing the width/height parameter and watching the effect on CPU usage. Figure 11-1 shows one possible configuration of this example. Clicking the Test button in the interface will provide a consistent performance measurement as it tumbles the model in space and updates the Frame Rate field upon finishing. The fact that the routine that modifies the vertex data and the fact that GL_QUADS is used rather than GL_QUAD_STRIPS are efforts to make the updates more costly and push on the CPU harder. Again, the point of this example is to load the system in various ways and move the performance bottleneck around so that you can get a feel for how to manage vertex submission in your own applications.

Efficient Handling of Texture Data

Many applications are far more texture intensive than vertex intensive these days. Here are some things to keep in mind when you are handling large quantities of texture data.

Formats and Types

The number of pixel types and formats in OpenGL has been on the rise since its inception. This increase has been driven, to a large extent, by scientific and entertainment visualization work in which the data is acquired from a device

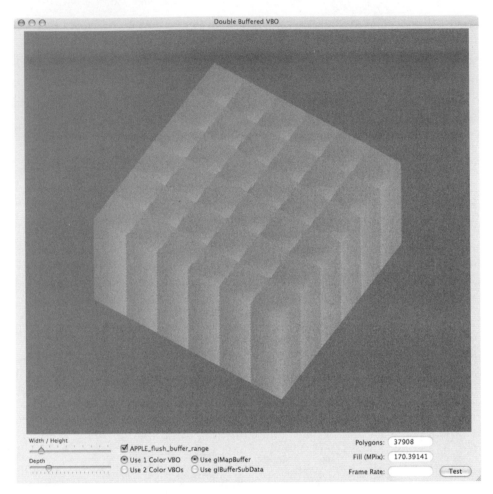

Figure 11-1 Vertex Submission Example Application

that works natively with the pixel format. The video acquisition of YCBCR-formatted data is a good example. Another is high-fidelity single-component pixel data used for medical imaging. In Mac OS X, there are about two dozen pixel types; more than a dozen pixel formats can be specified for OpenGL.

Consider the architecture of OpenGL on the Mac OS with regard to handling pixel data: The Mac OS implementation provides an abstraction layer over multiple types of graphics hardware, each with its own capacity for handling various types of pixel data. If an application requests a pixel format/type pairing that cannot be handled natively by the graphics hardware, the hardware driver will make a request of the Mac OS OpenGL layer to convert the pixel data from the requested format into the hardware's native format.

Depending on your application's performance needs, this can be a very expensive operation indeed! Imagine that you're uploading a stream of pixel data to the graphics card, but instead of free flowing at close to PCI-express limits between system memory and graphics device, it stops to perform a format/type transformation on the way there. At best, you've introduced a memcpy of the pixel data into your pixel path. At worst, the conversion is a very expensive one and is costly just from a CPU time perspective.

Determining which effective path you're on for the pixel format and type you're using is a matter of measuring the performance. The large matrix of changing possibilities between what the graphics hardware desires and which paths are tuned within the OpenGL framework is an unbounded problem over time. In a macroscopic sense, measuring OpenGL performance in general falls in the same category. It must be benchmarked.

The key to high-performance drawing with pixel data is to match the most common formats and types of the graphics hardware such that a format/type transformation does not take place. The tricky part is that the precise formats/types that are handled natively are not very well published.

As a rule, the canonical 4-component, 8-bits-per-component types are very well served. For any hardware made as recently as 2001, both ATI and NVIDIA graphics hardware natively support GL_BGRA, GL_UNSIGNED_INT_8_8_8_8_REV pixels. They will also handle GL_RGB and GL_RGBA formats with the type GL_UNSIGNED_BYTE. The 2001 cutoff date is somewhat arbitrary, of course. It's mostly a date chosen to represent "reasonably new" hardware that gives a great deal of coverage for the Mac computers that are running OS X.

For 16-bit formats, graphics parts from both vendors have an affinity for the GL_UNSIGNED_SHORT_1_5_5_5_REV type with a type of GL_BGRA. They also natively support the 16-bit YCBCR format with a gravity toward the GL_UNSIGNED_SHORT_8_8_REV_APPLE type. This type is essentially meant for high-streaming performance to the graphics device for video feeds.

The very latest and highest-performance discrete graphics chips will handle 4-component, 32-bit single-precision floating-point pixels or texels throughout the pipeline without costly conversions.

Pixel Pipeline and Imaging Subset State

In addition to the state involved with formats and types, the performance of pixel data throughput will greatly be affected by any pixel transform state that is enabled in the OpenGL pixel pipeline. The OpenGL 1.0 specification in combination with the imaging subset state yields numerous stages in the pixel pipeline for applying scales, biases, lookups, color matrices, convolutions, and so on. If these "non-default" states are enabled, your pixel upload performance will very likely suffer simply because these states are rarely used and, therefore, are not represented in the silicon of the graphics hardware installed on the systems. As a result, these stages take the pixel upload off the fast path and require modification by the CPU.

Alignment Considerations

It is quite important on any modern CPU architecture to pay attention to pixel data alignment. Alignment is such an important consideration that, in the opinion of the authors, it more often than not usurps video memory usage as a primary performance consideration.

The most common misconception is the notion that, because alpha is not needed, the developer should use RGB pixels rather than RGBA pixels to save space. This does, indeed, save space in host memory, but it may not save any space in VRAM considering that the silicon contains pathways for all four components and doesn't really care whether you are using all four as far as performance is concerned. I can't recall the last time I witnessed an application running faster with RGB pixels than with RGBA pixels.

The worst part of the RGB pixels is the alignment. They are 3 bytes long—need we say more? Thinking out loud: "Let's see, how many RGB pixels fits in a 16-byte SIMD register?" Answer: $5^{1}/_{3}$. Not much logic works on $5^{1}/_{3}$ pixels at a time, so there definitely needs to be some slower, special-case handling of these pixel fragments when you invoke any transformation logic that uses the vector units. You can be certain that as far as vector processing is concerned, it's a lot faster to handle 4 pixels atomically than it is to handle $5^{1}/_{3}$ pixels piecemeal.

The other alignment consideration is the base address of your pixel buffer to OpenGL. Is it 16-byte aligned? Unless you've done something to tweak the pointer, it should be. Malloc on OS X always returns 16-byte-aligned addresses in the worst case. For allocations exceeding a page size, the malloc returns page-aligned addresses.

What else can affect alignment? How about using glPixelStore() to affect the unpacking of your pixel data? If your pointer address is aligned on a 16-byte boundary and you specify a GL_UNPACK_SKIP_PIXELS value of 3, then your base address is effectively on a 12-byte boundary when you are using 4-byte pixels.

Another performance problem can result if you have specified a GL_UNPACK_ROW_LENGTH that is greater than the image size. In this case, if you have a base address in the image somewhere in this big buffer that is 16-byte aligned, and the image dimension is, for example, 9 RGB unsigned byte pixels wide, then the right end of each scanline of the image is 27 bytes past the beginning. Because the buffer is not tightly packed in memory using the big row length, this non-aligned, ragged, 27-byte-aligned right side of each scanline of the image will require special (in not so politically correct terms, "slow") handling.

Textures

More than 5400 valid combinations of texture formats, types, and internal formats can be specified via `glTexImage()` calls of OpenGL on the Mac OS. A great deal of engineering has been done to increase the effective texture upload performance on the Mac. If, however, you don't choose wisely on your internal format and external format/type, your texture upload performance may fall victim to the same pitfalls described for the pixel format/type transformations discussed in the previous section. Certainly, any pixel pipeline state that would cause `glDrawPixels()` or `glReadPixels()` to be slow may have the same effect on your texture upload performance.

Recall that the internal format parameter of a `glTexImage()` call is a format "request." That means the implementation will try to honor it but does not have to. Ultimately, the request will be honored if the graphics hardware natively supports the requested format. Note, however, that the fact that the graphics hardware natively supports an internal format does not mean the texture upload performance for the requested internal format will be fast. It may undergo an expensive CPU transformation to go from the format/type to the native internal format.

Compressed Textures

Graphics hardware from both ATI and NVIDIA supports S3TC compressed types natively but not compression of other formats into these S3TC types in hardware. If you specify a compressed internal format along with an uncompressed external format, your texture data will undergo compression on the CPU before it is handed off to the GPU.

The Mac OS texture compressor offers very high performance—at least 60MB/s per CPU core—on modern Mac systems. Although this is a very high number, it is not comparable to the realizable upload bandwidth of PCI Express, which exceeds 2GB/s. If the cited numbers satisfy your texture upload performance requirements, you're free to use OpenGL to compress your textures on upload. If not, it is advisable to pre-compress your textures and use the `glCompressedTexImage()` API to upload them.

Alignment Considerations

On the upside, the precedent for having power-of-two-sized textures relieves some of the alignment problems you might see in the pixel paths. On the downside, texturing can aggravate the alignment problem when you are doing `glTexSubImage()` calls. By its very nature, `glTexSubImage()` replaces an arbitrary region of pixels within the texture. The curse word in the previous sentence is "arbitrary" when it comes to alignment concerns.

In short, you should try to subtexture such that the replacement of texels falls on natural alignment boundaries if possible. Sometimes it can't be done, but it's always worthy of consideration.

Shaders

Shader performance, like many features of OpenGL, depends on the generation of graphics hardware used. The introduction of shaders meant that graphics hardware had to transition from fixed-function silicon, to hybridized silicon consisting of both fixed-function and programmable silicon, to all-programmable silicon. On modern graphics hardware, a fixed-function state is handled using programs that are generated by the framework and/or driver when that state is specified through the API.

There is a fair amount of residual wisdom from the hybridized time, when it made sense to use fixed-function state wherever possible for performance reasons. The confusion was somewhat compounded by the different paths chosen to implement programmability by the different graphics vendors. Fortunately, the industry has since found good footing with GLSL. R300- and NV30-class hardware and better generally produce the same performance results for programs encoding what used to be a fixed-function state in shader programs. Programmability is here to stay, and it seems likely that performance efforts for shaders will at least keep pace with what had been traditionally known as fixed-function state.

Aside from the performance comparisons of shaders versus fixed-function state, all of the standard rules apply when you are dealing with shaders. In general, you should avoid state changes whenever possible. With the introduction of GLSL, and its stages of specifying, compiling, linking, and using shader programs, the need to minimize state changes in this area should be obvious.

Tools

Apple, as a company, is committed to a great platform experience. As a user, this means an intuitive interface, consistency between applications, good aesthetic choices, and so forth. As a developer, platform experience is about great tools that offer all of these same merits. OS X has really hit its stride as a great development and tuning platform, and the proof is in the development tools provided for it.

System Tools

Shark

Shark, formerly known as Shakiri, is a system performance characterization tool. Shark allows numerous types of statistical sampling of virtually anything running on your system. If your binaries have not had their symbols stripped away and your source files are available, Shark profiles can correlate performance sampling values at the source and assembly levels. This tool will show you the breakdown of time spent in your application, time spent in system libraries, and even time spent in the Mach kernel. Shark is capable of sampling either PowerPC or x86 binaries, and it can provide valuable information on your application's performance on those different hardware architectures.

Getting useful information from Shark couldn't be any easier:

1. Start your application.
2. Start Shark.
3. Click the Start button.
4. Time elapses . . .
5. Click the Stop button.

At this point, Shark will generate a table showing sampling times for the routines used in your application's call stacks.

Using Shark is a snap in its simplest form (as described above). Becoming an expert on all the intricacies of Shark is another matter, however. Thankfully, most developers merely need to scratch the surface of Shark's capabilities. For those interested in more detail, the Shark user manual is an excellent resource; you'll find lots more information there. Suffice it to say that if you are suffering a performance problem in your code, Shark is the most comprehensive tool for examination and evaluation of those problems.

Activity Monitor

`Activity Monitor` is useful for monitoring the CPU activity of your application. One favorite feature in this tool is the ability to switch the icon view in the dock to CPU history. You'll notice that both bars show activity on single-threaded applications that use the multithreaded OpenGL engine. In fact, `Activity Monitor` is a good tool to verify that you've successfully enabled this engine.

`Activity Monitor` is also useful for sampling applications. In particular, if you see an application hang and wish to report it to Apple, use `Activity Monitor` to sample the hung process and submit your sample to Apple in the bug report.

Quartz Debug

`Quartz Debug` allows for configuration and debugging of settings for the Quartz window server. Some of the more interesting features you'll want to check out are the Window List tool and the User Interface Resolution tool. The User Interface Resolution tool allows you to emulate displays having different resolutions. As resolution independence is a standard feature of Leopard, it is very important to qualify your application.

Graphics Tools

OpenGL Profiler

The OpenGL Profiler is probably the best thing about developing OpenGL applications on Mac OS X. This diagnostic tool is best in class for evaluating the OpenGL state behavior of your application or, perhaps even better, for analyzing another OpenGL application that you have to debug!

When OpenGL Profiler reached version 3.0, it really hit its stride. This marked improvement over the version 2.x series boasts a greatly improved interface and reliable "attach to" functionality for running applications.

OpenGL Profiler Main Window

For our tour of this application, let's start with the main start-up window. We've expanded the "Launch Settings" arrow for Figure 11-2.

You will probably find the "Launch Settings" drop-down menu of greatest interest. This menu provides an incredibly powerful feature—the ability to test the behavior of your application against graphics devices other than the one installed in your system. In addition, this menu allows for a quick, easy comparison of the behavior of your application with the Apple Software Renderer. This is a great thing to check out if you suspect there is a bug in the OpenGL software itself. If the output is different, it probably indicates the presence of a bug you should report to Apple.

Also notice the "Use custom pixel format" check box. This option allows you to build a custom pixel format so that you can do a quick comparison of your application with a different pixel format configuration.

There are two modes of operation for profiling: launching the application from Profiler and attaching to a running application. When an application is launched from Profiler, it retains the history of the application and its arguments for use in the future. It's a simple session mechanism but is often overlooked in other applications even though it is immensely useful. Adding or deleting applications

Figure 11-2 OpenGL Profiler Main Window with Launch Settings Open

from the launchable list is done using the plus and minus icons. If you select the "Attach to application" option, the launchable application list will switch to a list of currently running processes that are candidates for being attached to.

Now, let's go through the Views menu in Profiler, which is where we find the substance of the application.

Breakpoints View

From the authors' perspective, the Breakpoints view is the mothership of all views (Figure 11-3). It is here that OpenGL Profiler steps out of the realm of being a mere analysis tool and becomes a full-fledged debugger. The power of Profiler is realized when the Breakpoints view is used in conjunction with the other views to refine logical or performance problems in your application.

First things first: What's the worst thing about OpenGL error state management from a developer's perspective? If you answered this question the way many others do, you said, "You can't tell where the error occurs without instrumenting the code with `glGetError()` calls." The Breakpoints view allows you to break on a GL error. When one occurs, you get a stack trace and the precise GL function that generated the error—solid time saver, indeed.

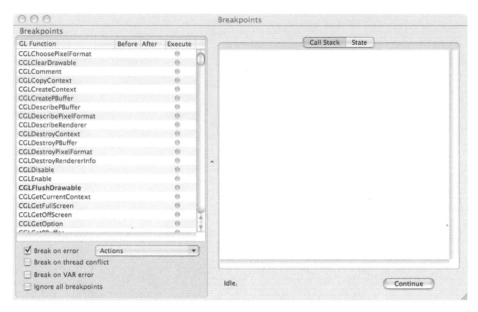

Figure 11-3 OpenGL Profiler Breakpoints View

The next most useful thing in the authors' opinion is the ability to delimit frames of rendering with breakpoints. Most OpenGL applications follow a cycle in making GL state changes that starts at the beginning of a rendered frame and ends at the end of the rendered frame. Very often, all state changes that need to be evaluated when debugging or doing performance evaluation will occur in a single frame.

If you look at the Breakpoints view, you'll notice that CGLFlushDrawable is set in a bold font. This is because it is so special! CGLFlushDrawable is the OS X version of swapping buffers and indicates that a frame has completed rendering. Here's where the combination of view usage becomes useful: By setting a breakpoint before CGLFlushDrawable, clearing the Trace and Statistics views, and then clicking "Continue" to resume execution, you will get precisely one frame's worth of GL function calls as a trace and as a collection of statistics. This often simplifies the debugging and performance process such that it yields the essential information only without any duplicate state changes.

In addition to collecting the trace and the statistics, the Breakpoints view provides state change information since the last breakpoint was encountered. If you click the "State" tab on the rightmost pane of the Breakpoints view window, all GL state settings that have changed since the last breakpoint was encountered will appear in a red typeface. All unchanged states remain in the normal black typeface. This distinction allows you to quickly review state changes for a frame. You may be surprised at how often you see state changes that you hadn't anticipated.

Now we leave the raw utility class of operations in the Breakpoints view and get to the "it's just plain cool" functionality. Specifically, the Breakpoints view allows you to execute a script before or after each invocation of a specified GL function. Generally speaking, there's no way to upload new data to GL in the same way an application can with memory buffers, but you can make any GL function calls that modify the GL state machine.

Let's consider an example. Suppose you have a rendering logic problem between a call to `glTranslated()` and a call to `glLineWidth()`. You could attach a script to be executed after the call to `glTranslated()` to set the current color to green. You could then attach a script to be executed before the call to `glLineWidth()` to set the current color to white. After attaching these scripts and continuing execution, you would know that all geometry rendered in green was subject to the logic problem and all geometry rendered in white was not.

Aside from GL function and GL error breakpoints, the Breakpoints view allows breaking on thread conflicts and vertex array range errors. Thread conflicts occur when multiple threads concurrently modify the same GL state. This often arises with multithreading and the use of `NSOpenGLViews` that internally must modify GL state. These implicit state modifications are often not anticipated by users of this Cocoa class.

Statistics View

The Statistics view accumulates and displays statistics on a per-GL-function basis (Figure 11-4). This view is useful in characterizing your application's usage patterns related to the OpenGL API. Often, having this information yields surprises and allows for reworking the application to achieve better performance.

For each OpenGL function called, both the execution time and the percentage of time spent inside the implementation to execute the call are shown. Generally speaking, if the percentage of time spent inside OpenGL is large, it indicates that the logical path being followed for your usage of the GL function is suboptimal. Large percentages of time spent in GL generally indicate a great deal of intermediate processing of the vertex or pixel/texel data before it is uploaded to the graphics hardware. This is known as being "off the fast path."

Trace View

The Trace view allows you to record all OpenGL calls for your application on a per-context basis (Figure 11-5). You can then filter the trace and save these results. One of the more informative exercises using the Trace view is to set a breakpoint in `CGLFlushDrawable` and continue to capture a single frame's

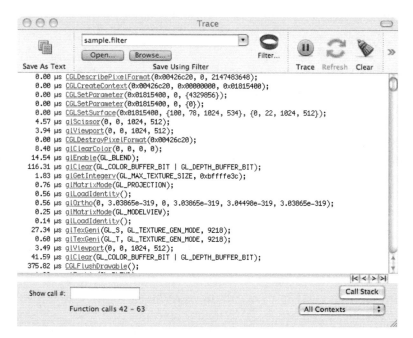

Figure 11-4 OpenGL Profiler Statistics View

worth of tracing data. The key difference regarding what the Trace view can provide you relative to what the Statistics view can deliver is the order of OpenGL calls, which, of course, can make all the difference when it comes to performance tuning.

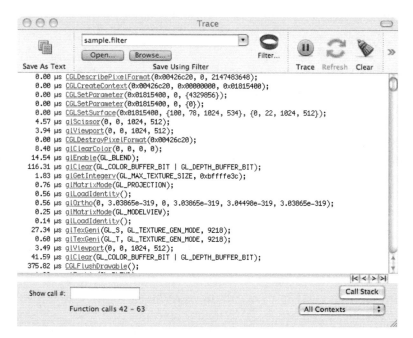

Figure 11-5 OpenGL Profiler Trace View

Resources View

The Resources view allows inspection of textures and vertex or fragment programs that have been submitted to the GL API (Figure 11-6). The ability to inspect these resources can be immensely valuable in debugging. If, for instance, a texture image has been procedurally generated and has never been viewed prior to being applied as a texture, you can evaluate the data in its raw form before its application as a texture to geometry and any transformations it may have undergone in the process. This can assist you in deciding whether rendering anomalies are a result of the texture generation/loading process or rather are part of the rasterization process.

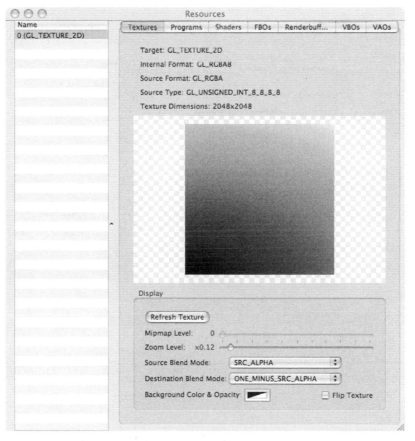

Figure 11-6 OpenGL Profiler Resources View

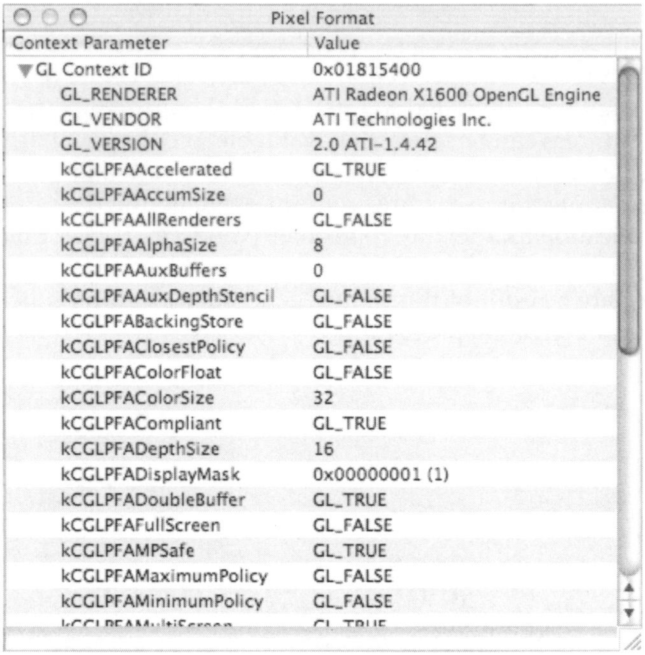

Figure 11-7 OpenGL Pixel Format View

Pixel Format View

The Pixel Format view is a nice time saver. It shows a comprehensive list of pixel format attributes for each context of the currently attached or launched application (Figure 11-7).

Buffer View

The Buffer view allows inspection of the various planes that constitute a GL framebuffer (Figure 11-8). At present these include the back buffer, the alpha buffer, the depth buffer, and the stencil buffer. It will be interesting to see how this view changes with the use of framebuffer objects and stereo rendering.

Scripts View

The Scripts view allows composition and saving of scripts (Figure 11-9). These are attached to and executed before or after breakpoints.

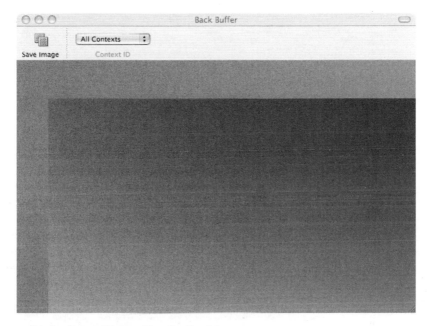

Figure 11-8 OpenGL Profiler Buffer View

OpenGL Driver Monitor

The OpenGL Driver Monitor is used to monitor various parameters of the graphics devices available on your Mac (Figure 11-10). To use this tool, first choose a driver from the Monitors menu, Driver Monitors submenu. Next, click

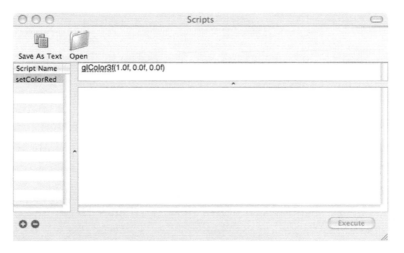

Figure 11-9 OpenGL Profiler Scripts View

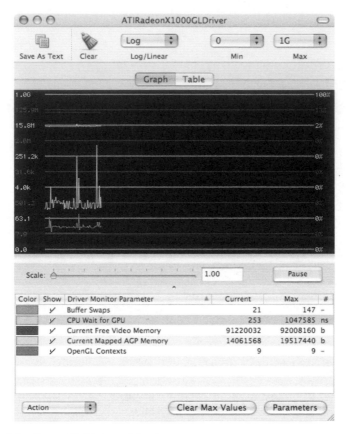

Figure 11-10 OpenGL Driver Monitor

the "Parameters" button at the bottom-right corner of the main window. You'll see a long list of anything you could want to know about data traffic, resource allocations, and various other parameters of the driver. One parameter of particular interest is "CPU Wait for GPU," which tells you whether your application is GPU bound and your application is stalled waiting for a response.

Driver Monitor also allows you to check the video memory currently available.

Pixie

Pixie is a tool that magnifies a portion of the screen (Figure 11-11). You can select a multiplier to vary the degree of magnification. Pixie is a great tool for inspecting individual pixels of your graphics application window.

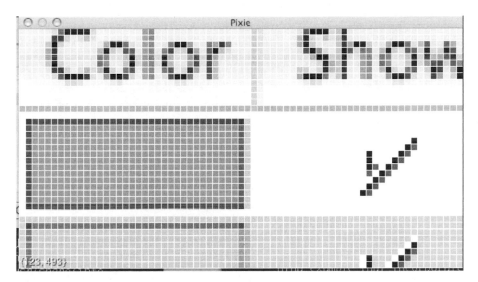

Figure 11-11 Pixie

Putting It All Together

In this section, the rubber meets the road. We're going to guide you through a performance-tuning example that incorporates many of the tuning techniques introduced in this chapter. The example is called please_tune_me, and you will find it in the examples folder that accompanies this book. In this folder are six source files, ptm1.c through ptm6.c. They feature an increasing level of optimization, with ptm1.c being the baseline and performing poorly and ptm6.c performing very well.

Each stage of optimization is a response to many of the most common performance-tuning questions and problems discussed on the Mac OS X OpenGL list. It's quite worthwhile to follow this example incrementally through every stage.

We encourage you to use Apple's stellar Filemerge tool to compare successive versions in this series of examples. This will make the changing code easy to follow.

About Please Tune Me

Please Tune Me may beg the question, "Why so complex?" The answer: because it's a more comprehensive approach to looking at performance tuning. By taking a naive implementation of an application that does more than draw a triangle to the screen, we're hoping to guide you through an environment that is a closer match to real-world performance tuning.

Please Tune Me goes heavy on texturing and geometry to give it some real-world weight. Here's some pseudocode describing this application:

- Create a color gradient texture for the textured quad mesh referenced below.
- Clear the entire application window with alpha set to 0.0.
- For some number of iterations, do:
    - Set the viewport to the left half of the application window.
    - Draw a randomly placed quad with an alpha value of 1.0.
    - Draw a textured quad mesh such that it fills the entire viewport.
    - Use blending to discard all fragments from the mesh rendering that do not lie within a previously drawn quad (where the framebuffer alpha is now 1.0).
    - Set the viewport to the right half of the application window.
    - Source the left half of the window (random quads/mesh) as a texture.
    - For all remaining texels of this texture that are still black:
        * Apply a gray color ramp to the texture.
        * Draw a teapot using texgen to apply the texture.

As the application runs, the teapot goes from gray, to a patchwork of textured regions and gray, to fully textured. A snapshot of this application can be seen in Figure 11-12.

Please Tune Me 1

Let's get started with `ptm1.c`. Compiling and running this example on our test system, we get less than $\frac{1}{2}$ a frame per second performance. Let's use OpenGL Profiler to figure out where our application is spending its time. Please note that in all example uses of Profiler, your results will vary from our test system to some degree. The results should be similar to Figure 11-13.

Notice the monsterous 89 percent of our time being spent in `glBegin()`. You'll often see a disproportionate amount of time devoted to `glBegin()` because of deferred validation. Notice, too, the 6 percent chunk at `glTexImage2D()`. This 6 percent is the time required to copy the texture data from application memory to OpenGL memory. Recall that OpenGL must keep copies of your data to be in compliance with the specification unless some extension relaxes that requirement (which many Apple extensions do).

The 89 percent time spent at `glBegin()` is primarily due to programming mistake numero uno in `ptm1.c`: use of a texture type that is not native to

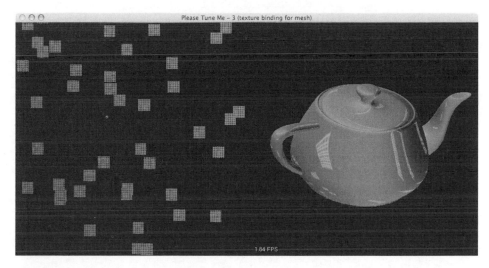

Figure 11-12 Performance-Tuning Exercise Application: Please Tune Me

the graphics hardware. In `ptm1.c`'s case, this texture type is `GL_UNSIGNED_SHORT_4_4_4_4`. Often OpenGL programmers will use packed types such as this because they don't require the fidelity of 8 bits per component and wish to save space. However, because this type is not native to the hardware, a very costly transformation needs to take place to translate this data into a hardware native form. This costly transformation is happening at `glBegin()` time because that is when you first use the texture.

GL Function	# of Calls	Total Time (µsec)	Avg Time (µsec)	% GL Time ▼	% App Time
glBegin	12	18260959	1521746.66	89.12	67.60
glTexImage2D	11	1236677	112425.18	6.04	4.58
glVertex2f	1,911,971	400169	0.21	1.95	1.48
glReadPixels	5	304281	60856.25	1.48	1.13
glTexCoord2f	1,911,947	106575	0.06	0.52	0.39
glEvalMesh2	160	71704	448.15	0.35	0.27
CGLFlushDrawable	6	35604	5934.06	0.17	0.13
glBitmap	50	21515	430.32	0.11	0.08

Total elapsed GL function time: 20490519.91 µsec

Estimated % time in GL: 75.85%

Show slice: < 9 of 9 >   Context ID: All Contexts

Figure 11-13 `ptm1` OpenGL Statistics

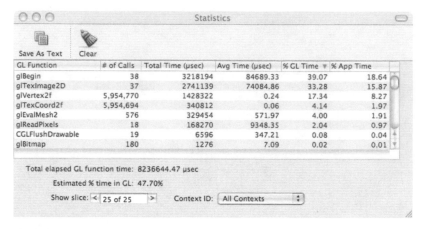

GL Function	# of Calls	Total Time (µsec)	Avg Time (µsec)	% GL Time ▼	% App Time
glBegin	38	3218194	84689.33	39.07	18.64
glTexImage2D	37	2741139	74084.86	33.28	15.87
glVertex2f	5,954,770	1428322	0.24	17.34	8.27
glTexCoord2f	5,954,694	340812	0.06	4.14	1.97
glEvalMesh2	576	329454	571.97	4.00	1.91
glReadPixels	18	168270	9348.35	2.04	0.97
CGLFlushDrawable	19	6596	347.21	0.08	0.04
glBitmap	180	1276	7.09	0.02	0.01

Total elapsed GL function time: 8236644.47 µsec

Estimated % time in GL: 47.70%

Show slice: |<| 25 of 25 |>| Context ID: | All Contexts ▲▼ |

Figure 11-14 `ptm2` OpenGL Statistics

Please Tune Me 2

Moving on to `ptm2.c`, we've remedied the texture type problem by replacing `GL_UNSIGNED_SHORT_4_4_4_4` with `GL_UNSIGNED_BYTE`. Again, we have twice the storage requirements but the type is hardware native. Running `ptm2` on our test system, we see more than one frame per second: Not earth-shattering, but a 200 percent improvement at least over the performance of `ptm1`.

If we're going to shatter earths, we need to keep tuning. Figure 11-14 shows an OpenGL Profiler look at `ptm2`.

Notice that the landscape has changed profoundly. As you improve certain areas of the code, other areas that were previously minor, such as the `glTexImage2D()` call at 6 percent become significant. We've reduced our `glBegin()` hit to 39 percent, but now our `glTexImage2D()` call has ballooned to 39 percent. We also have a new player in the list: `glVertex2f()` is weighing in at 17 percent OpenGL time.

Please Tune Me 3

To address the `glTexImage2D()` problem we saw in `ptm2.c`, `ptm3.c` moves the texture definition logic out of the rendering loop and into the initialization routine. In its place, we use texture binding. In effect, we've replaced immediate mode logic with retained mode logic. Making this retained mode change gave us a nice performance boost of 100 percent, moving us to nearly two frames per second. Still not a galactic contender, but we can now see the teapot tumbling.

Let's see what Profiler has to say about `ptm3` in Figure 11-15. With `ptm3`, we're seeing a nice fadeaway of `glTexImage2D()`. There's a new rogue at the top of

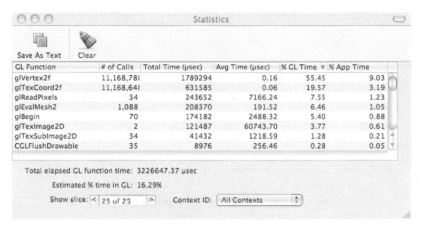

Figure 11-15 ptm3 OpenGL Statistics

our list now: glVertex2f() accounts for more than 55 percent of the time spent in OpenGL. Perhaps we can apply a retained mode technique for the glVertex2f() problem as well.

Please Tune Me 4

Please Tune Me 4 takes a huge stride forward relative to ptm3. By encapsulating the huge number of mesh vertices in a display list, we've avoided a tremendous amount of data copying, bus traffic, and function call overhead through OpenGL. Display lists are a very easy way to get big performance gains when rendering static geometry.

Making the display list change resulted in about an 1800 percent gain in performance—in the vicinity of 36 frames per second. Our little application is growing up! At this point, looking for more almost seems greedy, but let's indulge. Figure 11-16 shows the profile of ptm4:

The great thing about Profiler is the number of surprises it can uncover in your software. We've heard innumerable times, "I didn't even know I was calling that!" Often, the revelations are more subtle. In this case, glReadPixels() has made its way to the top of the list. Fortunately, there are ways to address this problem.

Please Tune Me 5

To subdue the glReadPixels() problem, ptm5 introduces pixel buffer objects (not to be confused with pbuffers). Pixel buffer objects (PBOs) can be used as

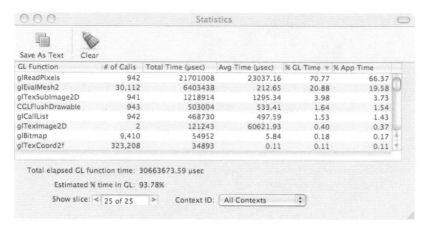

Figure 11-16 `ptm4` OpenGL Statistics

retained mode containers of pixel or texture data, which can then be sourced for rendering by texturing calls or `glDrawPixels()`.

In this case we've established the PBO as a container for reading the contents of the left side of the application window for later use as a texture on the teapot. Because this is a VRAM-managed resource, the readback operation is extremely fast. Notice that with the binding of the PBO, the data argument for `glReadPixels()` is 0 because the PBO is now being used as the destination for the read.

With the texture contents stored in the VBO, we still need to map the object and update it to preserve the "gray ramp" color teapot semantics described earlier. This is simply a matter of mapping, modifying, and unmapping the PBO. Later, when we wish to texture with the VBO, we bind it by using `GL_PIXEL_UNPACK_BUFFER` rather than the `GL_PIXEL_PACK_BUFFER` binding that we used when reading the pixels. Using PBOs for readback and as a texture source has brought Please Tune Me to more than 60 frames per second. Pretty soon we'll have to change the name to "Please Admire Me."

So what does our profile look like now (Figure 11-17)? We see what appears to be some more deferral overhead in the big spike at `CGLFlushDrawable`. We also have a big chunk sitting at `glEvalMesh2()`, which is a result of our call to `glutSolidTeapot`. Sticking with things under our immediate control, despite our PBO usage, we're still seeing a 16 percent hit in `glReadPixels()`.

Figure 11-17 ptm5 OpenGL Statistics

Please Tune Me 6

The final installment in our quest for ultimate performance is ptm6, which involves an architectural change. Sticking with the glReadPixels() track and considering some of the earlier performance tips, is there any way we can avoid reading this data back and touching it with the CPU altogether?

The answer is yes, and a fragment shader is the key to achieving this optimization. Simply put, during readback of the pixel data we apply a gray ramp to the texture data where it does not contain the colored-mesh readback information. A fragment shader with a texture sampler can easily evaluate this condition and apply the gray color for us.

Notice that we also change the filtering mode on the teapot texture to GL_NEAREST. This way we don't get any interpolation bleed-through when attempting to sample our texture and assign our gray color.

By eliminating the readback path altogether, "Please Admire Me" (ptm6) reaches frame rates in excess of 100 frames per second.

We've left one exercise for the reader. For ptm6.c, what could be done to improve the efficiency of the mesh rendering? We'll give you a hint: There's a more efficient way to draw quadrilaterals in OpenGL without using the GL_QUADS token to glBegin().

Summary

Many of the steps required to build a high-performance OpenGL application on OS X are shared with other platforms. Measures such as minimizing state changes, using retained mode rendering, and including other OpenGL "best practices" are platform-agnostic. To these known axioms, the Mac OS X OpenGL implementation is an industry leader with its plethora of asynchronous data submission interfaces and multithreaded OpenGL engine. Adding these capabilities to the great OpenGL diagnostic, performance, and debugging tools on OS X makes the platform first in its class for producing an optimally performing OpenGL application.

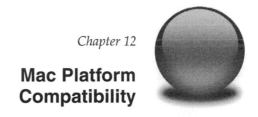

Chapter 12

Mac Platform Compatibility

Mac OS Versions

Mac OS X has evolved significantly over its life span, but OS X has featured OpenGL as a key piece of its foundation since day 1. As Mac OS X evolved, the operating system itself has assumed increasingly more heavy usage of the OpenGL layer, and the performance, features, and quality of the graphics subsystem have continually improved. In this chapter, we'll discuss which graphics and OpenGL pieces have changed and been added in various versions of Mac OS X since 10.0. We'll also explore the compatibility of the various OpenGL drivers and hardware, and introduce some ideas that will help you manage the evolution of OpenGL hardware and software.

10.0 through 10.1

In the beginning, there was 10.0. It was released in March 2001, and lo, it was good. But slow. But good! Versions 10.0 and 10.1 were Apple's first releases of Mac OS X and represented substantial leaps forward in architecture and design from OS 9 and earlier. In their first versions, however, they had rough spots and were not entirely complete. Because of the rapid evolution of the early OS X versions, OpenGL also evolved a lot in these early versions. Some would argue that Mac OS X wasn't really usable until 10.2; others would insist that the OpenGL implementation really firmed up around 10.3; and so on. We're not taking sides in that particular flamewar, so we'll focus our discussions on where things are today, and what you need to know to develop applications for the future. At the time of the writing of this book, considering targeting OpenGL applications for versions 10.0 and 10.1 is really a bad idea: These versions, and their OpenGL implementations, are so old as to be utterly obsoleted by later versions. They served their purpose well at the time and we appreciate their efforts, but time marches on, and so do we.

10.2 (Jaguar)

Jaguar was released in August 2002 and proved to be a really solid, fast, and finally almost complete version of Mac OS X. In the span of a little more than a year and a half, Mac OS X had improved from a fast but new operating system to a stable, fast, and widely supported operating system. Its performance had improved dramatically, too. Among the performance features added was an enhancement to its graphics layer Quartz, known as Quartz Extreme. Quartz Extreme promised (and mostly delivered) a great performance boost by offloading numerous UI elements to the graphics hardware. This was the first step Apple would publicly take that yielded insight into how the UI and window manager would evolve in the future.

10.3 (Panther)

Panther was released in October 2003. Apple continued to release numerous performance and feature enhancements, but among the most notable for graphics developers was the acceleration of UI elements through hardware (GPU) rendering. Version 10.3 added a few other features for OpenGL developers, including the ability to share a full-screen context with a windowed context on the Mac. As we've described earlier, context sharing means that resources in one context, such as textures and VBOs, can be used by another context without incurring extra memory overhead. Version 10.3's ability to share full and windowed contexts meant a resource optimization for applications that needed both modes to be supported.

Another new feature with 10.3 was the introduction of hardware-accelerated pixel buffers. Pixel buffer operations are known on many platforms as pbuffers, and on Mac OS X a specific extension exposed these hardware-accelerated off-screen render targets. That extension, which was named `GL_APPLE_pixel_buffer`, was really the underpinning of how Apple itself achieved UI acceleration.

10.4 (Tiger)

At the end of May 2005, Apple released Mac OS X 10.4, also known as Tiger. This particular evolution of the operating system offered some significant enhancements for those in the graphics world. In particular, Tiger brought high-level programmable shading languages to the Mac, the latest OpenGL Architecture Review Board extensions, and a continuing movement toward hardware-based acceleration of all elements of the UI through a technology known as Quartz 2D Extreme. Aside from the obvious performance benefits the later trend can provide to user experiences through the windowing system, it raises an interesting point for your application to consider: You are not alone. What we mean by this statement is that your application and the window system itself share the resources of the graphics card. As a consequence, both the graphics memory and the graphics bandwidth are in use by the UI and your application simultaneously. Thus you have fewer resources in both areas when it comes time to run your application, which has performance consequences. Another way of looking at this same problem is to state that your application should "play nicely" with the graphics hardware, as it will compete for resources with the window system. To do so, use best software practices, draw only when you need to, download data when only absolutely necessary, and so on. Not only will your application performance benefit from judicious use of graphics resources, but so will the rest of the user experience.

Beginning with version 10.4.4, Apple began officially supporting and shipping Intel-based Macs. This shift in the underlying processor marked the beginning of the latest processor transition for the Mac. Apple and Mac developers have weathered numerous processor transitions over the years, including switches from Motorola 680X0 processors to Motorola PowerPC 60X series processors to IBM/Motorola G3/G4/G5 processors and now to Intel processors. Why did Apple make this change? Theories abound, but a quote from Caroline Schoeder sums up one point of view: "Some people change when they see the light, others when they feel the heat." Said differently, the G5 was one hot processor— literally! Where there's heat, there's power being consumed, which has meant problems for laptop processors. The PowerBook platform, upon which I'm typing this very sentence, had relatively little performance gain for more than 2 years. Obviously, something had to change, to keep portables in the game.

But we digress! Apple has been willing to change binary formats and host platform many times over the years, but only most recently, with the change to Intel, has a true multiplatform binary been possible. A regular, native, PowerPC application can now run on an Intel processor through an emulation layer known as Rosetta. Rosetta essentially translates PowerPC code into Intel code at runtime, and only with relatively high-performance modern CPUs has it been possible to do this at runtime. The details behind this code translation layer aren't important, but suffice it to say that the performance of application running under Rosetta isn't nearly as good as the performance of a natively compiled application. It's good, to be sure—even remarkably good—but for performance-critical applications (and a typical OpenGL application is) native code is the only way to go. We'll have more to say on this later.

Beginning with 10.4.4, Apple developers no longer have the luxury (as with prior versions of 10.X) of assuming that they're running on a PowerPC chip—the possibility exists that an application may be running on either chip. Developers must account for this possibility because it affects many things, among them endianness, vector code acceleration, and inline-assembly tweaks. Primarily, however, it impacts performance.

10.5 and Beyond

Apple has announced its next revision in the Mac OS X sequence, 10.5, also known as Leopard. We know Leopard will fully support PowerPC and Intel Macs. Likely it will be faster, better, and more feature-complete in its OpenGL implementation. At least OpenGL 2.1 will be supported. Even more computation may be offloaded to the GPU, so that graphics developers need to be all the more conscientious about their place in the universe: Your application may not be the only one expecting to use the GPU and, in fact, may always be operating in conjunction with other GPU-intensive applications, specifically those within the Mac OS itself. However, if applications are well written and aren't resource gluttons, they should continue to perform well.

OpenGL Platform Identification

We've just talked a bit about the various changes evident among the versions of Mac OS X through the last few years, but let's not talk about how you can manage that change right now. In Chapter 13, we'll see a key way of managing change between OpenGL versions and ways of evolving your OpenGL functionality gracefully. But what do you do if something graceless is happening, for example, with a particular platform. For that matter, what is the definition of the OpenGL platform? We'll look at these questions, and even provide answers to them, in this section.

Earlier in this book we discussed the ways in which OpenGL is integrated with various window systems and APIs on the Mac. We looked at AGL, CGL, GLUT, and Cocoa, yet underpinning all of these systems was the same OpenGL code. Independently of how the image gets to the screen, the way we generate the image is the same—pure, sweet, light, graphics goodness: OpenGL. The windowing layer above OpenGL is an obviously essential element in using a particular platform. Yet OpenGL graphics commands are distinct, separate, and orthogonal to windowing systems. That is a key piece of what makes the original-design OpenGL so powerful.

Necessarily, then, we need ways of querying pieces of information about OpenGL itself, independently of the window system in which it integrates, and this information can be used to define the OpenGL. The OpenGL platform, as defined by the OpenGL specification, is the unique combination of two strings queried through the `glGetString` call. The OpenGL function `glGetString`

Table 12-1 glGetString Tokens

Token	Information
GL_VENDOR	The company responsible for this OpenGL implementation. Technically, despite what this string reports (frequently ATI or NVIDIA), Apple maintains the OpenGL driver and is the key contact for any questions or problems. This string can provide a useful hint in determining the underlying hardware used by this context.
GL_RENDERER	A specific name defining the hardware used by this OpenGL context.
GL_VERSION	OpenGL version information. Fields are space delimited within this string. The first field contains a version number of either the major.minor or major.minor.sub style. Additional fields are optional after this first one.
GL_EXTENSIONS	Extensions available on this platform. The list is space delimited.

accepts the tokens defined in Table 12-1 and can be used to get the results for the renderer and version; these results, when combined, uniquely define a target OpenGL graphics environment. Keep in mind that, as with any OpenGL call, you must invoke this query only from an active context.

So what are some results for this command? A sampling of a few graphics cards in our possession yielded strings like these:

- 1.5 ATI-1.4.18
- 1.1 APPLE-1.1

These strings can easily be parsed for extraction of the OpenGL version number and, therefore, for checking of baseline functionality, as seen in Chapter 13. But the entirety of the string, version, and renderer label completely define an OpenGL platform. On the Mac, it means that we're using a specific code path within a renderer. This is a useful piece of information to know not only when filing bugs, but also when fixing them in your own code. You can check this string at runtime. If some particular well-known problem exists in that renderer, you can then avoid that rendering path.

Mac OS Version Identification

We've seen how to query our OpenGL environment to determine its platform— now what about a particular version of the Mac OS itself? Can we determine its version, and when it is appropriate to use for functionality queries and testing? Turns out that there's a Carbon method that's been around since time immemorial for exactly this purpose. This method can tell you a lot of information on a lot of aspects of your running Mac system, but we'll use it for just the version number here. That Carbon call is `Gestalt`.

It has been said that brevity is the soul of wit, so we may therefore assume that the documentation of what the `Gestalt` method does is among the wittiest on the Mac. The documentation pages say that `Gestalt` "obtains information about the operating environment." Now, that's just the overview to the function, but really all `Gestalt` does is return information about your Mac environment. There is copious documentation on the zillions of queries that it can perform, but our token to query is `gestaltSystemVersion`. This query returns a `long` value with a hexadecimal representation of the Mac version. Note, however, that this value encodes the version in a somewhat stylized form, which is not directly usable as a value. For example, the return value for this function on Mac OS X 10.3.1 would be `0x1031` and on 10.4.4 would be `0x1044`.

We coded a quick little version in Example 12-1, which unpacks the major (in 10.X.Y, the X value) and the minor (in 10.X.Y, the Y-value) and returns the raw result. To use this function in your own application, make sure you include the `CarbonCarbon.h` header file and link against the Carbon framework.

Example 12-1 Unpack the OS X Version Number

```
long macOSXVersion( unsigned int *major, unsigned int *minor)
{
    long version = 0;
    Gestalt( gestaltSystemVersion, &version);
    *minor = version&0xf;
    *major = version&0xf0>>4;
    return( version );
}
```

A quick point of interest, for the curious: Which versions of Mac OS X have existed and been released? Apple maintains a complete list, including version numbers and build numbers, in Article Number 106176 [3]. Apple also maintains a really nice list of releases of hardware and software together in Article Number 25517 [11]. These pieces of information may prove useful when you are developing code that targets particular pieces of hardware and when your customers and clients need to debug your application.

When should you use this kind of query? If you're writing an application that must run on multiple versions of Mac OS X, and you're using some feature that you think might be available only on a particular version of the operating system, then this is what you'd do. There aren't a lot of reasons why you might search out version information, but working around a bug is one of them. Using undocumented API calls is another, but that wouldn't be a good idea in general. Finally, you expressly *don't* want to use this functionality to check for features with Cocoa applications. Cocoa has a well-defined mechanism (part of its overall runtime goodness) for inquiring as to whether a particular object or class responds to a particular method. These `respondsToSelector` and `instancesRespondToSelector` methods are thoroughly documented within Apple's developer documentation.

Summary

In this chapter we saw some of the differences between the various versions of Mac OS X, and we learned how to identify both the running Mac version and the OpenGL platform. With the combination of these identifying markers, you're well positioned to build features for specific combinations of Mac platform and OpenGL platform, to work around bugs, and to enable and disable features as appropriate. In Chapter 13, we'll dig into the details of customizing OpenGL rendering for particular versions of OpenGL. Taken in combination, these two chapters will show you how to exercise complete control over which features run on which platforms, for OpenGL and the Mac OS.

Chapter 13

OpenGL Extensions

Overview

In this chapter we'll discuss a design feature of OpenGL known as OpenGL extensions. We'll describe how these extensions work, how to discover which ones are available, and how to determine exactly how extensions operate. We'll also describe a few libraries for working with extensions that make your life as a developer easier. But first, what are extensions, and why do they exist?

Extensions are a mechanism that the OpenGL Architecture Review Board created for OpenGL to allow custom features beyond the scope of a particular version of OpenGL. They enable the creation of new features, modify existing features, expose capabilities on hardware that wasn't present when the current version of OpenGL was ratified, and more. In essence, an OpenGL extension describes features beyond the scope of the current base OpenGL version. That's part of why extensions exist—but there's another reason, and a fundamental one at that. If you'll indulge a minor rant, here's the more exhaustive scoop on the why of OpenGL extensions.

One complaint frequently leveled against OpenGL is that it is lagging the feature curve or is somehow farther off the leading edge than other APIs. The people who make such complaints often use other platforms and other APIs (we won't name names—cough ... Direct3D ... cough) and usually obtain new versions of their APIs every year or so. This is regarded as "progress" and developers who are enthralled with this model are usually quite excited to have access to new features. Unfortunately, making frequent changes to the underlying API requires developers to change code, implement new design patterns, and stay late at work. That's not such a great thing, especially if you're one of those developers.

Not only is the perception that other APIs advance more rapidly than OpenGL false, but OpenGL evolves in a way that developers have access to both features

253

and a compatibility path with older code. Thanks to a lot of really good up-front design in the OpenGL specification, OpenGL doesn't cause a major compatibility headache for the developer with each version[1] and, in fact, it handles growth and change in a very elegant and evolutionary fashion. The OpenGL mechanism for adding new features and evolving the API is known as the OpenGL process and is the focus of this chapter. We'll see how extensions are incorporated into OpenGL from a graphics vendor's perspective, which in turn yields insight into our second key goal in this chapter—how to use OpenGL extensions effectively.

Extension Design and API Integration

OpenGL extensions exist for a few key reasons:

- To allow OpenGL to evolve as fast as hardware developers push it
- To keep the core OpenGL API stable
- To give developers a consistent mechanism for accessing new features and capabilities
- To support feature, API, and usage compatibility across a wide variety of API versions and vendor hardware

These design parameters mean that if you work on the Mac, and on Linux, using whichever vendor's graphics hardware, you always use a very similar mechanism to access specific features of that hardware. Another implication is that if you are working on a platform that supports OpenGL 1.4, but the graphics hardware in that box has features that are not yet found in OpenGL 1.4, the vendor will provide extensions that enable you to use the full capabilities of that graphics card. Furthermore, if you stick to writing to the base of a core OpenGL version (say, 1.4) you can be assured that your results will be correct (barring bugs) on a variety of platforms, provided all of those platforms support that same version. Not to beat this point to death, but the OpenGL extension mechanism—and by implication, the core design of OpenGL—exists to help developers quickly write software that works wherever an application needs to be along the feature-functionality continuum.

Before we explore the actual extension mechanisms and methods, we should explain how extensions become parts of core OpenGL. An evolutionary process

---

1. This argument is the topic of an ongoing debate among OpenGL and DirectX programmers and all we've just done is pour a little more gasoline on the fire. Of course, the truth of the situation lies somewhere in the middle. However, despite the intense feelings on both sides, OpenGL has a well-defined and clear mechanism for handling growth and has done so very successfully for quite a long time.

takes once-bleeding-edge features and, over time, migrates them so that they become part of the OpenGL standard. Thus your application that uses extensions to OpenGL today may in the future be able to satisfy its needs using a particular version of core OpenGL.

But let's back up a step and describe how the core OpenGL specification evolves. There are many paths to adding functionality to the core of OpenGL, but the OpenGL API itself largely evolves through the process defined below. This process may be familiar to some, as it's modeled on School House Rock's "How a Bill Becomes a Law." We kid, of course, but the process is fairly democratic, and open to all good ideas from members of OpenGL's governing body, the OpenGL Architecture Review Board. Here's the process for a hypothetical new feature:

1. A new hardware or software feature exists.
2. A vendor creates an OpenGL extension: `GL_APPLE_new_feature_name`. This is known as a *vendor extension*.
3. A specification is published describing tokens and API entry points.
4. Time elapses . . .
5. Other vendors adopt the vendor extension, and `GL_APPLE_new_feature_name` becomes available on several platforms, at which point it is promoted from a vendor extension to an "EXT" extension.
6. Several vendors lobby the OpenGL Architecture Review Board to standardize the EXT extension as `GL_ARB_new_feature_name`. The extension is then known as an "ABB" extension.
7. Time elapses. . . .
8. The extension's purpose and utility become very clear to many developers and vendors.
9. A quorum of vendors lobbies the OpenGL Architecture Review Board again to include this ARB extension in the next version of the official OpenGL specification.
10. The extension is incorporated into core OpenGL X.Y.
11. The extension may or may not continue to exist in versions beyond OpenGL X.Y.

Of course, not all steps in this process are required, nor do all extensions wend their way through this entire process. Many never make it past the stage of a vendor defining and implementing a vendor-specific extension. Only if an extension is really useful to a wide variety of developers does it survive to become part of the OpenGL specification.

One further note: Even if you find an extension useful, but it's not yet an OpenGL Architecture Review Board extension, you may still use it with hope for its future. Even when an extension grows up, moving from an EXT to an ARB (sometimes from vendor straight to ARB) and finally into the specification itself, the older ways of identifying it will still exist. Specifically, the OpenGL specification says this on extension promotion:

> ARB extensions can be promoted to required core features in later revisions of OpenGL. When this occurs, the extension specifications are merged into the core specification. Functions and enumerants that are part of such promoted extensions will have the ARB affix removed.
>
> GL implementations of such later revisions should continue to export the name strings of promoted extensions in the EXTENSIONS string, and continue to support the ARB-affixed versions of functions and enumerants as a transition aid.

Now that we've seen the process that an extension goes through from concept to core OpenGL, what happens in the middle? That is, what does an extension define and provide, how do you determine what's available, and how do you implement an extension? Let's look at these issues in order.

Extension Styles and Types

OpenGL extensions have many different forms and usage patterns. Some extensions define new tokens for use with existing functions. One example is GL_ARB_texture_mirrored_repeat, which defines a new token for use with the glTexParameter suite of calls, allowing a new type of GL_TEXTURE_WRAP style: GL_MIRRORED_REPEAT_ARB. Other extensions define new API functions. A good but complex example is the extensions for the OpenGL Shading Language (GLSL). This language actually consists of a suite of extensions, including GL_ARB_shader_objects, GL_ARB_vertex_shader, GL_ARB_fragment_shader, and GL_ARB_shading_language_120. These extensions define both tokens (e.g., GL_OBJECT_COMPILE_STATUS_ARB) and API entry points (e.g., glCompileShaderARB, glLinkProgramARB).

In essence, then, there are two styles of extensions:

- Extensions that define only tokens
- Extensions that define API entry points and (optionally) tokens

This classification is important to understanding how to use particular extensions. Token-only extensions are a bit easier to use, as no special runtime function binding needs to occur, and you can simply pass these tokens to your existing OpenGL commands. For those extensions defining entry points, a slightly more complex procedure is necessary first to safely determine the function pointers and then to use them. We'll get into that issue soon. First we'll look at how to pick an extension from the many choices available, especially as some come in several versions even on the same platform!

Identification, Selection, Query, and Usage

Deciding which extension to use can warrant entire books by itself. The sheer number and similarity of the many extensions in existence makes this a daunting process. In this section we'll explain how you determine which extensions are available and how you decide which one is preferred in your particular case. Though there's no quick answer given all the parameters you must consider, there's always the phrase you might hear running through your head when shopping for a yacht (a problem the authors would love to have): "If you have to ask, you can't afford it." We're kidding again, but the point is that while owning and using a yacht may have certain benefits, it's an expensive proposition. Likewise, using OpenGL extensions carry a variety of direct and indirect costs, including development time, compatibility evaluation, and testing. As should be obvious by now, extensions can be vendor-, platform-, and driver-specific, and your development, test, and maintenance costs will inevitably increase as you try to manage that complexity. Thus the first rule of thumb is to be very thorough in your exploration of the core OpenGL API to determine whether there's a way to meet your needs using just the base API. If you must use extensions, however, you must then choose among the many options that exist. To guide you in this process, we'll explore some of the criteria to decide which extension to use.

We typically begin by deciding what our priority for using this particular extension will be. For example, are we most interested in performance, cross-platform availability, or ease of development? Each of these tacks (if we may be allowed to continue the sailing metaphor) implies a different priority regarding which extensions to investigate. We'll focus on each in turn, and suggest strategies for choosing among the various options.

Selecting Extensions

Whether your application is to be deployed on a single Mac platform (for example, a desktop system only), across the entire Mac line, or even on multiple platforms, your deployment target will most likely evolve over time. Making any assumptions about what's available in OpenGL at the moment you build and ship your software is a poor idea. As the saying goes, "Trust, but verify." Probably the safest, best, and easiest way to deploy a cross-platform application is to rely solely on a baseline version of OpenGL to provide all of the application's functionality. For example, choose a baseline of OpenGL 1.5 and use features only natively defined therein—no extensions. If you can stick to that criterion, you're in really good shape because a simple combination of compile-time and runtime checks will get you access to all the features you require.

In a real-world application, you'll likely want to use some newer OpenGL features in subsequent revisions to your application, so you may have access to these features on only some platforms, and in extension form. In this case, we recommend you choose extensions based on the OpenGL Architecture Review Board extension evolution process. By this, we mean that the OpenGL ARB extension process defines the evolution of an extension, from concept to core OpenGL. To be explicit, in a cross-platform or even a cross-Mac application, the most compatible ways of choosing which features and extensions to use are, in order:

1. Features satisfied by the core OpenGL version
2. Features satisfied by an ARB extension
3. Features satisfied by an EXT extension
4. Features satisfied by a vendor extension (e.g., ATI, nV, sGI)

In essence, there are three steps to choosing which extensions your application will use. First, choose which fundamental features your application needs, and which combinations of core OpenGL versions and extensions satisfy those needs. Decide which of those combinations will be the preferred path, the alternative path, and the fallback. The fallback may not actually satisfy those features, so instead of the feature you want, you should choose a plausible standby visualization—for example, simple texture versus shaded surface. Second, write code to make sure your application will compile, regardless of which OpenGL tokens are available in the headers on the system on which you're building. This means you should protect reserved tokens by using a combination of preprocessor tokens. Third, write code for runtime validation of the features and fallback path you're interested in using.

We'll now look at this process concretely and with code. Our first step is to choose the extensions and the preferred combination of OpenGL version and extensions, an alternative combination of OpenGL version and extensions, and a fallback visualization, if neither the preferred nor the alternative path is available. In this example, we will begin with our standby quad visualization code and decide to shade it.

What combination of extensions and versions will satisfy our needs? Well, we look at the latest OpenGL specification for guidance. The OpenGL specification is available at the OpenGL website [2]; for this example, we'll use the OpenGL 2.0 specification [1] as our baseline. Shading is supported natively in this version, so our preferred path will be to use OpenGL 2.0. We then look back in earlier versions referenced by the specification, and find that prior to this version of OpenGL, shading existed only as extensions. Because we're likely to use shaders in combination with multiple textures, we look at where we can satisfy that need as well, and we find that multitexture is a core capability of OpenGL 1.3.

Thus our alternative path will be OpenGL 1.3 plus the required extensions for shading, `GL_ARB_shading_language_100`, `GL_ARB_program_objects`, `GL_ARB_vertex_shader`, and `GL_ARB_fragment_shader`.

For simplicity, we will handle only this alternative rendering path in our application. Handling OpenGL 2.0 and OpenGL 1.3 requires a fair bit of API management, as the entry points for shading are similar, but different enough that there's a fair bit of confusion. We could continue to use the extension,[2] even if we were using OpenGL 2.0 , so we'll just present basic principles, follow the 1.3 path, and provide one fallback.

Good! So far we've chosen and figured out two of our three path elements. The final step is determining a fallback visualization. We will not explore the depths of OpenGL Shading Language shading, nor all the ways you could possibly simulate versions of your shaded visualization via OpenGL techniques. Instead, we'll again opt for a simple solution: We'll write shaders to transform the quad as the standard OpenGL pipeline would, and color it with a constant color. For illustration purposes, we will color our quad green if no shading is available (our fallback visualization) and color it yellow if shading is available. It's not a shiny, bumpy, infinitely detailed, anti-aliased shader, but it gets the point across.

The second step is to write the combination of preprocessor token-checking operations to ensure that, regardless of the machine on which we build our application (even one without proper extension headers), the application still builds properly. This may be something you want to leave broken (at least for now) because if you do build your application in an environment without proper tokens, you won't get the behavior you want from your application on any platform. We explicitly handle this possibility by adding an `#error` message in the case that our OpenGL extension preprocessor checks fail. It will warn us that the environment is not configured properly.

Next, we look at the tokens we need, based on our criteria for our OpenGL environment defined earlier. Table 13-1 shows our combination of preferred and alternative rendering path preprocessor tokens. There's a fairly straightforward naming convention for preprocessor tokens in OpenGL, as the table illustrates.

---

2. Apple, in a very vague and informal way, in TechNote 2080 [6] says, "No extension should ever be removed from the extensions string," as part of a larger discussion about when an extension should be used and when a core version of OpenGL should be used. Theoretically and currently, you can continue to use the shader extensions, even in the latest version of OpenGL. However, as we've seen with PowerPC, and with lots of API changes over the years, all good things must come to an end: While this is the case today, it may not always be. The authors recommend that you try to use core OpenGL features whenever possible, and modernize your code to take advantage of these features directly, rather than hoping that your extensions will always exist.

Table 13-1 Preprocessor Tokens for Extension Usage

Path	OpenGL Token	Extension Token
Preferred	GL_VERSION_2_0	None
Alternative	GL_VERSION_1_3	GL_ARB_shading_language_100, GL_ARB_program_objects, GL_ARB_vertex_shader, GL_ARB_fragment_shader
Fallback	Any	None

But in code, how do we wrap things? Well, anywhere code uses either tokens or API entry points specified by these extensions, we need to check for their existence prior to using that code. These tokens come from different places on different platforms. On the Mac, all of the necessary extension tokens and OpenGL version information are included with the gl.h header file. On other platforms, such as Windows, Linux, and other versions of Unix, a similar situation may exist or there may be a companion glext.h header file. The Mac also has a glext.h header file, although the baseline gl.h header files already include these tokens.

At this point in the discussion, it turns out that bootstrapping the rest of the way to a functional chunk of code is required to fully explain and demonstrate how to use preprocessor and runtime checks. We're in a bit of "chicken or egg" bind, so we will simply show the code for shading setup without further ado. We're going to look at Example 13-1. We'll gloss over a few runtime details here, and focus on the preprocessing elements for now. We'll circle around to the runtime checks momentarily.

First, let's look at an overview of this example. The code does three things, two of which we've seen before. The shading section begins by checking the method hasShaderExtensions to see if our platform has shader extension support. We won't dig into the hasShaderExtensions check now, as we're just looking at compile-time checks in this section. What do we see within this block? Essentially, we validate that our compiler and header support at least OpenGL 1.3 and the required shader extensions. Within that block, the API and token definitions for baseline OpenGL 1.3 and all the shader extensions are defined. Things get more complex when we try to intermingle various versions of OpenGL support. With OpenGL and shading, in particular, some of the API entry points change—which is why we're not looking at that issue here. Within the block, then, we do the things necessary to load, compile, link, and bind our shaders. These are all fairly commonplace shader operations, and the interested reader can find a much more detailed discussion of how those pieces work in a companion book in this series [21].

Finally, an `else` clause performs our preprocessing checks. We took this tack because if we fail to compile this code, no shader code will ever be executed—even on platforms that support it! Our preprocessing checks really just validate that we know how to build our application so that it can move on to the next step—runtime checking for these extensions, which we look at in the next section.

Example 13-1 Querying for Extensions in a Valid OpenGL Context

```
- (void) prepareOpenGL
{
    // setup projection
    glMatrixMode( GL_PROJECTION );
    glLoadIdentity();
    glOrtho(-1,1,-1,1,-1,100);

    // do we have shading extensions?
    NSLog( @"Has OpenGL Shader: %d\n", [ self hasShaderExtensions ] );

    if( TRUE == [ self hasShaderExtensions ] )
    {
        //
        NSBundle *res = [ NSBundle mainBundle ];
        NSString *fragsource = [ NSString stringWithContentsOfFile:
            [ res pathForResource:@"test" ofType:@"frag" ] ];
        NSString *vertsource = [ NSString stringWithContentsOfFile:
            [ res pathForResource:@"test" ofType:@"vert" ] ];

        const char * fragsource_c = [ fragsource UTF8String ];
        const char * vertsource_c = [ vertsource UTF8String ];

#if defined( GL_VERSION_1_3 ) && \
    defined( GL_ARB_shader_objects ) && \
    defined( GL_ARB_shading_language_100 ) && \
    defined( GL_ARB_vertex_shader ) && \
    defined( GL_ARB_fragment_shader )

        vertexShader =
            glCreateShaderObjectARB( GL_VERTEX_SHADER_ARB );
        fragmentShader =
            glCreateShaderObjectARB( GL_FRAGMENT_SHADER_ARB );

        glShaderSourceARB( vertexShader, 1, &vertsource_c, NULL );
        glShaderSourceARB( fragmentShader, 1, &fragsource_c, NULL );

        glCompileShaderARB( vertexShader );
        glCompileShaderARB( fragmentShader );

        programObject = glCreateProgramObjectARB();

        glAttachObjectARB( programObject, vertexShader );
        glAttachObjectARB( programObject, fragmentShader );
```

```
            glLinkProgramARB( programObject );
            glUseProgramObjectARB( programObject );

#else
#error "NO shading will be available."
#endif
        }
        // add a timer to oscillate the modelview
        NSTimeInterval ti = .1;
        [ NSTimer scheduledTimerWithTimeInterval: ti
                                         target: self
                                       selector: @selector(angleUpdate:)
                                       userInfo: nil
                                        repeats: YES ];
}
```

Utilization and Binding

An astute reader will notice that in the prior section we just checked that the API entry points exist in headers at compile time. If our OpenGL library doesn't actually export those entries, we'll fail at link time or runtime with some form of unresolved symbol error. That's not a good thing for a well-behaved application to do, so how can we ensure at runtime that we've got a valid environment (as defined by our OpenGL level and extensions) in which to run? We perform a variety of checks, specifically those shown in Examples 13-2 and 13-3.

The basic process for ensuring that our runtime environment is valid is this: Query the version number, and query the extension list to confirm that our shading extensions are available. Because these are runtime checks, they must take place within a valid OpenGL context, so we perform them within prepareOpenGL, seen in Example 13-2. We first check whether our running OpenGL version is inclusively greater than 1.3, our baseline version for OpenGL functionality.

Example 13-2 Querying the OpenGL Version Number

```
- (float) openGLVersionNumber
{
    NSString *versionstring =
        [ NSString stringWithUTF8String:
            (char*)glGetString( GL_VERSION ) ];
    NSArray *versioncomponents =
        [ versionstring componentsSeparatedByString: @" " ];
    return( [ [ versioncomponents objectAtIndex: 0 ] floatValue ] );
}
```

The next code fragment, in Example 13-3, uses our extension dictionary to query for four key components of the OpenGL Shading Language. Each of these

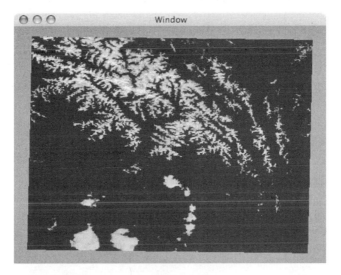

Figure 13-1 Shader Extension Application Results if Successful (Texture courtesy of NASA's Earth Observatory.)

extensions implies a combination of tokens, API entry points, and functionality.[3] This code first builds a list of OpenGL extensions, queried by the call `glGet-String( GL_EXTENSIONS )`, and then wrangles this list into a dictionary, as shown in Example 13-4. We simply look up a value in the dictionary (for example, `GL_ARB_vertex_shader`), and if a `nil` comes back, we don't have the extension. Conversely, if all our extension queries succeed, then we're off and running. Example 13-3 calls the `hasShaderExtensions` method and, upon its success, calls the various methods required to configure the shaders. If your environment is configured with the baseline OpenGL and shading extensions, you'll see a result like that in Figure 13-1; if not, you'll see our "fallback" rendering, the baseline material color, as in Figure 13-2.

Example 13-3 Querying for OpenGL Shader Extensions

```
- (BOOL) hasShaderExtensions
{
    BOOL has_shading = FALSE;
```

---

3. Because of some peculiarities in the Apple's implementation of this shading language, only the first three are really necessary to use shading. The last extension, `GL_ARB_shading_language_100`, defines whether the language is fully supported, and different graphics vendors interpret this differently. Apple interprets it to mean that while the shading stuff works, its implementation (at the time of this writing) is not completely compatible with the language flavor defined in that extension. Other vendors expose this token despite the completeness or capability of their implementations. Details, details. A truly portable application would ensure that all four tokens were available and run only if that is the case.

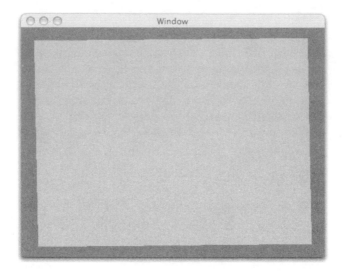

Figure 13-2 Shader Extension Application Results if Unsuccessful

```
float versionfloat = [ self openGLVersionNumber ];
if ( versionfloat >= 1.21 )
{
    NSDictionary *extdict = createExtensionDictionary();
    BOOL has_vs = [ extdict objectForKey:
        @"GL_ARB_vertex_shader" ] != nil;
    BOOL has_fs = [ extdict objectForKey:
        @"GL_ARB_fragment_shader" ] != nil;
    BOOL has_so = [ extdict objectForKey:
        @"GL_ARB_shader_objects" ] != nil;
    BOOL has_lang = [ extdict objectForKey:
        @"GL_ARB_shading_language_100" ] != nil;
    has_shading = has_vs && has_fs && has_so;
}
return( has_shading );
}
```

Example 13-4 Creating a Dictionary of All Extensions

```
NSDictionary * createExtensionDictionary()
{
    NSString *extstring =
        [ NSString stringWithUTF8String:
            (char*)glGetString( GL_EXTENSIONS ) ];
    NSArray *extensions =
        [ extstring componentsSeparatedByString: @" " ];
    NSDictionary *extdict =
        [ NSDictionary dictionaryWithObjects: extensions
                                    forKeys: extensions ];
    return( extdict );
}
```

One final note about extensions that export API entries: What happens at runtime? We've seen how we check for the validity of a particular extension at compile, link, and runtimes, but where are the symbols defined on the platform on which we're now running? What guarantees do we have about symbol definitions being valid? On the Mac, there's an implicit guarantee that if you have the extension defined and are linked with the OpenGL library, you'll have proper symbol resolution for all symbols exported by that extension. That's all there is to it—if you're a Mac-only developer, life is pretty easy.

What about other platforms? What about a "standard" way of resolving symbols across a variety of platforms? It turns out there are a variety of ways to look up symbols at runtime on the Mac. The technique we need here is a query of our loaded address space for a symbol matching the one that we want to use. In our series of examples, we're interested in building shaders, so we'll look for the symbol for glCompileShaderARB prior to using it. We'll focus on only the most modern techniques for symbol resolution in this chapter, as we're making this discussion as forward-looking as possible. If you need to target version 10.3 or earlier, there are well-documented techniques for querying and binding symbols [5]. In version 10.4 and beyond, Apple has integrated the dlopen/dlsym standard Unix-like technique for symbol loading and binding. It's pretty easy to do, so let's take a look how it works.

The two functions dlopen and dlsym constitute a standard external symbol addition and resolution package, integrated natively in 10.4 and found as part of an external dlcompat library in 10.3. The nice thing about this API is that you can find it on many other platforms, including Linux and most versions of Unix. The two functions have detailed manual pages, which you can read for exhaustive detail on how they operate. The overview of their function is simple, though. The first function, dlopen, links and loads a dynamic chunk of code. The second function, dlsym, finds and resolves a named symbol within that code. Thus in Example 13-6 first we use dlopen to get a handle to our running application, and then we use dlsym to resolve the passed-in function name. If we get a NULL back, the symbol doesn't exist and we shouldn't call it, unless we want a hasty exit from our application.

Two final notes on the dl* calls. First, notice that we symmetrically dlclose at the end of our resolveSymbol function. This is absolutely a good and necessary thing to do, but for performance reasons, you'd prefer to dlopen/dlclose once and resolve a lot of symbols in the middle. For our example, we do it for every symbol, within our resolveSymbol method, as a demonstration, and for simplicity. There isn't a huge performance penalty, however, because you don't/shouldn't/wouldn't call these methods each time you need a symbol. Instead, you would cache the result of resolveSymbol (which is a function address) and simply use those cached results later in your run loop.

The second note on these calls relates to the symbol names. Function names within libraries are changed (or, in compiler terms, mangled) into another form stored within those libraries. The mangling scheme is usually something you can learn about and figure out, but the `dl*` calls are designed to work with the human-readable versions of these names. For example, in one current version of the OpenGL library on one of our development machines, the symbol corresponding to the API entry `glCompileShaderARB` is named `_glCompileShaderARB`. The string you'd pass to the `dlsym` call would *not* be this mangled name, but rather the human-readable function name. The `dlsym` call would then mangle and resolve the name appropriately.

Now let's see the code that uses the `dlopen`/`dlsym`/`dlclose` API from start to finish. First, in Example 13-5 we extend our class definition to provide storage for the symbols. We allocate space for each of the symbols we use in our `prepareOpenGL` method, as seen in Example 13-8. Looking at this code segment, we see that we have the same preproccessor checks as before but add one more runtime check to see if we've successfully bound the symbols we require to proceed. If we pass the extension check, we call `resolveShaderSymbols`, as seen in Example 13-7, to resolve and cache the function entry symbols, and finally we invoke our shader code. The code in Example 13-7 simply calls the method we constructed earlier, `resolveSymbol`, to check whether each named symbol is available.

There's a lot of code here, but it really does three simple things, in a general form that you can follow for your own extension wrangling:

1. Resolve symbols for each extension API entry.
2. Validate that *all* symbols exist together, for complete definition and usage of that extension.
3. Store extension function pointers and use them later.

Example 13-5 Storage for the Discovered Symbols

```
@interface MyOpenGLView : NSOpenGLView
{
    bool hasShader;
    float time;
    float angle;
    GLhandleARB vShader, fShader, programObject;

    GLhandleARB (*myglCreateShaderObjectARB)( GLenum );
    void (*myglShaderSourceARB)();
    void (*myglCompileShaderARB)();
    GLhandleARB (*myglCreateProgramObjectARB)();
    void (*myglAttachObjectARB)();
    void (*myglLinkProgramARB)();
    void (*myglUseProgramObjectARB)();
}
```

```
- (BOOL) resolveShaderSymbols;
- (BOOL) hasExtension: (NSString*) ext inExtensions: (NSArray*) exts;
- (BOOL) hasShaderExtensions;
- (float) openGLVersionNumber;
- (void) angleUpdate: (NSTimer*) tt;
- (void) reshape;

@end
```

Example 13-6 Opening a Segment for Symbol Lookup

```
void * resolveSymbol( char * symname )
{
    void *lib = dlopen( (const char *)0L, RTLD_LAZY | RTLD_GLOBAL );
    void *sym = dlsym( lib, symname );
    dlclose( lib );
    return( sym );
}
```

Example 13-7 Looking Up Symbols

```
- (BOOL) resolveShaderSymbols
{
    myglCreateShaderObjectARB =
        resolveSymbol( "glCreateShaderObjectARB" );
    myglShaderSourceARB =
        resolveSymbol( "glShaderSourceARB" );
    myglCompileShaderARB =
        resolveSymbol( "glCompileShaderARB" );
    myglCreateProgramObjectARB =
        resolveSymbol( "glCreateProgramObjectARB" );
    myglAttachObjectARB =
        resolveSymbol( "glAttachObjectARB" );
    myglLinkProgramARB =
        resolveSymbol( "glLinkProgramARB" );
    myglUseProgramObjectARB =
        resolveSymbol( "glUseProgramObjectARB" );

    return( myglCreateShaderObjectARB &&
            myglShaderSourceARB &&
            myglCompileShaderARB &&
            myglCreateProgramObjectARB &&
            myglAttachObjectARB &&
            myglLinkProgramARB &&
            myglUseProgramObjectARB );
}
```

Example 13-8 Our Application's OpenGL Initialization Code

```
- (void) prepareOpenGL
{

    // setup projection
    glMatrixMode( GL_PROJECTION );
```

```
    glLoadIdentity();
    glOrtho(-1,1,-1,1,-1,100);

    // do we have shading extensions?
    if( ( TRUE == [ self hasShaderExtensions ] ) &&
        ( TRUE == [ self resolveShaderSymbols ] ) )
    {
        // load shader from disk (bundle)
        NSBundle *res = [ NSBundle mainBundle ];
        NSString *fragfile = [ res pathForResource:@"test"
                                            ofType:@"frag" ];
        NSString *vertfile = [ res pathForResource:@"test"
                                            ofType:@"vert" ];
        NSString *fragsource =
            [ NSString stringWithContentsOfFile: fragfile ];
        NSString *vertsource =
            [ NSString stringWithContentsOfFile: vertfile ];

        const char * fragsource_c = [ fragsource UTF8String ];
        const char * vertsource_c = [ vertsource UTF8String ];

#if defined( GL_VERSION_1_3 ) && \
    defined( GL_ARB_shader_objects ) && \
    defined( GL_ARB_shading_language_100 ) && \
    defined( GL_ARB_vertex_shader ) && \
    defined( GL_ARB_fragment_shader )

        vShader = myglCreateShaderObjectARB( GL_VERTEX_SHADER_ARB );
        fShader = myglCreateShaderObjectARB( GL_FRAGMENT_SHADER_ARB );

        myglShaderSourceARB( vShader, 1, &vertsource_c, NULL );
        myglShaderSourceARB( fShader, 1, &fragsource_c, NULL );

        myglCompileShaderARB( vShader );
        myglCompileShaderARB( fShader );

        programObject = myglCreateProgramObjectARB();

        myglAttachObjectARB( programObject, vShader );
        myglAttachObjectARB( programObject, fShader );

        myglLinkProgramARB( programObject );
        myglUseProgramObjectARB( programObject );

#else
    #error "No shading available."
#endif
    }

    // add a timer to oscillate the modelview
    NSTimeInterval ti = .1;
    [ NSTimer scheduledTimerWithTimeInterval: ti
                                      target: self
                                    selector: @selector(angleUpdate:)
```

```
                          userInfo: nil
                          repeats. YES ],
}
```

We've now seen how to determine which extensions to use; when they're appropriate; when you should use the baseline OpenGL versus extensions; which checks to perform for compile-, link-, and run-time correctness; and how to dynamically bind symbols. In essence, we've taken the complete tour of OpenGL extension selection and usage and shown how a lot of plumbing fits together. We'll now look at a simpler way to do things—that is, letting someone else do all the work for us in a cross-platform extension toolkit.

Extension Management Libraries

In prior sections we looked at native ways of dealing with extensions on the Mac, from the compile-time to runtime means of checking and using them. During this exploration, we made clear some of the complexity that is extension (and version) management in OpenGL, and we offered advice on some ways to manage that complexity. All of the express ways of managing extensions—from preprocessor token checks to dynamic symbol loading and executing—are perfectly fine for managing extensions. In fact, if you're using only a few extensions, manually checking for them may be the easiest way to get up and running, as our example has shown. However, if you write a large application and use a variety of extensions, you'll eventually end up writing a lot of code just to manage extensions. At that point, you might start to wonder why you bothered in the first place because you're spending a lot of time writing infrastructure and not a lot of time writing the next Killer App. Fortunately, a variety of people over the years have encountered this same OpenGL extension management issue, and decided to do something about it.

In this section, we'll present two toolkits with capability for extension management: GLUT and an open-source project called the GL Extension Wrangler (GLEW). GLEW and GLUT both wrap up the techniques we've discussed earlier, not just for the Mac but on a variety of platforms. Both are a great way to get up and running with extensions to OpenGL without writing the infrastructure yourself. Other choices are also available out there, in the wilds, as every few years someone else decides to take a crack at writing the definitive extension management toolkit. Apple even has its own version of something like GLEW, though it's just example code. Apple has written a little tool it calls glCheck. If you're interested in learning the details of ways of managing extensions, it's worth a look [6].

Because GLEW and GLUT are supported on multiple platforms, those tools are preferable, in the authors' estimation. However, all OpenGL extension and feature management toolkits tend to perform the same basic functions, so at the time of this writing, GLEW will be our preferred toolkit due to its comprehensive nature and modernity. Now, if you're roped into thinking, "Man, 'insert-extension-management-API-name-here' stinks (GLEW, for example); I guess I'll just have to rewrite my own toolkit from the ground up," we hope you'll at least first consider trying to work with the authors of the package you choose in an effort to make it better.

Okay, we now step down from our high horse. Let's first look at the tool GLEW and then explore an example in which we use it in an application.

GLEW

GLEW is a toolkit comprising a library for extension management and a few tools for introspection of system graphics capabilities. GLEW is a cross-platform tool that will build on Windows, Linux, various UNIXes, and, of course, the Mac. In addition to handling extensions for OpenGL, GLEW manages extensions for window system layers such as WGL for Windows and GLX for X-Windows systems. Our focus on using GLEW here will be on the OpenGL extension management aspects of the library.

GLEW builds and maintains a list of current OpenGL extension tokens and extension API entry points upon initialization of the library. The token list GLEW builds can be used to directly query whether a particular extension exists; if you prefer, you can also perform functional queries to test for groups of functionality. GLEW names tokens for extensions by defining a companion token to the extension of interest in which the GLEW prefix replaces the GL prefix. For instance, as per our earlier shader example, GLEW defines `GLEW_ARB_fragment_shader` to correspond to the `GL_ARB_fragment_shader` extension. If this token exists, a user is able to use all the functionality that this extension provides.

GLEW also provides all the basic compile-time definitions needed for an application—for example, the tokens defined by a particular extension. At runtime, when the library is initialized, GLEW resolves the symbols for each of the functions defined by a particular extension. It does so by exploiting the same Core foundation methods that we used to do this task ourselves earlier. However, GLEW does this for each and every extension known in the universe (or at least known to GLEW as of the version you're using).

In summary, GLEW defines all aspects of the extensions known to it at the time the library was created, including both extension tokens and extension functional bindings. That's a fair bit of complexity, but it's nicely wrapped, and using the library to query extensions is very straightforward.

To use GLEW in an application, there are several ways of accomplishing the same tasks. We'll look at one approach that's a close analog of the way we previously investigated shader support in an earlier example. The basic process is this:

1. Initialize the library: `glewInit()`.
2. Query for a particular extension: `if ( GL_TRUE == GL_ARB_shader_objects)`.
3. Use that extension and its API calls: `glCreateProgramObjectARB()`.

We'll perform those steps in conjunction with using OpenGL Shading Language shaders with our basic example as before. We begin with our prior example but change the headers from including the GL extensions to including the GLEW header, as shown in Example 13-9. The only caveat with GLEW is that because of the way it manages extensions, it must include its header before any other OpenGL header, as our example does.

Next, we modify our `prepareOpenGL` routine to initialize GLEW, and then prepare our shaders as before, pending success. As you look at the code for Example 13-10, you'll notice that the only difference between this version and our last version is that we initialize GLEW. We preserve our compile-time checks, on the off-chance that we're building under some broken environment; this strategy will help us catch that error early. The runtime aspects are identical to the earlier code: We just call the various OpenGL shading functions. Simple enough, so we look at the next place where we had extension information—namely, the method that checks whether the extension is valid, found in `hasShaderExtensions` (Example 13-11).

Example 13-9 GLEW Headers

```
#include <GL/glew.h>
#include <OpenGL/gl.h>
#include <GLUT/glut.h>
```

Example 13-10 Our Application's OpenGL Initialization Code Using GLEW

```
- (void) prepareOpenGL
{
    GLenum err = glewInit();
    if ( GLEW_OK != err )
    {
        NSLog( @"GLEW Error: %s\n", glewGetErrorString( err ) );
    }
    NSLog( @"Status: Using GLEW %s\n", glewGetString( GLEW_VERSION ) );

    glMatrixMode( GL_PROJECTION );
    glLoadIdentity();
    glOrtho(-1,1,-1,1,-1,100);
```

```
    // do we have shading extensions?
    NSLog( @"Has OpenGL Shader: %d\n", [ self hasShaderExtensions ] );
    if( TRUE == [ self hasShaderExtensions ] )
    {
        NSBundle *res = [ NSBundle mainBundle ];
        NSString *fragsource = [ NSString stringWithContentsOfFile:
                [ res pathForResource:@"test" ofType:@"frag" ] ];
        NSString *vertsource = [ NSString stringWithContentsOfFile:
        [ res pathForResource:@"test" ofType:@"vert" ] ];

        const char * fragsource_c = [ fragsource UTF8String ];
        const char * vertsource_c = [ vertsource UTF8String ];

#if defined( GL_VERSION_1_3 ) && \
    defined( GL_ARB_shader_objects ) && \
    defined( GL_ARB_shading_language_100 ) && \
    defined( GL_ARB_vertex_shader ) && \
    defined( GL_ARB_fragment_shader )

        vertexShader =
            glCreateShaderObjectARB( GL_VERTEX_SHADER_ARB );
    fragmentShader =
            glCreateShaderObjectARB( GL_FRAGMENT_SHADER_ARB );

    glShaderSourceARB( vertexShader, 1, &vertsource_c, NULL );
    glShaderSourceARB( fragmentShader, 1, &fragsource_c, NULL );

    glCompileShaderARB( vertexShader );
    glCompileShaderARB( fragmentShader );

    programObject = glCreateProgramObjectARB();

    glAttachObjectARB( programObject, vertexShader );
    glAttachObjectARB( programObject, fragmentShader );

    glLinkProgramARB( programObject );
    glUseProgramObjectARB( programObject );
#else
#error "No shading extension information in headers"
#error "NO shading will be available. Only fallback"
#error "rendering provided in this binary."
#endif
    }

    // add a timer to oscillate the modelview
    NSTimeInterval ti = .1;
    [ NSTimer scheduledTimerWithTimeInterval: ti
                                      target: self
                                    selector: @selector(angleUpdate:)
                                    userInfo: nil
                                     repeats: YES ];
}
```

The method `hasShaderExtensions` doesn't really do anything conceptually different from the action of our prior example, but the methodology is slightly different. We first check our version number, but we don't create an extension dictionary; GLEW has already done that for us, and we can directly use the code it provides. Thus we can directly check for the GLEW analog extensions we described before—namely, those corresponding to our OpenGL extensions. This method either succeeds or fails based on the existence of these extensions. Back in `prepareOpenGL`, we use these extensions if the method is successful.

Example 13-11 Query for Shader Extensions Using GLEW

```
- (BOOL) hasShaderExtensions
{
    BOOL has_shading = FALSE;

    float versionfloat = [ self openGLVersionNumber ];
    if ( versionfloat >= 1.21 )
    {
        BOOL has_vs = ( GL_TRUE == GLEW_ARB_vertex_shader );
        BOOL has_fs = ( GL_TRUE == GLEW_ARB_fragment_shader );
        BOOL has_so = ( GL_TRUE == GLEW_ARB_shader_objects );
        BOOL has_lang = ( GL_TRUE -- GLEW_ARB_shading_language_100 );
        has_shading = has_vs && has_fs && has_so;
    }

    return( has_shading );
}
```

That's all there is to do as far as determining whether an extension exists and using it with GLEW goes. It's simple, it's compact, and it's comprehensive. It's also highly recommended if you have to take the plunge into the depths of OpenGL extensions.

GLUT

Another approach to extension testing and management is to use the GLUT API. GLUT performs many features in a cross-platform fashion, but one of these, which is not directly related to window management, is extension resolution and binding. GLUT provides two entry points that allow quick and easy testing of named-extension existence and function binding:

- `glutExtensionSupported( EXT_string)` : Return non-zero if the extension exists, and zero if it does not.
- `glutGetProcAddress( glExtensionNameARB)` : Return a function pointer for the named extension if it exists, and `NULL` otherwise.

These two API entries together constitute a complete set of extension testing and API binding operations for extension functions in a cross-platform fashion.

If the complexity of GLEW isn't something you need, and writing GL-level management isn't your bag either, these tools may be just what you're looking for.

In Example 13-12, we present C code for checking the OpenGL version number, as a component of our example shading extension tests adapted for GLUT. In Example 13-13, we reimplement our Cocoa shader test using the GLUT extensions. As you can see, the code is very similar to that used for both Cocoa and raw GL.

Example 13-12 Query for OpenGL Version Information Using GLUT

```
float openGLVersionNumber()
{
    char *versionstring = (char*) glGetString( GL_VERSION );
    std::string vs( versionstring );
    return( atof( vs.substr( 0, vs.find( " " ) ).c_str() ) );
}
```

Example 13-13 Query for Shader Extensions Using GLUT

```
bool hasShaderExtensions()
{
    bool has_shading = false;

    float versionfloat = openGLVersionNumber();
    if ( versionfloat >= 1.21 )
    {
        bool has_vs =
            glutExtensionSupported( "GL_ARB_vertex_shader" );
        bool has_fs =
            glutExtensionSupported( "GL_ARB_fragment_shader" );
        bool has_so =
            glutExtensionSupported( "GL_ARB_shader_objects" );
        bool has_lang =
            glutExtensionSupported( "GL_ARB_shading_language_100" );
        has_shading = has_vs && has_fs && has_so;
    }

    return( has_shading );
}
```

The second piece of extension resolution performed by GLUT is the optional binding of functions from the active GL library. The entry point glutGetProcAddress allows this binding with a simple API. You just pass in the name of your entry point of interest, and a non-NULL result indicates success and the function pointer.

As we mentioned earlier, Apple has an implicit policy of not requiring explicit function lookup if the extension exists. Sometimes, however, your infrastructure for a cross-platform application may require this capability. GLUT is probably not the best layer for performing this task because you'll probably end up linking in GLUT as an additional framework. Your memory footprint may increase, as might your load times. The `dlopen`/`dlsym` route is preferable, given that Apple probably does something like this internally in its implementation of this function. Although various implementations of GLUT exist in source form, all of them indicate that `glutGetProcAddress` works only for Windows and X11. However, despite the fact that Apple doesn't document this function in the manual pages, this API really does work, and yields correct results. If you so choose, this is another option for GL function binding.

Summary

Whatever your level of OpenGL programming, sooner or later extensions will be part of your future. And when you do have to use them, there are a number of ways of addressing how to efficiently manage their complexity. In this chapter on OpenGL extensions, we explored a variety of aspects of extensions on Mac OS X. We looked at the particulars of how to find, choose, and use extensions through native OpenGL mechanisms. We also explained how to perform the same process with external extension management tools. Finally, we covered both approaches with an eye toward Mac specifics but remained grounded in the reality of multiplatform development.

At this point, you should be conversant in extensions, and well prepared to use them to make your application faster, more well rounded through advanced features, or more compatible with a variety of platforms. Extensions are a necessary part of keeping your application up-to-date on the feature and compatibility curve of OpenGL development on the Mac.

X11 APIs for OpenGL Configuration

X11 (X Window System, Version 11) is a network-transparent window system that is widely used on Unix-based workstations. It is a client/server-based windowing environment where a single server services multiple "client" windows of applications written for X11.

The first windowing system on which OpenGL was supported was X11. This windowing interface to OpenGL is called GLX. GLX running under X11 is analogous to Cocoa or Carbon running under the Quartz windowing system of the Mac.

X11 was introduced to OS X in OS 10.2 (Jaguar). The X11 server runs within the Quartz windowing system in either full-screen mode or windowed mode. The X11 server also takes care to present some widgets and UI elements in the Aqua style so that even if your application is just a simple port of another X11-based application, at least some of the UI elements are rendered in the Mac style. This behavior makes the X11 environment a possible alternative to a full-scale port. However, no native Mac user will be fooled because X11 doesn't have nearly the visual richness of the native Mac UI elements. A better path to bringing an OpenGL/X11 application to the Mac may be to start with the simple port, work out some of the OpenGL bugs, and, as time and budget permit, rework the UI in native Cocoa or Carbon.

In this appendix we'll examine the capabilities, APIs, and behavioral characteristics of using OpenGL on the Mac under GLX and X11.

Installation

X11 is available as an install option on OS X install disks versions 10.3 and later. The system requirements for installing X11 are as follows:

- 256MB RAM
- 200MB of available hard disk space
- A built-in display or a display connected to an Apple-supplied video card

When the installation is complete, X11 is launched using the `/Applications/ Utilities/X11.app` application. In the Application menu, you'll find the familiar "xterm" application. Xterm will set up the X11 execution environment for you and makes it easy to launch your X11 applications. If you need more information on configuring your X11 environment, see Apple's comprehensive guide on its website [9].

Like most X11 distributions, the X11 install comes with the Athena and Xt widget sets. If your application uses another widget set (most commercial applications do), you'll have to do a bit more installation work to configure your Mac.

One of these widget sets, Motif, is quite popular in the commercial X software world. Motif is a layer above raw X11 that provides a variety of higher-level, object-oriented (though not C++) rendering widgets. Many large-scale applications use Motif in the Unix world, and a compatible version of Motif for Mac OS X, called OpenMotif, can be downloaded from the OpenMotif website [20]. This version of OpenMotif requires a complete compile process, however, so you may prefer to use a precompiled version. IST makes a variety of packaged versions of OpenMotif for many platforms, including an installer `.dmg` for OS X. Despite this not being an official Open Group version of OpenMotif, installing from the disk image is considerably easier than building Motif from scratch. IST's version of this packaged OpenMotif can be downloaded from the company's website [17].

Building X11 Applications on OS X

Once the software is installed, building your X11 applications on OS X is similar to building them on any other Unix platform. By definition, this means that your X11 application builds will look different from standard native OS X application builds. Specifically, you will be linking against libraries in `/usr/lib` rather than specifying frameworks.

Following is a sample makefile from our `x11_simple` example for an OpenMotif/OpenGL application on OS X (Tiger):

```
# Object files
CXXOBJS = main.o oglMotif.o

default: oglMotif

# Compile
$(CXXOBJS): %.o: %.c++
```

```
g++ -g -Wall -I/usr/OpenMotif/include \
    -I/usr/X11R6/include -c $< o $@

# Link
oglMotif: $(CXXOBJS)
g++ -g -o $@ $(CXXOBJS) -L/usr/X11R6/lib \
    -L/usr/OpenMotif/lib -lGL -lGLw -lXm -lXt -lX11

clean:
rm -f *.o oglMotif
```

Note the -I and -L options of the compile and link lines, respectively. They refer to the default installation directories for both X11 and OpenMotif. Also note the lack of any -framework options. You cannot mix and match references to the Mac OS X OpenGL libraries for an X11 application.

As far as the build process goes, X11 on OS X is quite straightforward. It probably will not require many changes for the Mac when bringing applications from other platforms running Unix.

X11 Color Models

X11 shows its age (or seniority, if you prefer) with the prevalence of color index rendering. Two X11 color models use color index (or color mapped) rendering: PseudoColor and DirectColor. PseudoColor is the more common of these two and represents each pixel in the framebuffer as an index into a single colormap. DirectColor, by contrast, has a separate color map for red, green, and blue. As you would expect, each pixel in the framebuffer contains an index for each of the three color maps.

If you wish to run an application that uses the PseudoColor model, you can launch X11 in 256-color mode. To do so, select the output tab from the X11.app preferences pane, and select "256 colors" from the Colors drop-down menu. You must restart X11.app for this change to take effect.

The TrueColor color model stores a maximum of four color component intensity values in the framebuffer—one each for red, green, blue, and alpha. Modern graphics applications typically use this color model.

By default, X11.app is configured to take the color setting from the display. The display setting is typically millions for 24-bit color. This setting is appropriate for TrueColor X11 applications.

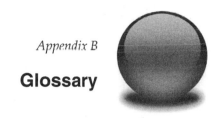

Appendix B

Glossary

API Acronym for application programming interface. An API is a set of functions, classes, and tokens used to define a particular set of software tools. OpenGL is an API for graphics.

ARB See *OpenGL Architecture Review Board*.

Context sharing Reusing resources from one OpenGL context in another OpenGL context.

Deferred validation The caching or postponement of data or state changes in OpenGL until these changes are required at drawing time.

Direct memory access A hardware-to-hardware fetching of data. In the context of graphics, it usually entails the GPU fetching data from a region of specially mapped or reserved host system memory.

Display capture To take over a particular display as part of a full-screen application.

Fragment A collection of all framebuffer state information for a single pixel. A fragment may have some or all of color, alpha, depth, stencil, and other related data. The data associated with a fragment is defined when the drawable or surface for the framebuffer containing this fragment is constructed.

Framebuffer A destination buffer to which the results of OpenGL rendering are written.

Frame rate quantization A description of the artifact observed when analyzing the performance of double-buffered OpenGL windows, where the frame rate moves between discrete states defined by integer divisors of the monitor refresh rate. For example, a 60Hz monitor refresh may cause a double-buffered application to run at 60Hz, 30Hz, or 20Hz.

GLSL Acronym for OpenGL Shading Language.

GLX The OpenGL and X-Windows interface layer. The GLX specification describes how OpenGL contexts and drawables interact with X-Windows widgets and windows.

Immediate mode rendering Rendering with objects passed from the host to the GPU on a per-frame basis. Compared to retained mode rendering, immediate mode rendering implies more function-calling overhead in each rendering frame in addition to more bus bandwidth used with each frame.

OpenGL Architecture Review Board The standards body that defines which features, functionality, and APIs appear in core OpenGL versions, extensions, and associated specifications.

OpenGL Shading Language The high-level shading language employed by OpenGL.

Red Book The familiar name for the OpenGL programming guide.

Retained mode rendering Rendering with objects already cached on the GPU. Typically `glBind ... Object` calls invoke retained mode rendering. Display lists are another form of this style of rendering.

Throughput The data transfer rate that an application achieves for a particular form of data over some data path. In graphics, throughput typically refers to the rate at which data can be transferred from main memory to the graphics processor.

vbl-sync Vertical blanking synchronized is a configuration option of graphics applications that ties the redrawing of the framebuffer to the refresh rate of the display device.

Virtualized desktop A single, continuous desktop that may span multiple, potentially heterogeneous graphics devices. Dragging windows among the displays attached to these graphics devices is seamless and continuous.

The Cocoa API for OpenGL Configuration in Leopard, Mac OS X 10.5

Cocoa, also known as AppKit, is the Objective-C API for writing modern Mac OS X applications. Cocoa provides a high-level, object-oriented set of classes and interfaces for the OpenGL subsystem and for user–interface interaction. Cocoa is the modern successor to the NextStep API from NeXT Computer; the company's initials explain the "NS" prefix on all of the class definitions and data types. Cocoa provides a more object-oriented API than any other option on the Mac, which is useful for building UIs, handling events, and functioning as an interface to OpenGL.

We presume you're reading this appendix with a fundamental understanding of the Objective-C language and basic Cocoa, so we won't spend any time reviewing core Cocoa concepts like the Objective-C language, views, actions, outlets, Interface Builder, and so on. We also assume you've already read one of the many good books on these key background elements of Cocoa. If not, we've got a reference or two for you in Appendix D. In the following sections, we'll explore two ways of creating a Cocoa-based application: one that relies heavily on Interface Builder and one that requires more code but yields a bit more flexibility and capability. We'll also tackle some advanced OpenGL topics concerning off-screen rendering, context sharing, and more.

This appendix is a repeat of the earlier chapter focused on Cocoa and OpenGL but with a focus on Leopard. Though all the basic concepts from that chapter still apply, Leopard does it a bit differently. Because of that, rather than trying to integrate the two, we've broken them into two tracks. If you're on Tiger or earlier, read Chapter 8, but if you're using Leopard, check out this appendix.

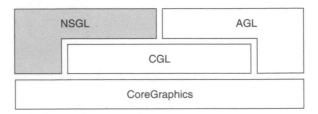

Figure C-1 AppKit API and Framework in Overall OpenGL Infrastructure on the Mac

Overview

The AppKit OpenGL API is part of the overall Apple OpenGL infrastructure. It constitutes a layer above CGL but also has the ability to reach down into both CGL and lower layers. Figure C-1 shows where the AppKit (also known as Cocoa or NSGL) API and framework reside relative to other API layers.

The AppKit framework is typically found at /System/Library/Frameworks but may also be in a path specific to your SDK installation. As with other APIs, linking against AppKit requires specification of this framework path (Table C-1).

NSOpenGLView

In this section, we will create an XCode project showing how to create a custom view to handle OpenGL rendering using a Cocoa UI element. This project will be a foundation project that we will return to when we create other examples with increased functionality throughout this appendix. We'll begin with the overall project setup and creation—so launch XCode, and we'll get started.

Create a new XCode project of type Cocoa Application. This action will create your project, set it to link properly against the Cocoa frameworks, and create a sample main program from which we'll begin. If you do not feel like walking through the steps or would like to see the finished product first, check out the sample code from our website (www.macopenglbook.com).

Open the Resources folder, and double-click on the MainMenu.nib icon. This will open the NIB file for this project in Interface Builder. Now switch to Interface Builder.

Table C-1 AppKit Cocoa Headers, Frameworks, and Overview

Framework path	/System/Library/Frameworks/AppKit.framework
Build flag	-framework AppKit
Header	#include<AppKit/NSOpenGL.h>

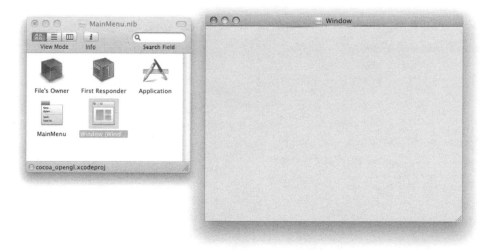

Figure C-2 Window and NIB Ready to be Edited in Leopard Interface Builder.

In the `MainMenu.nib` window, double-click on the `Window` icon, and you'll see the window that will be your application window open. Position and scale it as you like, and you should end up with something like Figure C-2 when finished.

Next bring up the `Library` and `Inspector` tools, both available in the `Tools` menu. Navigate to the `Inspector` icon in the `Library` window and drag the custom view out and into our window. Position and scale the view within the window to suite your tastes. Finally, in the `Inspector` window, name your class something sensible, like `MyOpenGLView`. Your results should look similar to Figure C-3.

So what did we just do? We told Interface Builder that we wanted to create a CustomView, arrange it in the window, and name it. We're trying to get a custom OpenGL view, specifically the `NSOpenGLView` class. It provides the integration between OpenGL and Cocoa. By subclassing it, we become able to customize many aspects of its behavior, including pixel format selection and context sharing. But we're getting ahead of ourselves. First we've got to get `MyOpenGLView` into a form where we can write some code.

We'll now use Interface Builder to instantiate a default object when the NIB file is loaded, bind it to our CustomView and create some sample code.

First, let's create an instance of our class. Return to the `Library` window and find the blue cube icon. This stands for an arbitrary object to be instantiated on

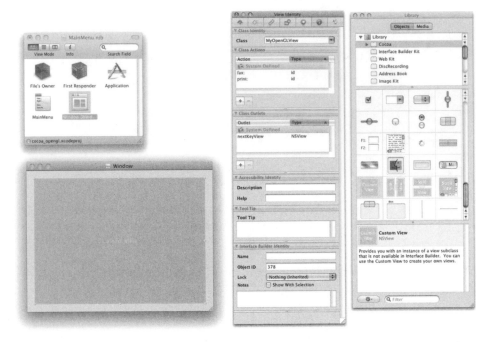

Figure C-3 Selection, Layout, and Specialization of a CustomView in Interface Builder

our behalf. Drag that out and into the MainMenu window. Select the blue cube, and look in the Inspector window. Type in the Class entry the name of our custom view, MyOpenGLView. This creates a custom object, of our custom view type in the NIB, and will recreate that when the NIB gets instantiated at runtime. You should see something like Figure C-4.

Now let's create the actual headers and code. In Interface Builder go to the File menu and choose Write Class Files. This will prompt you to create files for both the header and the source for this view. Accept the defaults, placed within your project directory. Finally, drag those files into your XCode project and we're set to start coding. The final step in this setup operation is to change the CustomView to derive from NSOpenGLView, the base Cocoa View class for rendering OpenGL content. To do so, open the code you've just generated within XCode, and change the MyOpenGLView.h header so your project and code look like Figure C-5.

We could have handled all of this setup, configuration, and routing programmatically—but this book isn't about Cocoa plumbing, so we'll stay at this level for now. In a later section, we'll explore Cocoa configuration of a

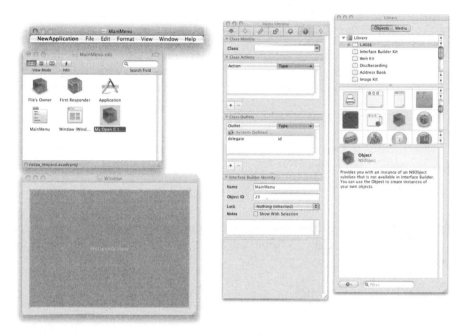

Figure C-4 Create and Bind an Instance of our CustomView

Figure C-5 Custom View Derivation and Project Files in XCode 3.0

generic NSView, which allows us a bit more flexibility. For now, switch back to XCode and we'll dig into the code.

In XCode, open the file MyOpenGLView.m. We'll now begin adding methods to handle key elements of the OpenGL render cycle. We start by adding a method to select pixel formats. This code performs pixel format selection in three steps:

1. A structure is created containing a list of pixel format configuration parameters.
2. That structure is passed to an NSOpenGLPixelFormat constructor to create a new pixel format object.
3. That pixel format object is passed on to the base NSOpenGLView method for finishing the initialization of this view.

Either add the code yourself to your project or grab it from the sample code provided in Example C-1. Compile and run the code, and you should have a window!

Example C-1 Configuration of an OpenGL View in initWithFrame

```
#include <OpenGL/gl.h>
#include <GLUT/glut.h>

#include <math.h>
#import "MyOpenGLView.h"

@implementation MyOpenGLView

- (id) initWithFrame: (NSRect) frame
{
    time = 0;
    angle = 0;

    GLuint attributes[] =
    {
        NSOpenGLPFAWindow,
        // choose among pixelformats capable of rendering to windows
        NSOpenGLPFAAccelerated,
        // require hardware-accelerated pixelformat
        NSOpenGLPFADoubleBuffer,
        // require double-buffered pixelformat
        NSOpenGLPFAColorSize, 24,
        // require 24 bits for color-channels
        NSOpenGLPFAAlphaSize, 8,
        // require an 8-bit alpha channel
        NSOpenGLPFADepthSize, 24,
        // require a 24-bit depth buffer
        NSOpenGLPFAMinimumPolicy,
        // select a pixelformat which meets or exceeds these requirements
        0
    };
```

```
NSOpenGLPixelFormat* pixelformat =
    [ [ NSOpenGLPixelFormat alloc ] initWithAttributes:
        (NSOpenGLPixelFormatAttribute*) attributes ];

if ( pixelformat == nil )
{
    NSLog( @"No valid OpenGL pixel format" );
    NSLog( @"matches the attributes specified" );
    // at this point, we'd want to try different sets of
    // pixelformat attributes until we got a match, or decide
    // we couldn't create a proper graphics environment for our
    // application, and exit appropriately
}
// now init ourself using NSOpenGLViews
// initWithFrame:pixelFormat message
return self = [ super initWithFrame: frame
                    pixelFormat: [ pixelformat autorelease ] ];
}
```

"But wait," you say, "what about the rest of the key OpenGL configuration pieces: the context and the drawable or surface?" By subclassing NSOpen-GLView, you're getting the last two pieces configured for you, you lucky dog—no extra work required. The base NSOpenGLView class creates a context from the pixel format you passed in, and it creates a drawable such that it can be visualized in the window we created with our CustomView back in Interface Builder. Later, however, we'll go through the process of specializing an NSView so we can do the fun bits in creating a context and a drawable, too. This step is necessary if you want to do more advanced context things, such as share data with another context. More on that in later sections.

Moving along, now that you know how to choose a pixel format, it's probably an appropriate time to discuss what the various flags mean to an NSOpenGLPixelFormat. These flags are generally well documented by Apple, but we're including a list of all the flags in one spot for handy reference here. Take a look at Tables C-2 and C-3, see which values make sense for your application, and try a few in the code we've just developed. Table C-3 contains a fair bit of exposition on these flags, including what the various values mean and how you might use them—it's worth a quick read.

Table C-2 Selection Policies and Behaviors

Policy	Description
Match	Choose only from the set of pixel formats that match exactly.
Closest	Choose a match closest to the size specified, but not necessarily an exact match.
Minimum	Require a match of at least this size. Can choose larger sizes.
Maximum	Require a match of at most this size. Prefers larger sizes.

Table C-3 Common Pixel Format Qualifiers for Use with
`NSOpenGLPixelFormat`

Token	Description
NSOpenGLPFAAllRenderers	Look in entire set of renderers to find a match.
	Type: Boolean
	YES: Search entire set of available renderers, including those that are potentially non-OpenGL compliant.
	Default: YES
	Policy: Any
NSOpenGLPFADoubleBuffer	Double buffer requirements.
	Type: Boolean
	YES: Search only for a double-buffered pixel format. NO: Require a single-buffered pixel format.
	Default: NO
	Policy: Any
NSOpenGLPFAStereo	Stereo requirements.
	Type: Boolean
	YES: Require a stereo pixel format. NO: Require a monoscopic pixel format.
	Default: NO
	Policy: Any
NSOpenGLPFAAuxBuffers	Auxiliary buffer requirements.
	Type: Unsigned integer
	Number of auxiliary buffers required by this pixel format.
	Default: NA
	Policy: Smallest
NSOpenGLPFAColorSize	Color bits requirements.
	Type: Unsigned integer
	Number of color buffer bits required by all color components together.
	Default: If this token is not specified, a `ColorSize` that matches the screen is implied.
	Policy: Closest
NSOpenGLPFAAlphaSize	Unsigned integer: The value specified is the number of alpha buffer bits required.
	Default: If no value is specified, pixel formats discovered may or may not have an alpha buffer.
	Selection policy: Pixel formats that most closely match this size are preferred.

Token	Description
NSOpenGLPFADepthSize	Unsigned integer: The value specified is the number of depth buffer bits required.
	Default: If no value is specified, pixel formats discovered may or may not have a depth buffer.
	Selection policy: Pixel formats that most closely match this size are preferred.
NSOpenGLPFAStencilSize	Unsigned integer: The value specified is the number of stencil planes required.
	Selection policy: The smallest stencil buffer of at least the specified size is preferred.
NSOpenGLPFAAccumSize	Unsigned integer: The value specified is the number of accumulation buffer bits required.
	Selection policy: An accumulation buffer that most closely matches the specified size is preferred.
NSOpenGLPFAMinimumPolicy	YES: Change to the selection policy described.
	Selection policy: Consider only buffers greater than or equal to each specified size of the color, depth, and accumulation buffers.
NSOpenGLPFAMaximumPolicy	YES: Change to the selection policy described.
	Selection policy: For non-zero buffer specifications, prefer the largest available buffer for each of color, depth, and accumulation buffers.
NSOpenGLPFAOffScreen	YES: Consider only renderers capable of rendering to an off-screen memory area that have a buffer depth exactly equal to the specified buffer depth size. An implicit change to the selection policy is as described.
	Selection policy: NSOpenGLPFAClosestPolicy
NSOpenGLPFAFullScreen	YES: Consider only renderers capable of rendering to a full-screen drawable. Implicitly defines the NSOpenGLPFASingleRenderer attribute.
NSOpenGLPFASampleBuffers	Unsigned integer: The value specified is the number of multisample buffers required.
NSOpenGLPFASamples	Unsigned integer: The value specified is the number of samples for each multisample buffer required.
	(*Continued*)

Table C-3 Common Pixel Format Qualifiers for Use with
`NSOpenGLPixelFormat` (*Continued*)

Token	Description
NSOpenGLPFAColorFloat	YES: Consider only renderers capable of using floating-point pixels. `NSOpenGLPFAColorSize` should also be set to 64 or 128 for half- or full-precision floating-point pixels (Mac OS 10.4).
NSOpenGLPFAMultisample	YES: Consider only renderers capable of using supersample anti-aliasing. `NSOpenGLPFASampleBuffers` and `NSOpenGLPFASamples` also need to be set (Mac OS 10.4).
NSOpenGLPFAAuxDepthStencil	If present, searches for pixel formats for each `AuxBuffer` that has its own depth stencil buffer.
NSOpenGLPFARendererID	Unsigned integer: ID of renderer.
	Selection policy: Prefer renderers that match the specified ID. Refer to `CGLRenderers.h` for possible values.
NSOpenGLPFAAccelerated	YES: Modify the selection policy to search for pixel formats only among hardware-accelerated renderers.
	NO (default): Search all renderers, but adhere to the selection policy specified.
	Selection policy: Prefer accelerated renderers.
NSOpenGLPFAClosestPolicy	YES: Modify the selection policy for the color buffer to choose the closest color buffer size preferentially. This policy will not take into account the color buffer size of the current graphics devices. NO (default): No modification to selection policy.
NSOpenGLPFABackingStore	YES: Constrain the search of pixel formats to consider only renderers that have a back color buffer that is both the full size of the drawable and guaranteed to be valid after a call to a buffer flush. NO (default): No modification to the pixel buffer search.
NSOpenGLPFAWindow	YES (default): Search only among renderers that are capable of rendering to a window.
	Note: This attribute is implied only if neither `NSOpenGLPFAFullScreen` nor `NSOpenGLPFAOffScreen` is specified.
NSOpenGLPFAPixelBuffer	YES: Rendering to a pixel buffer is enabled.

In particular, pixel format selection can have a profound impact on both the performance of and the video memory usage by your application. Keep in mind that choosing pixel formats with more capabilities may lead to slower performance than choosing pixel formats with fewer options and smaller buffers. For example, if you have a choice between a pixel format with a color buffer size of, say, 8 bits per color component (32 bits total) or one with a color buffer represented as a 32-bit floating-point number per component (128 bits total), it's pretty clear that writing to a single pixel in your drawable requires four times the bandwidth just for color. We'll get into these performance implications later and explore issues like this one in more detail. For now, just realize that a good rule of thumb for choosing pixel formats is to choose the one that most closely matches your application's needs.

We'll finish this Cocoa example by adding a few more useful methods to our code. These will allow two more key tasks—namely, context setup (that is, things you might do in an OpenGL application, such as, `glEnable` certain states and bind textures) and drawing.

The first of these methods, which is named `prepareOpenGL`, is defined to be the first opportunity that your class will have to make some OpenGL calls. `prepareOpenGL` will be called once a valid pixel format, context, and drawable are all available, so you can go ahead and call anything you'd like there. Keep in mind that this method will be called only once, so from that point on, you'll have to manage your OpenGL state changes on the fly.

The second method to implement is `drawRect`. This method will be called every time a scene redraw is necessary; you will do the bulk of your OpenGL work there. As part of the `drawRect` signature, you will be handed an `NSRect` containing the current origin and size of the drawing area, in pixels.

With that introduction out of the way, we'll simply point you at the code (Example C-2) to add to your `MyOpenGLView.m` file, somewhere between the `@implementation` and `@end` tokens. Once you've added this code, recompile and run the code again, and you should see something like Figure C-6.

Example C-2 Cocoa `drawRect` Rendering Method with Sample OpenGL Content

```
- (void) drawRect: (NSRect) rect
{
    // adjust viewing parameters
    glViewport( 0, 0, (GLsizei) rect.size.width,
                      (GLsizei) rect.size.height );
    glClearColor( 0, .5, .8, 0 );
    glClear( GL_COLOR_BUFFER_BIT | GL_DEPTH_BUFFER_BIT );

    glMatrixMode( GL_MODELVIEW );
```

Figure C-6 Teapot Rendered with `NSOpenGLView` with Subclass

```
    glLoadIdentity();

    glTranslatef( 0, 0, -1 );

    GLfloat green[ 4 ] = { 0, 1, 0, 0 };
    glMaterialfv( GL_FRONT_AND_BACK,
        GL_AMBIENT_AND_DIFFUSE, green );
    glutSolidTeapot( .5 );

    [ [ self openGLContext ] flushBuffer ];
}

@end
```

If you see a teapot—success! In this section, we've explored one of the ways to configure a Cocoa OpenGL Surface, delved into the details of how to specify a pixel format, and constructed a functional application. This should serve as a starting point in your exploration of Cocoa, pixel format selection, and OpenGL rendering in these frameworks. In the next section, we'll examine how you create a custom `NSView`-derived class for even more flexibility.

NSView

Now that we've seen what `NSOpenGLView` can do for us, let's create our own `NSView`-based application to expose some of the functionality that `NSOpenGLView` performed behind the scenes. Why expose this extra complexity? You may want to take this path if your application features many OpenGL views of the same data. The technique we'll demonstrate here allows you to share data between these multiple views. But whatever your needs, this exploration will show you how to attach a context to an NSView, getting at the guts of how contexts are created, and then do some rendering. If you need precise management of a context, this is the way to do it in a Cocoa application. We'll end up exactly where we did before, with a cozy teapot on a calming blue background. We'll also begin where we did last time as well, in XCode. Launch it, and we'll get started.

We begin with the big picture—an overview of where we're going in this section. If you'd like to try to do this chunk on your own before the walkthrough, we encourage you to apply what we did in the last section to create a custom view. This time, however, we'll create our subclass based on NSView. Here are the steps:

1. Create a custom View in Interface Builder, named to your liking.
2. Create a custom Object in your NIB, using this same class name.
3. Export this code into XCode.
4. Change the class derivation to NSView this time.
5. Write code to create the teapot and handle the OpenGL initialization.

We won't say any more about how to accomplish the XCode project setup and configuration at this point, but rather will leave you to try to figure it out on your own. The walkthrough here will take you through all the details if you'd prefer to try it this way.

Create a new XCode project of type Cocoa Application. This action will create your project, set it to link properly against the Cocoa frameworks, and create a sample main program from which we'll begin. If you don't feel like walking through the steps or would like to see the finished product first, check out the sample code from our website (www.macopenglbook.com).

Open the Resources folder, and double-click on the MainMenu.nib icon. This will open the NIB file for this project in Interface Builder. Now switch to Interface Builder.

In the MainMenu window, double-click the Window icon, and drag a CustomView from the Library palette to the window. In the Inspector, name this custom view.

Now go back to MainMenu, and drag from the Library a custom Object into the MainMenu window. In the Inspector change its Class name to that of the custom view from the last step.

As before, we must create headers and code. From the File menu, Write Class Files, and then import those files (by dragging them) to your XCode project.

With that configuration out of the way, we move straight into the code phase. Save your `MainMenu.nib`, and switch to XCode. As before with the `NSOpenGLView`-derived project, we'll do many of the same things, including creating a pixel format and creating a subclassed version of `drawRect`. We'll also mimic some of the infrastructure automatically provided in `NSOpenGLView`, so you can see how it does its work. This time around, we'll present all the code in the final versions of both the header file (Example C-3) and the source file (Example C-4) first, and then walk you through each.

Example C-3 `MyView.h` Final Header

```
#import <Cocoa/Cocoa.h>

@interface MyView : NSView
{
    @private
        NSOpenGLContext *_context;
        NSOpenGLPixelFormat* _pixelformat;
}

- (NSOpenGLContext*) openGLContext;
- (void) prepareOpenGL;

@end
```

We begin by looking at the `MyView.h` header. We've inserted both a few member variables and a few methods. We've also created member variables to store pointers to our context and to our pixel format; we'll create code to initialize these variables in the source file. We also declare two methods, `openGLContext` and `prepareOpenGL`, named to emulate the behavior of the Cocoa-supplied `NSOpenGLView`. `openGLContext` will be used to return the current context or to create one if none exists. `prepareOpenGL` will be used as our first call to our OpenGL context to initialize the basic OpenGL functionality, as we did before for our `MyNSOpenGLView` class.

That's all there is to do in the header, so let's look at the source, see which other methods we've overloaded from `NSView`, and see how the code behind these signatures works.

Example C-4 `MyView.m` Final Code

```
#include <OpenGL/gl.h>
#include <GLUT/glut.h>

#import "MyView.h"

@implementation MyView

- (id)initWithFrame:(NSRect)frameRect
```

```
{
    NSLog( @"myView::initWithFrame" );
    if ((self = [super initWithFrame:frameRect]) != nil)
    {
        GLuint attributes[] =
        {
            NSOpenGLPFAWindow,
            NSOpenGLPFAAccelerated,
            NSOpenGLPFADoubleBuffer,
            NSOpenGLPFAColorSize, 24,
            NSOpenGLPFAAlphaSize, 8,
            NSOpenGLPFADepthSize, 24,
            NSOpenGLPFAMinimumPolicy,
            // select a pixelformat which meets or
            // exceeds these requirements
            0
        };
        _pixelformat = [ [ NSOpenGLPixelFormat alloc ]
            initWithAttributes:
                (NSOpenGLPixelFormatAttribute*) attributes ];

        if ( _pixelformat == nil )
        {
            NSLog( @"No valid OpenGL pixel format" );
            NSLog( @"matching attributes specified" );
        }
    }
    // init the context for later construction
    _context = nil;

    return self;
}

- (NSOpenGLContext *) openGLContext
{
    if ( _context == nil )
    {
        // if this is our first time to initialize
        _context = [ [ NSOpenGLContext alloc ]
            initWithFormat: _pixelformat shareContext: nil ];

        if ( _context == nil )
        {
            NSLog( @"No valid OpenGL context can be" );
            NSLog( @"created with that pixelformat" );
            /*
            we can fail a few ways:
                1 - bogus parameters: nil pixelformat,
                    invalid sharecontext, etc.
                2 - share context uses a different Renderer
                    than the specified pixelformat

            recovery techniques:
                1 - choose a different pixelformat
```

```
                2 -proceed without a shared context
            */
        }
    }

    return( _context );
}

- (void) lockFocus
{
    NSLog( @"myView::lockFocus" );

    // ensure we are ready to draw
    [ super lockFocus ];
    // get our context
    NSOpenGLContext *cxt = [ self openGLContext ];

    // ensure we are pointing to ourself as the Drawable
    if ( [ cxt view ] != self )
    {
        [ cxt setView: self ];
    }

    // make us the current OpenGL context
    [ cxt makeCurrentContext ];
}

- (void) prepareOpenGL
{

    NSLog( @"myView::prepareOpenGL" );

    glMatrixMode( GL_PROJECTION );
    glLoadIdentity();
    glOrtho(-1,1,-1,1,-1,100);
}

- (void) drawRect: (NSRect) rect
{
    // adjust viewing parameters
    glViewport( 0, 0,
        (GLsizei) rect.size.width, (GLsizei) rect.size.height );

    glClearColor( 0, .5, .8, 0 );
    glClear( GL_COLOR_BUFFER_BIT | GL_DEPTH_BUFFER_BIT );

    glMatrixMode( GL_MODELVIEW );
    glLoadIdentity();

    glTranslatef( 0, 0, -1 );

    GLfloat green[ 4 ] = { 0, 1, 0, 0 };
    glMaterialfv( GL_FRONT_AND_BACK, GL_AMBIENT_AND_DIFFUSE, green );
    glutSolidTeapot( .5 );
```

```
    [ [ self openGLContext ] flushBuffer ];
}

@end
```

In our `MyView.m` file, we start by looking at our `initWithFrame` overloaded method. This method is called when our object is getting constructed, with the desired layout of this particular view. As with our `MyNSOpenGLView` class, this method is where we set up our pixel format and prepare the rest of our class for subsequent use. In fact, the majority of the code in this method is identical to the code given earlier, with a slight inversion: We initialize the parent first and then, based on success there, create a pixel format. We end this method by initializing our `context` member to `nil` in preparation for configuring it later.

The next method, `openGLContext`, is the body of what we declared in the header. This method's intent is to hand the caller a pointer to the context used by this view. It begins by checking whether the existing context is empty; if so, it creates a context using the existing pixel format we created earlier and calls the `NSOpenGLContext` constructor `initWithFormat: NSOpenGLContext *`. This constructor takes two parameters: a pixel format and either another `NSOpenGLContext` pointer or `nil`. The pixel format parameter is used by the context to configure itself with any specific information that may affect OpenGL rendering, such as anti-aliasing or stencil capability. The second parameter, a different `NSOpenGLContext*`, is used in the case that the context passed back by this method will be shared with the context specified. Sharing a context will be explained in further detail later. For our example here, we simply pass in `nil`, indicating that we want a new context that does not share any resources with any other context. In this case, the only failure mode for this routine would be if the pixel format specified were invalid or `nil`. This routine ends by returning a pointer to the new context

The next method we will create is an overloaded method of `NSView` named `lockFocus`. `NSView` uses this method to make the current view the focus so that it's the target of whatever drawing commands follow. Quoting the Cocoa documentation, `lockFocus` "locks the focus on the receiver, so subsequent commands take effect in the receiver's window and coordinate system." This command essentially tells the windowing system that we will require some specific configuration to be set up and active before we render into this window.

Why do we need this? Well, every OpenGL context is essentially a snapshot of the entire OpenGL state used during rendering. Thus, if you've painstakingly configured some precise combination of OpenGL data, rendering paths, and other information, the same context in which you've done that work is likely the one in which you'd like your subsequent OpenGL commands to be executed.

Put more succinctly, you want your context to be active. In context parlance, this is known as "making your context current." `lockFocus` is the place in the Cocoa framework where your view is made current, and where you can then make your context current.

If we now look at our code, we can see that we need to overload this method to do the usual `lockFocus` work when we call our superclasses `lockFocus`. We then do work to get our OpenGL context and make it current. And that, as they say, is that: We've got a context, it's current, and we're ready to finish this exercise with two methods that we've seen before.

The last two methods we implement are identical to those we've used before. The `prepareOpenGL` and `drawRect` methods contain the same code as in the prior example. As before, they perform two tasks in your context—OpenGL initialization and rendering, respectively. With their completion, you're ready to build and run the application. You should see the same teapot against a blue background as in Figure C-6.

Additional Topics

So far, we've explored ways to render directly to the screen using Cocoa. Now we'll dig into how to render somewhere off-screen. There are many reasons why you might want to do this—for example, to create a cube map for reflection, to create shadow maps, or to create another form of dynamic texture. For off-screen rendering, we'll be building on the foundation from the Cocoa examples in previous sections, so if you've skipped to this point without reading those sections, you may want to review them to gather additional details.

Manipulating Images and Pixels in OpenGL

Before we get into specific techniques, let's talk about the various ways that an image of some sort can be moved around, rendered, and copied in OpenGL. OpenGL provides two main paths for pixel data:

- Pixel path
- Texture path

These two paths are very different in the way they're ultimately available to be rendered. The pixel path consists of two basic calls, `glDrawPixels` and `glReadPixels`, which allow for drawing and reading, respectively, of pixels from the current write and read buffers. These pixel path calls are 2D only and can read and write only screen-aligned data. By comparison, the texture path differs from the pixel path specifically in that texture data can be rendered in 3D. Because the texture path can also be used to render screen-aligned images as well, it is ultimately the more flexible of the two paths, so we'll focus on the texture path here. The *Red Book* [22] has lots of details on the imaging pipeline, if you'd like more information on that.

Any pixel data that you might want to render in an OpenGL scene, you can handle through textures. To do so, you would download that image as a texture using `glTexImage[123]D` calls. Let's provide an overview of this process and then translate it into code:

1. Create and configure a texture (`glGenTextures`, `glBindTexture`, `glTexImage2D`, `glTexEnv`, `glTexParameter`).
2. Bind that texture (`glBindTexture`).
3. Draw using that texture (`glBegin ... glTexCoord2f ... glEnd`).

This book isn't meant to teach you fundamental OpenGL rendering techniques, but the preceding sequence is essential to understand for two key reasons. First, texturing is the primary means by which you'll access the data you render to off-screen surfaces and the primary way by which you'll re-render those data in another form. Second, textures are chunks of data that are intimately bound to OpenGL contexts, and we'll need to know how to share data among contexts if we want to use textures rendered in one context in another context. Essentially, this section is a segue into sharing contexts, which is the topic we explore next.

Context Sharing

A key concept in many aspects of OpenGL rendering—on the Mac or otherwise—is what lives in an OpenGL context and how to efficiently use that data for multiple purposes. Essentially, a context contains all OpenGL state data associated with rendering, such as the viewport dimensions, active color, and rendering modes. A context also includes much heavier-weight items, such as texture objects and vertex objects.

Large objects consume nontrivial amounts of memory on a graphics card, so the designers of OpenGL anticipated the need to avoid duplicating resources among multiple rendering areas. This anti-redundancy capability is exposed at the window-system level as a feature called *context sharing*. This capability is typically requested when a new OpenGL context is created, after the first rendering context has been created and used. The context with items you wish to access is passed into some form of initialization for your new context, usually along with a pixel format. For two contexts to be compatible, their pixel formats must be compatible, which is why you see these two things specified together to successfully enable sharing.

What makes pixel formats incompatible? On the Mac, usually it's one thing—incompatible renderers. As a rule of thumb, if you can choose pixel formats that use the same renderers, you can share contexts created with those pixel formats.

So we've covered the how and why of sharing a context, but what, exactly, is shared when context sharing is enabled? Interestingly enough, most OpenGL objects are shared, but the overall context state is not. That's not entirely intuitive, but it correlates well with what people usually want to do. You save valuable card memory by reusing heavyweight objects in multiple spots, but still preserve the ability to customize each OpenGL view as needed. Specifically, the following entities are shared:

- Display lists
- Vertex array objects (VAOs)
- Buffer objects (VBOs, PBOs)
- Texture objects
- Vertex and fragment programs and shaders
- Frame buffer objects (FBOs)

Now that we have an overview of how context sharing works, let's walk through some code. For purposes of this example, we will build a two-windowed version of our earlier Cocoa example in which we created a custom context. In this case we'll modify the example to share the context between the two views and surfaces, render some shared data (a display list), and visualize the data in two views, each with a different-color background color. The plan is to demonstrate what is and what isn't shared in context sharing.

We begin by setting up a new project as we did for the simple Cocoa context example. The exact process isn't described here, except to say that you duplicate the steps from before but add a new window in your `MainMenu.nib` and create two custom `NSOpenGL`-derived views. Your results should look like Figure C-7.

Working in XCode, add an OpenGL framework dependency, and ensure that your frameworks and classes appear as shown in Figure C-8. Try building and running this application, knowing that we've not yet connected up the drawing or context sharing. On the off chance that you see only one window, make sure you've added the "Visible at Launch" flag to your Interface Builder properties, as in Figure C-9.

Finally, let's look at the code necessary for context sharing. There are a number of techniques for deciding which context to share, but one approach that is particularly nice, from an architectural perspective, is to use an "external" context provider. In this model, we configure and create a context in a separate class, and then share it with any OpenGL view that needs to render using its shared objects. In our example, we'll use the pattern of a singleton—that is, an object-based wrapper around a static object. This code is very straightforward, so we'll present it here and then discuss a bit more after presentation. The header code lives in Example C-5 and the source code is found in Example C-6.

Figure C-7 Two Views, Contexts Shared

Example C-5 Singleton Class Declaration for Managing a Shared Context

```
#import <Cocoa/Cocoa.h>
@interface SharedContext : NSObject
{

    NSOpenGLPixelFormat* _pixelformat;
    NSOpenGLContext * _context;
}

- (NSOpenGLPixelFormat *) pixelFormat;
- (NSOpenGLContext *) context;
+ (SharedContext *) instance;

@end
```

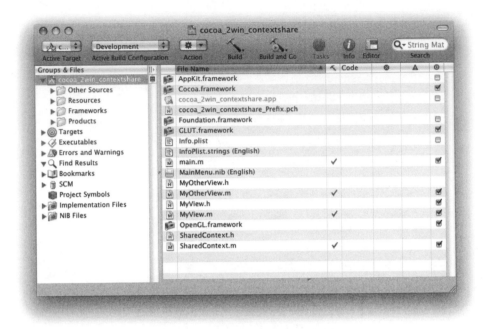

Figure C-8 Final Two Window XCode Contents

Figure C-9 Visible at Launch Enabled

Example C-6 Singleton Class Implementation for Managing a Shared Context

```objc
#import <AppKit/NSOpenGL.h>
#import <OpenGL/gl.h>

#import "SharedContext.h"

SharedContext *_sharedContext = nil;
@implementation SharedContext

- (id) init
{
    if (self = [super init])
    {
        _pixelformat = nil;
        _context = nil;

        GLuint attributes[] =
        {
            NSOpenGLPFAWindow,          // windowed pixelformats
            NSOpenGLPFAAccelerated,     // hw-accel pixelformat
            NSOpenGLPFADoubleBuffer,    // double-buffered pixelformat
            NSOpenGLPFAColorSize, 24,   // 24 bits for color-channels
            NSOpenGLPFAAlphaSize, 8,    // 8-bit alpha channel
            NSOpenGLPFADepthSize, 24,   // 24-bit depth buffer
            NSOpenGLPFAMinimumPolicy,   // meets or exceed reqs
            0
        };
        _pixelformat = [ [ NSOpenGLPixelFormat alloc ]
            initWithAttributes:
                (NSOpenGLPixelFormatAttribute*) attributes ];

        if ( _pixelformat == nil )
        {
            NSLog( @"SharedContext: No valid OpenGL pixel" \
                @"format matching attributes specified" );
            // at this point, we'd want to try different
            // sets of pixelformat attributes until we
            // got a match, or decided we couldn't create
            // a proper working environment for our
            // application
        }
        else
        {
            _context = [ [ NSOpenGLContext alloc ]
                initWithFormat: _pixelformat shareContext: nil ];
        }
    }
    return self;
}

- (NSOpenGLPixelFormat *) pixelFormat
{
    return( _pixelformat );
```

```
}

- (NSOpenGLContext *) context
{
    return( _context );
}

+ (SharedContext *) instance
{
    if ( _sharedContext == nil )
    {
        _sharedContext = [ [ SharedContext alloc ] init ];
    }
    return _sharedContext;
}

@end
```

If you're familiar with the singleton pattern, the `instance` method and idea should be familiar to you. If not, consult the classic *Design Patterns* book by the notorious Gang of Four [16]. Essentially, `instance` provides a handle to our static context manager object. Upon its creation, this object allocates a pixel format and a context based on that pixel format. This code should look familiar, as we've written code similar to it earlier in this book. The only caveat when writing context-sharing code of your own is to keep in mind that any context that is meant to be shared must be compatible with the other contexts. Compatibility implies many things, but chiefly that the destination pixel depth, color depth, and other factors are similar. We work around that problem in this example by first exposing a common pixel format through the `pixelFormat` method, and then using that method to construct our pixel format and context for each window's view.

Let's revisit the code we used for our custom OpenGL view example for initialization and setup. This code, with one minor twist, does everything we need and is presented in Example C-7.

Example C-7 Initialization of an OpenGL View with a Shared Context

```
@implementation MyView

- (id)initWithFrame:(NSRect)frameRect
{
    NSLog( @"MyView::initWithFrame" );

    if ((self = [super initWithFrame:frameRect]) != nil)
    {
        _pixelformat = [ [ SharedContext instance ] pixelFormat ];

        if ( _pixelformat == nil )
        {
```

```
                    NSLog( @"No valid OpenGL pixel format" \
                            "matching attributes specified" );
                    // at this point, we'd want to try different
                    // sets of pixelformat attributes until we
                    // got a match, or decided we couldn't create
                    // a proper working environment for our
                    // application
                }
        }

        // init the context for later construction
        _context = nil;

        return self;
}

- (NSOpenGLContext *) openGLContext
{
        if ( _context == nil ) // only if uninitialized
        {
                // if this is our first time to initialize
                _context = [ [ NSOpenGLContext alloc ]
                    initWithFormat: _pixelformat
                        shareContext: [ [ SharedContext instance ] context ] ];

                if ( _context == nil )
                {
                        NSLog( @"No valid OpenGL context can be" \
                                "created with that pixelformat" );
                        /*
                        we can fail a few ways:
                        1 - bogus parameters: nil pixelformat, invalid
                            sharecontext, etc.
                        2 - share context uses a different Renderer
                            than the specified pixelformat

                        recovery techniques:
                        1 - choose a different pixelformat
                        2 - proceed without a shared context
                        */
                }
        }

        return( _context );
}
```

As you can see in Example C-7, the only changes we made from our original custom view example are to use the [[SharedContext instance] pixelFormat] accessor to create a pixel format for this view and then, similarly, to use the [[SharedContext instance] context] accessor when constructing our context. We should always, of course, confirm that all pixel formats and contexts are successfully created for our production code as well. So, add code like this to your existing code and then make one

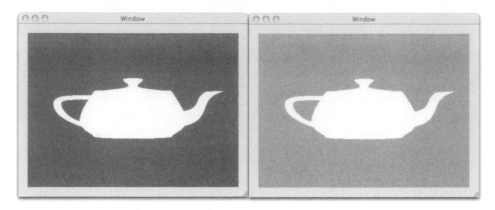

Figure C-10 Context Sharing: Two Windows Demonstrating Common Shared Data and Unshared (Clear Color) Context Data

last change—specifically, change the clear color in one of your custom View `drawRect` methods. If everything works as planned, your application should produce results like these shown in Figure C-10.

Remember that the OS X OpenGL implementation follows the conventions established in the GLX specification. Applications are responsible for synchronizing the state of objects between contexts. This implies that multithreaded applications with shared context establish mutex locks between the threads, use `glFlush` to flush pending commands that modify object state, and call `glBind` to realize changes to shared objects in other contexts. These may seem like a lot of steps, but they are usually worth the resulting resource conservation and performance gains.

In this section, we've seen how to configure context sharing in Cocoa, how to use it with a custom OpenGL view, and under which circumstances you'd want to share contexts. We've provided examples of how this sharing mechanism works in Cocoa, and we'll revisit this topic for AGL and CGL later. Context sharing is a key principle we'll use for a variety of on- or off-screen rendering techniques, so you'll likely revisit this section from time to time for hints when performing full-screen and off-screen rendering.

Full-Screen Surfaces

Every now and again, you might want to put your Cocoa OpenGL application into full-screen mode. There are lots of reasons why you might want to do this, and Apple often uses this approach for many of its applications. Apple software examples include QuickTime full-screen movie presentation, iPhoto/Finder slideshows, DVD playback, and FrontRow set-top display. The most common example of this technique in user software is found in games, usually where a game takes over the display for a complete and unobstructed experience of slaying dragons, flying through canyons at Mach 0.8, or conquering the galaxy. A rule of thumb to decide when full-screen rendering is needed is this: Any time you want to present a completely custom user interface, full-screen applications are one way to go. In this section we'll first tackle some plumbing details necessary to render full-screen OpenGL surfaces and then demonstrate how to create and use a full-screen OpenGL area.

Display Capture

One major reason for using a full-screen area is to coherently display some content without the distraction of other UI elements. A key element of this experience would be blocking interruption by other applications while in this mode. Apple provides hooks to allow an application to essentially take over the display, preventing other applications from presenting their content over the top. This behavior is known as *display capture*. Display capture exists at the Core-Graphics level of graphics, typically a 2D layer, and is not part of our discussion in this book. Nonetheless, the ability to capture the display is a useful—albeit not required—element of a full-screen application, even in Cocoa. Performing display capture is a very easy task, but entails strict ordering of the tasks. Essentially, the process proceeds as follows:

1. Capture the display.
2. Configure and display a full-screen window.
3. Handle events.
4. Release the display.

It's important to ensure that both event handling and teardown (or display release) occur. If they do not, you'll probably get into a deadlock of some sort—one in which either you can't do anything with your application or other applications move to the foreground, respectively. You're almost guaranteed to experience this problem once unless you're really listening to me here, and you'll never repeat the mistake—rebooting in the middle of your development cycle is a pretty good deterrent. The specifics of display capture and release are sketched out, in Example C-8. Please read Apple's developer documentation on the methods described here for additional information. Because these methods are so fundamentally simple, we will just show you the code and have you use it without further discussion.

Example C-8 Capturing and Releasing the Display

```
/*!
    Captures all displays, returning true/false for
    success/failure.
 */
bool capturedDisplaysLoop()
{
    bool error = false;
    CGDisplayErr err = CGCaptureAllDisplays();
    if (err != CGDisplayNoErr)
    {
        // failure - maybe another application is already
        // fullscreen
        error = true;
    }
    else
    {
        // your code here: open fullscreen window

        // your code here: event handler loop.

        // stay here until no longer in fullscreen mode.
        // upon exit, we transition back to windowed mode, and
        // release the display

        CGReleaseAllDisplays();
    }
    return( error );
}
```

For simplicity, we use the global form of display capture—that is, the form in which all displays are captured. You may have a need or a preference to control which display you capture more precisely. For those circumstances, Apple provides `CGDisplayCapture` and `CGDisplayRelease` to specify a particular display. And that's really all there is for display capture as it relates to OpenGL, except for the event-handling part, which we'll discuss next.

Event Handling

One key caveat to full-screen windows, regardless of the amount of OpenGL window-system integration, relates to event handling: Who's handling the events now that your window-system and UI elements are hidden? Yes, Virginia, this is another headache of full-screen windows, but you've got to do it. Otherwise, nothing will be handling events, making it very difficult to even quit your application. So what's an application to do, especially in Cocoa? As we do a number of times throughout the book, we will not go into the details of this operation, as numerous Cocoa books deal with this topic. Here we simply present Example C-9, in which code modeled closely on an Apple source example shows what you might do with events while you're in a full-screen mode.

Example C-9 Custom Controller Event-Handling Loop in a Full-Screen Context

```
stayInFullScreenMode = YES;
while ( stayInFullScreenMode )
{
    NSAutoreleasePool *pool =
        [ [ NSAutoreleasePool alloc ] init ];

    // Check for and process input events.
    NSEvent *event;
    while ( event =
        [ NSApp nextEventMatchingMask: NSAnyEventMask
                            untilDate: [ NSDate distantPast ]
                               inMode: NSDefaultRunLoopMode
                              dequeue: YES ] )
    {
        switch ([event type])
        {
            case NSLeftMouseDown:
                [ self mouseDown:event ];
            break;

            case NSLeftMouseUp:
                [ self mouseUp:event ];
            break;

            case NSLeftMouseDragged:
                [ self mouseDragged:event ];
            break;

            case NSKeyDown:
            {
                unichar cc =
                    [ [ event charactersIgnoringModifiers ]
                        characterAtIndex:0 ];
                switch ( cc )
                {
                    case 27: // escape key
                        stayInFullScreenMode = NO;
                    break;
                    default:
                    break;
                }
            }
            break;

            default:
            break;
        }
    }
}
```

The basic idea is that while in full-screen mode, no external UI controls (Cocoa or other) exist that have natural event-handling mechanisms, so you need to do whatever your application requires when an event occurs. This includes mouse handling, key handling, and external device (e.g., joystick, tablet) handling. Example C-9 does nothing more than simply handle the Escape key, quit the render loop, and return to windowed mode. The example deals specifically with key events, handling the Escape key by quitting full-screen mode, and calling out to other methods (not shown) for handling mouse events.

This structure and code should be enough of a basis for you to get started. If you need more detail, we provide a more comprehensive example on our website (www.macopenglbook.com).

Alternative Rendering Destinations

In the following sections we'll explore what it takes to render an intermediate image for use later in your application. You'll probably already know if this is something you're interested in. If not, let's discuss a case or two in which you might need to render intermediate results.

One example in which intermediate rendering results are useful is for rendering of reflections. Suppose you've got a scene with some watery bits and some shiny bits in it. Picture a rainy street scene with puddles and a car: The puddles would reflect the buildings across the street, and those shiny rims would reflect the buildings behind the viewer. To reflect something on those wheels and puddles, we have two options. One is to use a fake scene to create the reflections, and the other is to use the real scene. Obviously the real scene is the better option, so we'll need to generate a view of the scene that contains the images to be reflected. This would be the image that we'd render in our intermediate buffer.

In another example, we might want to render the same view of the street scene, but perhaps after the viewer hit his or her head on something—a painful simulation, to be sure! Perhaps your character was jogging and ran into a signpost. We want to render the scene slightly blurred and wavy regardless of the method of cranial impact. In this case, our intermediate scene would be the original street scene rendering. We would then take that image and run it through our `Blunt-Trauma.frag` shader.

Our example code will render scenes of similar complexity, or at least a teapot, to demonstrate this process, but the idea remains the same. The basic path for performing this render is as follows:

1. Render to an alternative destination.
2. Configure those results for use in the final scene render.
3. Render the final scene.

The following sections describe the various techniques available on the Mac for alternative destination rendering and subsequent reuse of those data. We'll prioritize these strategies in terms of their modernity, encouraging you to use the most modern of these, framebuffer objects, whenever possible. For a variety of reasons (not least of which are simplicity and performance), framebuffer objects are the best choice when your hardware supports them. However, as always with more advanced OpenGL features, the most modern features are not always supported on the hardware your customers have, so choosing fallbacks for those cases may require you to implement some of the other techniques. We cover the basics of each below. Dive in.

Framebuffer Objects

In this section we describe a modern and widely available technique for intermediate renders using framebuffer objects (FBOs). Rendering to FBOs is a technique born out of frustrations with the complexity of many of the other intermediate rendering techniques. FBOs were designed to provide a simple enable/disable mechanism that is familiar in usage to textures, and yet provide a great deal of flexibility in terms of what can be rendered and how to use it later. FBOs are an evolution from earlier extensions—namely, GLARBrendertexture. However, they are a vast improvement over the older techniques, as you'll hear shortly. FBOs are really the only choice for new applications, as they offer high performance, are flexible, and are easy to use.

That's our perspective on the matter, but for reference, you should defer to the extension specification as the authority. The specification declares:

Previous extensions that enabled rendering to a texture have been much more complicated. One example is the combination of GLARBpbuffer and GLAR-Brendertexture, both of which are window-system extensions. This combination requires calling glxMakeCurrent, an expensive operation used to switch between the window and the pbuffer drawables. An application must create one pbuffer per renderable texture in order to portably use GLARBrendertexture. An application must maintain at least one GL context per texture format, because each context can operate on only a single pixel format or FBConfig. All of these characteristics make GLARBrendertexture both inefficient and cumbersome to use.

GLEXTframebufferobject, on the other hand, is both simpler to use and more efficient than GLARBrendertexture. The GLEXTframebufferobject API is contained wholly within the GL API and has no (non-portable) window-system components. Under GLEXTframebufferobject, it is not necessary to create a second GL context when rendering to a texture image whose format differs from that of the window. Finally, unlike the pbuffers of

GLARBrendertexture, by changing color attachments, a single framebuffer object can facilitate rendering to an unlimited number of texture objects.

We believe that this extension is the best way to render to texture and authoritatively settles the question of what to use when performing a render-to-texture operation. Without further ado, let's walk through how to use FBOs for intermediate rendering and look at code to do so as well.

The overall algorithm for using FBOs is straightforward:

1. Build and initialize the target object to be used with this FBO. This object is typically a texture.
2. Build and initialize the FBO by attaching the target objects.
3. Bind the FBO and render the FBO contents.
4. Unbind the FBO and render the final scene using the target object.

We'll begin by revisiting our old standby Cocoa example and extending it to configure and render to an FBO. We will then use those results on our final rendered object. Example C-10 shows our custom view header, which indicates where we'll store our texture object and FBO IDs.

Example C-10 Custom View Header for FBO Example Code

```
#import <Cocoa/Cocoa.h>
#import <OpenGL/OpenGL.h>

@interface MyOpenGLView : NSOpenGLView
{
    GLuint fboID;
    GLuint textureID;
    float time;
    float angle;
}

- (void) angleUpdate: (NSTimer*) tt;
- (void) reshape;

@end
```

We next look at the code in our prepareOpenGL method. As before, this is the place where we create and initialize things that we need to set up once per context. We look at the entire prepareOpenGL method in Example C-11, so essentially we see the first two phases of our outlined FBO usage: build and initialization for both our target texture and our FBO. We begin by creating and initializing a texture object, which we'll both bind to our FBO and use in our final rendering. We then create an FBO and bind it to that texture for color rendering. Finally, after configuration, we unbind our current FBO (by binding the FBO ID of 0).

Example C-11 OpenGL Setup for FBO Rendering

```
- (void) prepareOpenGL
{
    glMatrixMode( GL_PROJECTION );
    glLoadIdentity();
    glOrtho(-1,1,-1,1,-1,100);

    // enable, generate, and bind our texture objects
    glEnable( GL_TEXTURE_2D );
    glGenTextures( (GLsizei) 1, &textureID );
    glBindTexture( GL_TEXTURE_2D, textureID );
    const unsigned int texdim = 64;
    const unsigned int nbytes = 3;
    char data[ texdim * texdim * nbytes ];
    memset( data, 0xff, texdim * texdim * nbytes );
    unsigned int ii;
    for( ii=0; ii<texdim*texdim; ii++ )
    {
        data[ ii*nbytes + 0 ] = 0xff;
    }
    gluBuild2DMipmaps( GL_TEXTURE_2D, // 0,
                    GL_RGB, texdim, texdim, // 0,
                    CL_RGB, GL_UNSIGNED_BYTE, data );
    glTexEnvi( GL_TEXTURE_ENV, GL_TEXTURE_ENV_MODE, GL_REPLACE );


    // generate & bind our framebuffer object to our texture object
    glGenFramebuffersEXT( 1, &fboID );
    glBindFramebufferEXT( GL_FRAMEBUFFER_EXT, fboID );
    glFramebufferTexture2DEXT( GL_FRAMEBUFFER_EXT,
                            GL_COLOR_ATTACHMENT0_EXT,
                            GL_TEXTURE_2D, textureID, 0 );
    glTexEnvi( GL_TEXTURE_ENV, GL_TEXTURE_ENV_MODE, GL_DECAL );
    glBindFramebufferEXT( GL_FRAMEBUFFER_EXT, 0 ); // unbind fbo

    // add a timer to oscillate the modelview
    NSTimeInterval ti = .1;
    [ NSTimer scheduledTimerWithTimeInterval: ti
                                      target: self
                                    selector: @selector(angleUpdate:)
                                    userInfo: nil
                                     repeats: YES ];
}
```

The OpenGL designers did a pretty good job of keeping the design clean and consistent with that of other objects in the OpenGL system. Specifically, note the parallels in the setup and configuration of FBOs and texture objects. In essence, you simply bind the FBO, do some rendering, and unbind the FBO. At that point, the texture bound to that FBO is ready to be used. We'll demonstrate this usage of the FBO next, even though we've really covered it all in the setup. It couldn't be much simpler. Example C-12 shows our drawRect routine.

Example C-12 Cocoa `drawRect` Routine for FBOs

```
- (void) drawRect: (NSRect) rect
{
    // render to offscreen
    glBindFramebufferEXT( GL_FRAMEBUFFER_EXT, fboID );
    [ self drawIntermediateContents ];
    glBindFramebufferEXT( GL_FRAMEBUFFER_EXT, 0 );

    // render to final
    [ self drawFinalContents ];

    // complete rendering & swap
    glFlush();
    [ [ self openGLContext ] flushBuffer ];
}
```

Finally, for interest, we present the code we actually draw with in those routines in Example C-13.

Example C-13 Cocoa Draw Methods for Contents of the FBO and the Final Render

```
- (void) drawIntermediateContents
{
    glClearColor( 1, 1, 0, 1 );
    glClear( GL_COLOR_BUFFER_BIT | GL_DEPTH_BUFFER_BIT );
    glMatrixMode( GL_MODELVIEW );
    glLoadIdentity();
    glTranslatef( 0, 0, 1 );
    glColor3f( 0, 1, 1 );
    glBegin( GL_QUADS );
    float ww = .9;
    float hh = .9;
    float zz = 0.0;
    glDisable( GL_TEXTURE_2D );
    glVertex3f( -ww, -hh, zz );
    glVertex3f( ww, -hh, zz );
    glVertex3f( ww, hh, zz );
    glVertex3f( -ww, hh, zz );
    glEnd();
}


- (void) drawFinalContents
{
    glClearColor( 0, .5, .8, 1 );
    glClear( GL_COLOR_BUFFER_BIT | GL_DEPTH_BUFFER_BIT );

    glMatrixMode( GL_MODELVIEW );
    glLoadIdentity();
    glRotatef( angle, 0, 0, 1 );

    glTranslatef( 0, 0, 1 );
    glColor3f( 0, 1, 0 );
    glBindTexture( GL_TEXTURE_2D, textureID );
```

```
        glEnable( GL_TEXTURE_2D );
        glBegin( GL_QUADS );
        float ww = .9;
        float hh = .9;
        float zz = 0.0;
        glTexCoord2f( 0, 0 );
        glVertex3f( -ww, -hh, zz );
        glTexCoord2f( 1, 0 );
        glVertex3f( ww, -hh, zz );
        glTexCoord2f( 1, 1 );
        glVertex3f( ww, hh, zz );
        glTexCoord2f( 0, 1 );
        glVertex3f( -ww, hh, zz );
        glEnd();
}
```

So what does our example do? Our goal is to render a textured quad to the screen, where the texture represents an intermediate rendered result. We begin by configuring our FBO and texture so that they refer to each other. In the render loop, we make the FBO active, clear to yellow, and then unbind the FBO. Because of the magic of FBOs, those results are now usable as a texture, so we render a textured quad to the screen. When we set up the texture environment parameters for texturing, we specified GLREPLACE to wholly replace any color on the quad with the texture image. If everything works as we've described (and it does), we should see the final rendered image as shown in Figure C-11.

Figure C-11 Results of Rendering to an FBO and Texturing a Quad with That Result (Texture Courtesy of NASA's Earth Observatory)

You can do a lot more with FBOs, including capturing other rendering results such as depth, stencil, and other render targets, but this kind of advanced usage is beyond the scope of this book. We refer you to the OpenGL framebuffer object extension for complete details.

Before we leave the topic of FBOs, we'd like to point out a few more reasons why FBOs are superior to other forms of off-screen rendering. First, FBOs consist of memory allocated on the graphics card itself that is directly usable in its target form—for example, as a texture. As a consequence, you avoid any off-card copies to and from the host: You can even avoid on-card copies in good implementations of the extension. Second, FBOs present a consistent, platform-agnostic interface. There just isn't a simpler interface to intermediate rendering than FBO, largely due to the evolutionary process by which OpenGL is developed. A variety of intermediate target rendering APIs and implementations were explored over the years, culminating in the design and implementation that exists today. FBOs are the best choice for modern rendering on the Mac. Third, FBOs avoid expensive context switching that can cost you a great deal of performance.

Copy-to-Texture

In this section we describe a very common and widely available technique known as render-to-texture. Render-to-texture is as simple as it sounds:

You simply render your intermediate scene, copy it to a texture, and then use that texture in your final render. Elegant, simple, and concise. There are, of course, details to deal with concerning how you target the texture into which you want to render and, in some cases, how you move pixels around the system into your final texture. Nevertheless, the process is largely as simple as described. Render-to-texture is interesting because it's a widely available technique and offers relatively high performance. There are problems with it, too: It's not as clean as the most modern OpenGL technique of FBOs, and there may be extra data copies. Overall, however, it works pretty well. Performance is pretty good, though not as consistently good as using FBOs. Even so, you may sometimes run into problems when using cards from different vendors on which this technique is actually moderately expensive. But if you can't use FBOs, and this is the best alternative available, you gotta do what you gotta do.

The essence of the render-to-texture technique is actually a bit simpler than the FBO example presented earlier. The code is virtually the same, but we omit the pieces of the rendering that relate to the FBO. We begin by looking at the header for our custom view (Example C-14).

Example C-14 Custom View Header for Copy-to-Texture Example Code

```
#import <AppKit/NSOpenGL.h>

#import <Cocoa/Cocoa.h>

@interface MyOpenGLView : NSOpenGLView
{
    GLuint textureID;

    float time;
    float angle;
}

- (void) angleUpdate: (NSTimer*) tt;
- (void) reshape;

@end
```

Because we're only going to render and copy into a texture, that's the extent of
the information we need to keep track of throughout our view class. We then
look at the initialization code, which is again very similar to the FBO example,
but now without the FBO configuration (Example C-15).

Example C-15 OpenGL Setup for Copy-to-Texture Rendering

```
- (void) prepareOpenGL
{
    glMatrixMode( GL_PROJECTION );
    glLoadIdentity();
    glOrtho(-1,1,-1,1,-1,100);
    glMatrixMode( GL_MODELVIEW );

    // enable, generate, and bind our texture objects
    glEnable( GL_TEXTURE_2D );
    glGenTextures( (GLsizei) 1, &textureID );
    glBindTexture( GL_TEXTURE_2D, textureID );
    const unsigned int texdim = 64;
    const unsigned int nbytes = 3;
    unsigned char data[ texdim * texdim * nbytes ];
    memset( data, 0, texdim * texdim * nbytes );
    unsigned int ii;
    for( ii=0; ii<texdim*texdim; ii++ )
    {
        data[ ii*nbytes + 0 ] = 0xff;
    }
    gluBuild2DMipmaps( GL_TEXTURE_2D, // 0,
                GL_RGB, texdim, texdim, // 0,
                GL_RGB, GL_UNSIGNED_BYTE, data );
    glTexEnvf( GL_TEXTURE_ENV, GL_TEXTURE_ENV_MODE, GL_REPLACE );
```

```
    // add a timer to oscillate the modelview
    NSTimeInterval ti = .1;
    [ NSTimer scheduledTimerWithTimeInterval: ti
                                     target: self
                                   selector: @selector(angleUpdate:)
                                   userInfo: nil
                                    repeats: YES ];
}
```

As before, our main drawRect routine does the bulk of the work—but here is
where the code differs from the FBO version. Let's look at it now in Example
C-16 and talk about the differences and caveats to this technique.

Example C-16   Cocoa drawRect Routine for Copy-to-Texture Rendering

```
- (void) drawRect: (NSRect) rect
{
    // setup and render the scene
    [ self drawIntermediateContents ];

    // copy it to a texture
    glBindTexture( GL_TEXTURE_2D, textureID );
    glCopyTexSubImage2D( GL_TEXTURE_2D, 0,
                         0, 0,
                         0, 0,
                         64, 64 );

    // render final scene
    [ self drawFinalContents ];

    // complete rendering & swap
    glFlush();
    [ [ self openGLContext ] flushBuffer ];
}
```

Notice two things in Example C-16. First, our draw routines are the same as the
FBO example, so we won't present them again. The first method draws the stuff
to be used as a texture, and the second draws the scene using the texture generated from the first method. Second, there is no binding or other redirection of
where this routine renders. Instead, we do all of the rendering in the back buffer,
and then copy it to a texture. This approach has one important implication: This
technique really works only for double-buffered visuals.

Another consequence of the way this technique works is that we're actually
copying the contents of the back buffer to a texture, so performance may be less
than that in the FBO case. Specifically, we perform this copy between each of
the [self draw*] methods. Thus performance is likely to be slower than
in the FBO case, but there's a lot of bandwidth available in modern graphics
hardware, so if you can spare it, this technique will be pretty efficient. But the
reason we're explaining this method at all is that the hardware on which you run

potentially might not support a real off-screen technique like FBO, so a technique like render-to-texture may be required.

And that brings us to the final point: This technique is window-dependent. You'll notice that we're copying only a fixed area of pixels from within our drawing surface in our example. If we wanted to capture the entire area, we'd have to monitor the size of the drawable area (using the `reshape` routine) and ensure that the width and height of the copy call were updated accordingly. Another way of looking at this problem is to consider texture resolution: You'll need a window at least as big as the texture size you want to use, because you're directly copying pixels from within it. Thus, if your user wants a window smaller than this texture size, either you have to fall back to a smaller-sized texture or you have to limit the window minimum size. At any rate, the hairy details of the bookkeeping surrounding pixel sizes are not the most fun part of this technique, and constitute another way in which FBOs are a better solution.

In this section, we've covered how to perform textured renders from the contents of a texture filled by another render. The technique is very portable, but carries some overhead concerning texture and window sizes, and has some performance limitations based on the underlying OpenGL operations. This technique is a capable fallback for when FBOs are not available.

Pbuffer, Off-Screen, and Other Intermediate Targets

There exist a variety of other ways of writing intermediate rendering results for reuse in later final renderings in your OpenGL application. Among these are pbuffers, off-screen render areas, and a variety of extensions for directly rendering into textures. Though many other choices are possible, we faced a difficult decision when writing this book—either to cover them all or to cover only a subset.

To free up some weekends, we chose the latter option. To be fair, since we began this project, the FBO extension has really come of age, and we would recommend it without hesitation for those cases when you need intermediate rendering. The other techniques that we do not cover here are all genealogical predecessors to the FBO extension and, in many ways, are inferior to it. Specifically, off-screen render areas, regardless of the interface (CGL, AGL, or Cocoa) are software renderers and so have only nominal performance. They should be avoided for interactive or real-time applications. Pbuffers are complex and unwieldy to implement. Although they often perform at native hardware speeds, the complexity of managing the interface is not worth the headache if you can write to a modern render target like an FBO instead.

The pure simplicity, flexibility and generality, and raw performance of what can be accomplished via FBO are unmatched by these alternative techniques.

If you've got older code that uses one of these approaches, a move to FBOs will likely both simplify and accelerate your code. Take the leap.

Summary

In this chapter, we explored how to create and configure Cocoa-based OpenGL rendering areas for on-screen windows and for various intermediate render targets. We saw how to create custom pixel formats, examined some of the flags that these pixel formats take, and demonstrated how to configure and initialize pixel formats. We also saw how to customize NSViews and NSOpenGLViews to use custom pixel formats and create contexts. We considered how to share data among multiple contexts, and we learned how to configure full-screen surfaces. Now that you know the fundamentals of OpenGL and Cocoa setup, you have a solid foundation from which to begin building your own Cocoa OpenGL applications.

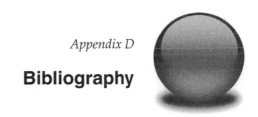

Appendix D

Bibliography

[1] The OpenGL Architecture Review Board. OpenGL 2.0 specification. `http://www.opengl.org/documentation/specs/version2.0/glspec20.pdf`.

[2] The OpenGL Architecture Review Board. OpenGL website. `http://www.opengl.org`.

[3] Apple Computer. About this Mac build information. `http://docs.info.apple.com/article.html?artnum=106176`.

[4] Apple Computer. Apple developer website. `http://developer.apple.com`.

[5] Apple Computer. Apple technote 1188: getprocaddress and openGL entry points. `http://developer.apple.com/qa/qa2001/qa1188.html`.

[6] Apple Computer. Apple technote 2080: understanding and detecting openGL functionality. `http://developer.apple.com/technotes/tn2002/tn2080.html`.

[7] Apple Computer. Apple texture range sample code. `http://developer.apple.com/samplecode/TextureRange/TextureRange.html`.

[8] Apple Computer. Apple Vertex performance sample code. `http://developer.apple.com/samplecode/VertexPerformanceTest/VertexPerformanceTest.html`.

[9] Apple Computer. Configuring and running X11 on Mac OS X. `http://developer.apple.com/opensource/tools/runningx11.html`.

[10] Apple Computer. Core video and QuickTime with OpenGL. http://developer.apple.com/samplecode/QTCoreVideo101/index.html.

[11] Apple Computer. Mac OS: Versions and builds since 1998. http://docs.info.apple.com/article.html?artnum=25517.

[12] Apple Computer. Quick Start guide for AltiVec. http://developer.apple.com/hardware/ve/quickstart.html.

[13] Apple Computer. SSE performance programming. http://developer.apple.com/hardware/ve/sse.html.

[14] Alex Eddy. OpenGL version, renderer, GLSL table. http://homepage.mac.com/arekkusu/bugs/GLInfo.html.

[15] Ron Fosner. *OpenGL® Programming for Windows 95 and Windows NT.* Boston, MA: Addison-Wesley, 1997.

[16] Erich Gamma et al. *Design Patterns: Elements of Reusable Object-Oriented Software.* Boston, MA: Addison-Wesley, 1995.

[17] IST. IST OpenMotif website. http://www.istinc.com/DOWNLOADS/motif_download.html.

[18] Mark J. Kilgard. *OpenGL® Programming for the X Window System.* Boston, MA: Addison-Wesley, 1996.

[19] Paul Martz. *OpenGL® Distilled.* Boston, MA: Addison-Wesley, 2006.

[20] OpenMotif. OpenMotif website. http://www.opengroup.org/openmotif/.

[21] Randi J. Rost. *OpenGL® Shading Language, Second Edition.* Boston, MA: Addison-Wesley, 2006.

[22] Dave Shreiner, Mason Woo, Tom Davis, and Jackie Neider. *OpenGL® Programming Guide, Fifth Edition.* Boston, MA: Addison-Wesley, 2006.

Index

Note: Information presented in tables and figures is denoted by t and f respectively.

A

Activity Monitor, 227
Advanced Graphics Port, 29, 30t
AGL. *see* Apple OpenGL
AGL_ACCELERATED, 99t
AGL_ACCUM_ALPHA_SIZE, 97t
AGL_ACCUM_BLUE_SIZE, 97t
AGL_ACCUM_GREEN_SIZE, 97t
AGL_ACCUM_RED_SIZE, 96t
AGL_ALL_RENDERERS, 95t
AGL_ALPHA_SIZE, 96t
AGL_AUX_BUFFERS, 96t
AGL_AUX_DEPTH_STENCIL, 98t
AGL_BACKING_STORE, 100t
AGL_BLUE_SIZE, 96t
AGL_BUFFER_SIZE, 95t
AGL_CLOSEST_POLICY, 97t
AGL_COLOR_FLOAT, 98t
AGL_DEPTH_SIZE, 96t
AGL_DOUBLEBUFFER, 95t
AGL_FULLSCREEN, 98t
AGL_GREEN_SIZE, 96t
AGL_LEVEL, 95t
AGL_MAXIMUM_POLICY, 97t
AGL_MULTISAMPLE, 98t
AGL_MULTISCREEN, 100t
AGL_NO_RECOVERY, 99t
AGL_NONE, 101t
AGL_OFFSCREEN, 98t
AGL_PBUFFER, 100t
AGL_PIXEL_SIZE, 97t
AGL_RED_SIZE, 96t
AGL_REMOTE_PBUFFER, 101t

AGL_RENDERER_ID, 99t
AGL_RGBA, 95t
AGL_ROBUST, 100t
AGL_SAMPLE_ALPHA, 99t
AGL_SAMPLE_BUFFERS_ARB, 98t
AGL_SAMPLES_ARB, 98t
AGL_SINGLE_RENDERER, 99t
AGL_STENCIL_SIZE, 96t
AGL_STEREO, 95t
AGL_SUPERSAMPLE, 98t
AGL_VIRTUAL_SCREEN, 100t
AGL_WINDOW, 100t
aglChoosePixelFormat, 93–94,
    95t–101t
aglCreatePBuffer, 110t
aglDescribePBuffer, 110t
aglDestroyPBuffer, 110t
aglGetPBuffer, 110t
aglSetPBuffer, 110t
aglTexImagePBuffer, 110t
AGP. *see* Advanced Graphics Port
alignment
    pixel data, 224–25
    texture, 225–26
alternative rendering destinations,
    109–13, 312–22
AltiVec engines, 28, 42–43
API layers, 15–16, 16f
APIs
    and surfaces, 15–16
    cross-platform, 48–49
    integration with, 254–55
    Mac-only, 46–49
    X11, 277–79

AppKit, 16, 16f, 20, 122–33, 123f, 124f, 125f, 126f
Apple Fence, 216–17
Apple Float Renderer, 13
Apple Generic Renderer, 13
Apple OpenGL, 16, 16f, 47
  alternative rendering destinations in, 109–13
  context sharing in, 107–9
  framebuffer objects in, 117–19
  full-screen application in, 91–101
  pbuffers in, 110–13, 110t, 113f, 208t
  renderers in, 104–7, 107t
  software layering in, 90–91, 91f, 91t
  windowed application in, 101–4
Apple Texture Range, 205–7
Apple Vertex Array Range, 205–7
APPLE_flush_buffer_range, 220–21
APPLE_vertex_array_range, 217–19
ARB. see Architecture Review Board (ARB)
Architecture Review Board (ARB)
  and extensions, 8–9
  creation of, 8
asynchronous calls, 204–7

B

best practice axioms, 196–201
BGRA pixel format, 10t
bitmap, to NSImage, 183–84
blend squaring, 10t
blending logical operations, 9t
Breakpoints view, 229–31, 230f
buffer flush, 205–7, 220–21
buffer sizing, 59–60
Buffer view, 234, 235f
bugs, in OS, 39–41
bus
  bandwidth, 30
  graphics, 29–30, 30t
  memory, 29

C

C (programming language), 2, 89–90
C++, 89–90
cache, in CPU, 25
CAD limitations, 27
CAE limitations, 27
central processing unit (CPU)
  and Activity Monitor, 227
  and clock rate, 28
  cache, 25

idle time minimization, 204–7
  northbridge of, 23–24, 24f
  southbridge of, 24, 24f
  transistors in, 23
CGL. see Core OpenGL (CGL)
CGLChoosePixelFormat, 58–59
CGLFlushDrawable, 230, 231–32
CGLRendererInfoObj, 72
Cheetah. see also OS X
  release of, 17t
clock rate, 28
Cocoa API in Leopard, 283–322
Cocoa Image, 174–84, 178f, 179t
Cocoa OpenGL, 47–48
color models, X11, 279
context enables, 64–65
context management, in CGL, 63–68
context parameters, 64–65
context sharing
  in AGL, 107–9
  in OpenGL, 141–49, 143f, 144f
  in OpenGL Leopard, 301–8
copy-to-texture, 114–17, 158–61, 318–21
Core Graphics, 16, 49
Core OpenGL (CGL), 16, 16f, 18, 47, 53–54, 54f, 55–87
  buffer sizing, 59–60
  ChoosePixelFormat, 58–59
  context management in, 63–68
  error handling in, 57
  global state functions in, 84–86
  macros in, 86
  pbuffer selection mode, 208t
  pixel format selection in, 57–63
  read-only parameters, 68
  read/write parameters in, 66–67
  virtual screen management in, 83–84
Core Video, 192
CoreFoundation, 37–38
CPU. see central processing unit (CPU)

D

Darwin, 33
data copy minimization, 201–2
data flow
  across contexts, 51–53, 76–77
  and hardware, 24–32
  unidirectional, 199–200
data management, 209–10

NSOpenGLView, 122–33, 123f, 124f, 125f, 126f, 284–93
NSSlider, 221
NSView, 133–40, 134f, 135f, 294–300

O

object-oriented programming, and state management, 197–98
Objective-C, 89, 121
off-screen drawables, 82
off-screen rendering, 161–62, 321–22
off-screen surfaces, 109–10
OpenGL
  advantages of, 3–4
  as specification document, 8
  debugging, 39–41
  feature support, 14–15
  graphics tools, 228–36, 229f, 230f, 232f, 233f, 234f, 235f, 236f, 237f
  history of, 7–8, 9f
  platform identification, 248–49, 249t
OpenGL Driver Monitor, 235–36, 235f, 236f
OpenGL Profiler, 228–34, 229f, 230f, 232f, 233f, 234f, 235f
OS 9, 2
OS requirements, 27–28
OS version identification, 249–51
OS X. *see also* Cheetah; Jaguar; Leopard; Panther; Puma
  10.0 through 10.1, 245–46
  filesystem, 38
  implementation of OpenGL specification, 11
  power management in, 34–38
  tools, 226–28
  version history, 17t, 33–34, 34t

P

Panther. *see also* OS X
  improvements of, 246
  QTKit in, 185
  renderer support, 12t
parallel extensions, 8
Pascal (programming language), 2
pbuffers, 78–81, 79t, 110–13, 110t, 113f, 161–62, 208t, 321–22
PCI Express, 29–30, 30t
pixel buffer objects, 11t, 241–42
pixel buffers, 78–81, 79t, 110–13, 110t, 113f
pixel data, from NSImage, 178–79, 179t
pixel data alignment, 224–25
pixel data processing, 26

pixel format
  and texture data handling, 221–23
  in AGL, 91–109
  in CGL, 57–63
  in GLUT, 167–70, 167f, 169t, 170t
Pixel Format view, 234, 234f
pixel manipulation, 140–41
pixel pipeline, 223–24
pixel types, 221–23
Pixie, 235, 236f
Please Tune Me, 237–43, 239f, 240f, 241f, 242f, 243f
plug-in architecture, 17–18, 18f
point parameters, 10t
polygon offset, 9t
power management, 34–38
PowerPC, 42–43
Profiler, 228–34, 229f, 230f, 232f, 233f, 234f, 235f
programmable shading, 11t
ptm1.c, 238–39, 239f
ptm2.c, 240, 240f
ptm3.c, 240–41, 241f
ptm4.c, 241
ptm5.c, 241–42, 242f
Puma. *see also* OS X
  release of, 17t

Q

QTKit, 184–88, 191–92
QTMovie, 186–87, 191–92
quad-buffering, 61
Quartz, 15, 16, 46–47
Quartz 2D, 31
Quartz Debug, 228
QuickTime, 184–92

R

range extensions, 205–7
read-only parameters, 68
read/write parameters, 66–67
render targets, 60–61
render-to-texture, 114–17, 158–61
renderer support, 12t–13t, 13–14
renderers, 18–21
  and intermediate rendering, 152–53
  choosing, 21
  definition of, 18
  drivers, 21
  hardware *vs.* software, 19
  in AGL, 104–7, 107t
  incompatibility of, 141–42

OpenGL® Titles from Addison-Wesley

OpenGL® Programming Guide, Sixth Edition
The Official Guide to Learning OpenGL® Version 2.1
OpenGL Architecture Review Board, Dave Shreiner, Mason Woo, Jackie Neider, and Tom Davis
0-321-48100-3

OpenGL® Programming Guide, Sixth Edition, provides definitive, comprehensive information on OpenGL and the OpenGL Utility Library. This sixth edition of the best-selling "red book" describes the latest features of OpenGL Version 2.1.

OpenGL® Shading Language, Second Edition
Randi Rost
0-321-33489-2

OpenGL® Shading Language, Second Edition, is the experienced application programmer's guide to writing shaders. Part reference, part tutorial, this book explains the shift from fixed-functionality graphics hardware to the new era of programmable graphics hardware and the additions to the OpenGL API that support it.

OpenGL® Library, Fourth Edition
0-321-51432-7

This special boxed set contains both *OpenGL® Programming Guide, Sixth Edition*, and *OpenGL® Shading Language, Second Edition*.

OpenGL® SuperBible, Fourth Edition
Comprehensive Tutorial and Reference
**Richard S. Wright Jr., Benjamin Lipchak,
and Nicholas Haemel**
0-321-49882-8

OpenGL® SuperBible, Fourth Edition, offers comprehensive coverage of applying and using OpenGL in your
day-to-day work. It covers topics such as OpenGL ES
programming for handhelds and OpenGL implementations
on multiple platforms, including Windows, Mac OS X, and
Linux/UNIX.

OpenGL® Distilled
Paul Martz
0-321-33679-8

OpenGL® Distilled provides the fundamental information
you need to start programming 3D graphics, from setting up an OpenGL development environment to creating
realistic textures and shadows. Written in an engaging,
easy-to-follow style, you'll quickly learn the essential and
most-often-used features of OpenGL, along with the best
coding practices and troubleshooting tips.

OpenGL® Programming on Mac® OS X
Architecture, Performance, and Integration
Robert P. Kuehne and J. D. Sullivan
0-321-35652-7

Apple's highly efficient, modern OpenGL implementation
makes Mac OS X one of today's best platforms for OpenGL
development. *OpenGL® Programming on Mac OS® X* is the
first comprehensive resource for every graphics programmer who wants to create, port, or optimize OpenGL
applications for this high-volume platform.

**Available wherever technical books are sold. For more information, including free
sample chapters, go to www.awprofessional.com.**

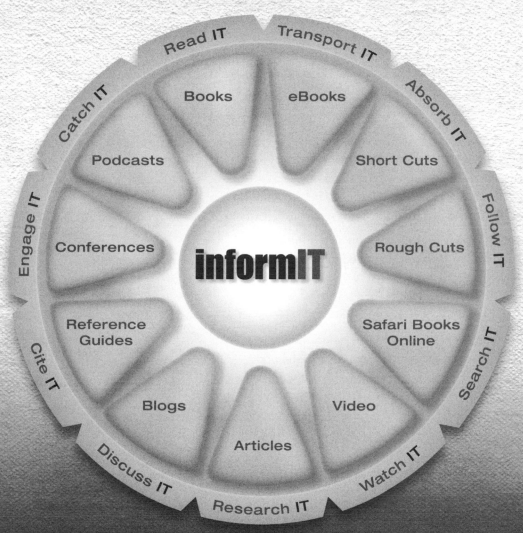

BOOKS ONLINE
ENABLED

THIS BOOK IS SAFARI ENABLED

INCLUDES FREE 45-DAY ACCESS TO THE ONLINE EDITION

The Safari® Enabled icon on the cover of your favorite technology book means the book is available through Safari Bookshelf. When you buy this book, you get free access to the online edition for 45 days.

Safari Bookshelf is an electronic reference library that lets you easily search thousands of technical books, find code samples, download chapters, and access technical information whenever and wherever you need it.

TO GAIN 45-DAY SAFARI ENABLED ACCESS TO THIS BOOK:

- Go to **http://www.awprofessional.com/safarienabled**
- Complete the brief registration form
- Enter the coupon code found in the front of this book on the "Copyright" page

Addison
Wesley

If you have difficulty registering on Safari Bookshelf or accessing the online edition, please e-mail customer-service@safaribooksonline.com.